A TIMES BARTHOLOMEW GUIDE

ROME

Authors: **Patrick Dubois, Soline Goux-Dietlin, Claire Maupas and Béatrice Labourel-Viterbo**
Translation: **Anthony Roberts**
Editors: **Lisa Davidson-Petty, Alexandra Tufts-Simon**
Photo credits: All photos by **Alain Durand**, except pp. 117 **(Roy-Explorer)**, 177 **(G. Chassagne-La Photothèque S.D.P.)** and 181 **(B. Richebe-La Photothèque S.D.P.)**.

This edition published in Great Britain by **John Bartholomew & Son Ltd. Duncan Street,** Edinburgh, EH9 1TA.
This guide is adapted from *à Rome,* published by Hachette Guides Bleus, Paris, 1988.

© Hachette Guides Bleus, Paris, 1989. First edition.
English translation © Hachette Guides Bleus, Paris, 1989
Maps © Hachette Guides Bleus, Paris, 1989.
Colour maps © TCI, Milan, 1989.

British Library Cataloguing in Publication Data
Rome. — (A Times Bartholomew guide)
 1. Italy. Rome: Visitors guides
 I. Dubois, Patrick II. à Rome. *English*
914.5′63204928

ISBN 0-7230-0327-0

Printed in France by Aubin Imprimeur, Ligugé.

A TIMES BARTHOLOMEW GUIDE

ROME

Published by
John Bartholomew & Son Ltd

▄▄▄ HOW TO USE YOUR GUIDE

Before you leave home, read the sections **'Planning Your Trip'** p. 23, **'Practical Information'** p. 27, **'Rome in the Past'** p. 45 and **'Rome Today'** p. 55.

The rest of the guide is for use once you arrive. It is divided into **itineraries** (the routes are indicated on maps of each itinerary) and includes sections on museums and architecture. A section called **'Rome Addresses'** is provided at the end of the guide, p. 196. It includes a selection of hotels, restaurants, bars and shops, organized by neighbourhood.

To quickly locate a site or practical information, use the **'Index'** p. 214.

To easily locate recommended sites, hotels and restaurants on the maps, refer to the map coordinates printed in blue in the text.

Example: III, AB2

▄▄▄ SYMBOLS USED

Sites, monuments, museums, points of interest

★★★ Exceptional
★★ Very interesting
★ Interesting

Hotels and restaurants

See p. 196.

▄▄▄ MAPS

▬▬ *CONTENTS*

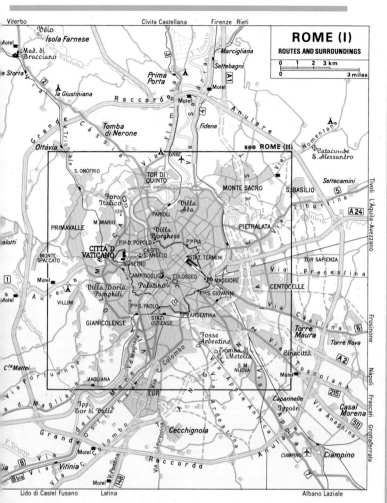

MAPS

ROME (II)

METROPOLITAN

- – – – – Route A
- – – – – Route B

CAVOUR ■ Station

⊡ Station interchange
□

Scale: 0 500 1000 1500 m / 0 1 miles

A

B

C

E

F

Campeggio

V. Cassia Nuova

Via Flaminia Nuo

Via Flaminia

TOR DI QUINTO

Via d. Foro

Via dell'Acqua Traversa

Camilluccia

Cassia

Cimit. Mil. Francese

FORO ITALICO

P⁰ Flaminio

M.lvio

Lung. d. Acqua Acetosa

S. ONOFRIO

Via Trionfale

Stadio Olimpico

Stadio Olimpico

Villa Madama

Villa Glori

P

R.

Pilsuds

TRIONFALE

Monte Mario 139

VITTORIA

Lung. d. Vittoria

Viale

see ROME (III)

PRIMAVALLE

Via Trionfale

Viale delle Milizie

Museo Naz. Villa Giulia

Borg

bm

Via della Pineta Sac

Via di Valle Aurelia

Viale G. Mazzini

FLAMINIO

Via Cipro

OTTAVIANO

Viale Angelico

LEPANTO

P⁰ d. Pópolo

Fincio

CITTÀ DEL VATICANO

Via Cola di Rienzo

SPAGNA

Via di Boccea

S. Pietro

P⁰ Risorg.

Castel S. Angelo

T.C.I.

P⁰ di Spagna

Via Cavour

BARB

AURELIO

Via Aurelia

Via Gregorio VII sw

S. Pietro F.S.

Lung. Tor di Nona

Montecitorio

Qui

VALCANNUTA

Via Aurelia Antica

Corso Vitt. Eman. II°

Corso

Navona

P⁰ Venezia

Campeggio

Via Aurelia

Campidoglio

VILLINI

Via di Leone XIII

Villa Doria Pamphili

Gianicolo

Lung. Farnesina

Lung. Aventino

S. Sabina

Via della Nocetta

GIANICOLENSE

Viale dei Quattro Venti

Viale Trastevere

Albani

P⁰ S.

PIRA

Via Donna Olimpia

Circonvallazione Gianicolense

Staz. F.S. Trastevere

Testaccio

St. Roma-Lido

Sta

see ROME (VI)

P⁰ d. Radio

GARBA

E

Via Portuense

G. Cibo

Via Casaletto

Via dei Colli Portuensi

E. Fermi

A. Meucci

F. Tevere

Via Ostiense

S. Paolo Fuori le M

S. PAOLO

Via del Trullo

V⁰ P. Colonna

Via Marconi

Via del Mare

LA PARROCCHIETTA

Via Portuense

Via dell'Imbrecciato

F

Via Ostiense

see ROME (VIII)

MAGLIANA

Autostrada

MAGLIANA

Pal. d. Civiltà d. Lavoro

Via della Magliana

TRULLO

E.U.R. MARCONI

E. U. R.

Pal. d. Congressi

Ab d. d.Tre

Sta

Civitavécchia km 71

Fiumicino km 28

Autostrada km 14 - Rieti km 77
Mentana km 23   A
Tivoli km 31   B
L'Aquila km 114   C
Palestrina km 39   D
Autostrada km 12 - Frosinone km 84   E
Frascati km 21   F

5 **6**

Aeroporto dell'Urbe

MONTE SACRO ALTO

TUFELLO

MONTE SACRO

M. Antenne Campeggio

Villa Ada (Villa Savoia)

PIETRALATA

S. Agnese Fuori le Mura

Costanza

NOMENTANO

P.za Bologna

Staz. Tiburtina F.S.

S. MARIA DEL SOCCORSO

REBIBBIA

P.za Mammolo

TIBURTINO

Cimitero di S. Lorenzo f.le Mura Campo Verano

REPUBBLICA

Staz. Termini F.S.

TERMINI

S. Maria Magg.

CAVOUR

COLOSSEO

Staz. Prenestina F.S.

V.lo Gordiani

PRENESTINO a LABICANO

VITTORIO EMAN.

S. GIOVANNI

S. Giovanni in Later.

MANZONI

V. La Spezia

P.za S. Giovanni

RE DI ROMA

P.za Metronio

PONTE LUNGO

Staz. Tuscolana F.S.

TOR PIGNATTARA

P.za Latina

CENTOCELLE

P.za S. Sebastiano

see ROME (V)

TUSCOLANO

Domine Quo Vadis?

C.ta ALBANI

ARCO DI TRAVERTINO

QUADRARO

P.za FURBA

Cat. di Domitilla

Fosse Ardeatine

N. QUADRATO

L. SESTIO

G. AGRICOLA

SABAUGUSTA

S. Sebastiano

Circo di Massenzio

CINECITTÀ

Cinecittà

Tomba di Cecilia Metella

ANAGNINA

E A T I N O

S. M. NUOVA

4 **5** Terracina km 103 **6**

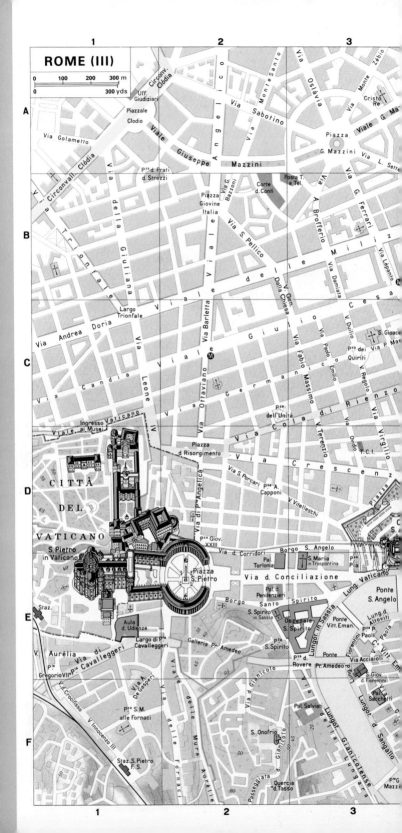

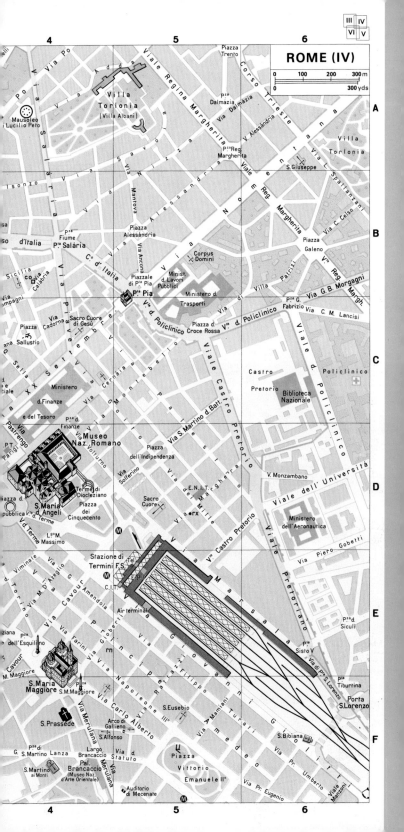

ROME (V)

ROME (VI)

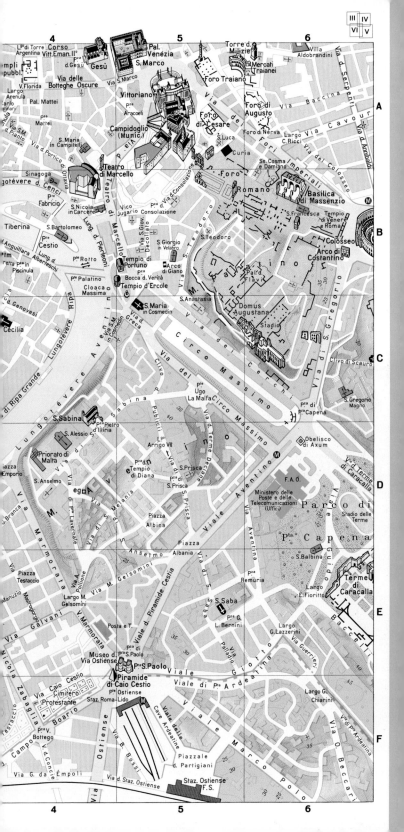

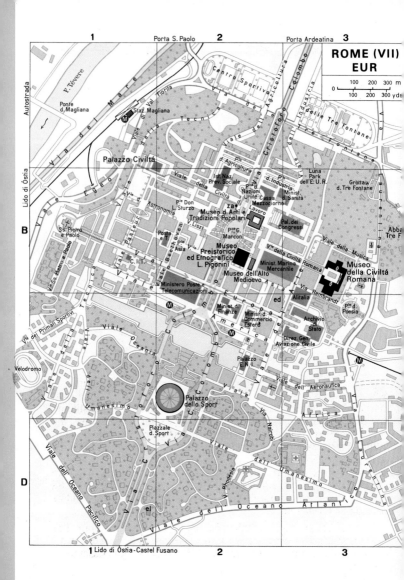

INTRODUCTION TO ROME

R ome has attracted Christian pilgrims since the earliest times. It was here that the head of the primitive church, St Peter, was martyred by the Emperor Nero; and it was here that Christianity first took root in the world. From the 16th to the 19th century, the elite of Europe flocked to Rome for intellectual enlightenment and, in the 17th century, Roman antiquity came to be recognized as the wellspring of the classical aesthetic. The Romantics came to meditate on grandeur, decadence and the fragility of human achievement in the shadow of the city's ruins. Today, people still come to Rome in vast numbers, attracted by its monuments and its position as a religious centre.

Yet Rome, today, is much more than a shrine or museum. The city's parks, Baroque palaces and fountains are only backdrops for the exuberant, almost anarchic city life that is quintessentially Roman.

Rome is a place of poignant, sometimes jarring contrasts: of popular trattorias, where working people come on Sundays to eat lunch with their families; of street workshops, where gilders, weavers and restorers ply their ancient crafts; of noisy, colourful open-air markets; and of crowded bars, where Romans gossip and argue for hours at a time. There is a negative side to all this vitality and excitement, however. Rome is noisy, beset by mammoth traffic jams, overwhelmed by unbridled advertising and intrusive media. It is also plagued by petty crime, attributable to a marked contrast between the lives of the rich and poor.

Modern Rome takes special pride in its own architectural confusion. Here, there is no such thing as anachronism; the various stages of the past are neither embalmed nor sentimentally preserved under glass. Instead, the landscape is one large cluster of accumulated history that is constantly being looted, rearranged and redefined by the encroachments of the modern city.

Rome in brief

Location: Rome is situated in central Italy, on the west coast, about 18.6 mi/30 km from Ostia on the Tyrrhenian Sea and 186 mi/300 km from the Adriatic Sea.

The province of Rome, which comprises the city and its inner and outer suburbs, is one of five provinces in the Region of Latium. The other four are Rieti, Latine, Viterbo and Frosinone.

The city itself lies in the alluvial valley of the Tiber River, 262.5 ft/80 m above sea level.

Distances: *Bologna:* 235 mi/379 km. *Florence:* 172 mi/277 km. *Genoa:* 311 mi/501 km. *Milan:* 355 mi/572 km. *Ravenna:* 227 mi/366 km. *Naples:* 136 mi/219 km. *Turin:* 416 mi/669 km. *Venice:* 328 mi/528 km. *London:* 1150 mi/1850 km. *Paris:* 932 mi/1500 km.

Population and land area: Central Rome has a population of 3 million; the total population of the city and suburbs is 5 million. The entire province of Rome (2065 sq mi/5350 sq km — roughly 30 % of the Latium region) contains about 7 million people.

Today, Rome's ethnic makeup is changing. Previously almost entirely Italian, the population now includes many new immigrants, the major groups being Poles, Turks, North Africans and Central Africans.

Language: Italian; French and English are also widely spoken.

Religion: Catholicism: Rome is the capital of the Catholic church. The Vatican, which is the world's smallest independent state (109 acres/44 hectares), enjoys extra-territorial status.

Political status: Rome has been the capital of Italy since 1870. Today, it is also the seat of the two legislative assemblies and the headquarters of the President of the Republic.

Resources: Latium is not heavily industrialized; its main economic activities are furniture manufacture, agriculture and public works. The major employers are the administration and the church. There are small mining and winegrowing sectors. Tourism is a major industry: in 1988, over 2.6 million foreigners visited Rome for at least two days.

There is nothing new in this. Constantine pillaged the monuments erected by his predecessors to embellish his great arch. The original Coliseum was cannibalized during the Renaissance in order to supply building material for the palaces of Roman aristocrats. And when Pope Urban VIII Barberini dismantled the bronze covering of the Pantheon for his baldachin at St Peter's, word passed through the city that 'what even the barbarians did not do, that the Barberini have done'.

In Rome, hybrid buildings are everywhere. The colonnades of the first Christian basilicas were borrowed from pagan temples. Castel Sant'Angelo was built over the Mausoleum of Hadrian. The church of San Clemente is Baroque on mediaeval on antique; Santa Maria degli Angeli stands squarely amid the Baths of Diocletian.

It is impossible to find a single definition for the city's many faces. There is probably no such definition; and, anyway, Rome reveals its charms slyly, sometimes in the least expected places, for example, at the monument to Victor Emmanuel II, that weird, surrealist 'typewriter' standing amid stately forums, palaces and churches. You will find the city's essence in the backstreets, in the imaginations of its artists and, above all, in its people.

PLANNING YOUR TRIP

WHEN TO GO

Rome is only 17 mi/28 km from the sea, on the plain of Latium. Thus the warm waters and the latitude combine to make Rome's climate typically Mediterranean. If possible, try to plan your trip for spring or autumn, when the city's mild temperatures and beautiful light will amply reward you. Winter in Rome is generally temperate, though on the rainy side; this is the season for opera and theatre, and at this time you will have the museums to yourself. If you are thinking of visiting Rome in July or August, at the height of summer, try to follow the sensible example of its citizens who take many siestas and retreat as often as possible into cool gardens and churches during the hottest hours of the day, and emerge only in the evenings to enjoy the out of doors. Many Romans go away in the month of August and, consequently, the pace of the city becomes less frantic, more easygoing: this is the best season to wander around Rome at your leisure. Make reservations well in advance if you plan to visit at Easter or Christmas, since the city is always full of pilgrims during major religious holidays. The principal hotels are also invariably full during the International Tennis Championships (see p. 42) and the International Horse Trials (see p. 42), two important social occasions that take place annually in the first and last weeks of May.

Weather table

Month	January	May	August	November
Average temperature	7° C/44° F	18° C/64° F	24° C/75° F	12° C/53° F
Average number of rainy days	8	10	2	9

GETTING THERE

Plane

Rome is easily accessible from most major cities. We list only a few of the many airlines that offer flights to Rome.

Canada

Air Canada, 500 Dorchester Blvd., Montreal, Québec 42Z 1X5, ☎ (514) 879 7000.

Alitalia, 2055 Peel St., Montreal, Québec H3A 1VB, ☎ (514) 842 5201; PO Box 115, Station A, Ottawa, Ontario K1N 8VI, ☎ (613) 237 1460.

The lovely via Guilia, a street with many antique dealers and art galleries.

Great Britain

Alitalia, 127/28 Piccadilly, London W1V 9PF, ☎ (01) 602 7111.

British Airways, 75 Regent St., London W1R 7HG, ☎ (01) 897 4000; 421 Oxford St., London W1R 1FJ, ☎ (01) 897 4000.

United States

Alitalia, 666 Fifth Ave., New York, New York 10103, ☎ (212) 582 8900; 421 Powel St., Suite 300, San Francisco, California 94102, ☎ (800) 223 5730.

Pan Am, 100 E. 42nd St., New York, New York 10019, ☎ (212) 687 2600.

TWA, 100 E. 42nd St., New York, New York 10019, ☎ (212) 290 2121.

Airport

Rome is served by the major international airport, **Leonardo da Vinci,** at Fiumicino, 30 mi/48 km from the city centre (☎ 60121). There is a regular bus service between the airport and the bus station on via Giolitti 36. Tickets for the bus may be obtained in the main concourse of the airport. Taxis are also available but the fares are very high. Avoid unofficial taxis—those without meters or taxi signs.

Train

Rome is linked to many major European cities by train. Calais, Lille, Brussels, Luxembourg and Strasbourg are directly connected to Rome by the Italia Express. Two daily trains, the Palatino and the Napoli Express, travel between Paris and Rome, and one daily train travels from Nice. Although trains are less expensive than regular full-fare flights, they now tend to be more expensive than charter flights.

The Italian railway system includes five different types of trains:

Super-Rapido: This train offers first class service only between large cities. Additional cost and reservations required.

Rapido: These are rapid trains with service between major cities. Additional cost and reservations required.

Espresso: First and second class service are provided to main stations.

Diritto: These trains stop at most stations. First and second class.

Locale: First and second class service to all stations.

Information and booking offices for seats and couchettes are open 7am-11pm in the larger stations. The state railways accept the Inter-Rail card, Eurailpass, Rail Europe Senior and other tickets approved under international conventions.

Car

If you plan to visit Rome by car, there are certain things that you should be aware of in advance. The main thing is that fuel in Italy is very expensive. However, for foreign travellers this problem is alleviated by free use of the road network, free help in case of emergency and coupons for fuel discounts. To take advantage of these offerings, one must obtain special packages at **ACIENIT (Italian Automobile Club-Italian National Tourist Office)** offices, which are located at national border stations. The packages contain coupons for discounts on fuel and free highway tolls, and can also be purchased before you leave home. The **Italian National Tourist Office** has many foreign offices (see p. 26).

▬▬ ENTRY FORMALITIES

Passport

To enter Italy, the visitor must have a valid national passport. For visitors from Great Britain, a document satisfactorily establishing identity and nationality is sufficient. If arriving by car, the visitor must have a valid driver's license, registration papers for the car, and car insurance (international green card).

Customs

The visitor may enter Italy with no more than 300 cigarettes or 150 cigarillos or 75 cigars, and with no more than 1.5 litres of alcohol (over 22 proof), 5 litres of wine, and 3 litres of other alcoholic beverages (under 22 proof).

Visitors are allowed to leave (without payment of tax, if there is no intention to resell) with 200 cigarettes or 100 cigarillos or 50 cigars; 1 litre of over-22-proof alcohol or 2 litres of under-22-proof alcohol and 2 litres of wine; 50 grams of perfume and 114 litres of eau de toilette; and 500 grams of coffee. Customs are more lenient toward visitors from the EEC, making it possible to leave with rather more than is listed. For visitors from other countries, however, these regulations are strictly enforced, except for cigars and cigarettes.

Animals

If the visitor wishes to enter with an animal, it must be in good health and must have been vaccinated against rabies between 20 days and 11 months before arrival.

Currency

The visitor is allowed to enter or leave with up to 400,000 lire. There are no limits on foreign currency, but if you plan to leave Italy with more than the equivalent of 1 million lire (per person), you should declare the amount imported on the 'V2' form that must be filled out at customs on arrival.

MONEY

The Italian currency is the lira. Banknotes are issued in denominations of 1000, 2000, 5000, 10,000, 50,000 and 100,000 lire; coins in 5, 10, 20 (now little used), 50, 100, 200 and 500 lire. San Marino and Vatican City coins are also in circulation in Italy. They are the same shape and weight as their Italian equivalents (and rather rare).

Exchange

Foreign currency may be changed at the frontier, in banks, international airports and major railroad stations. Exchange rates are the same throughout the country. For further information on currency exchange, see p. 29.

Banks

Banks are open to the public from 8.30am-1.30pm and from 2.45-3.45pm, except on Saturdays, Sundays and holidays. Bank holidays are New Year's Day, Easter Monday, April 25, May 1, August 15, November 1, December 8, December 25 and December 26. Half-day holidays (closing time at 11.30am) are August 14, December 24 and December 31. Bear in mind that in some banks exchange desks may be open shorter hours. Any amount of money may be sent from abroad to an Italian bank, but a charge will be made.

Traveller's checks

Traveller's checks can be changed in banks and are widely accepted by hotels, restaurants and shops. Credit cards are also widely accepted and may be used for hotels, transportation and other services. Many businesses display signs indicating which methods of payment (other than cash) are acceptable.

WHAT TO PACK

You will need warm clothing if you travel in winter. The spring and fall are the most agreeable times to visit Rome; during these seasons, a sweater or light jacket and raincoat will suffice. Summers in Rome tend to be hot and you will need lightweight clothes. As in any major city, comfortable footwear is essential.

BEFORE YOU LEAVE: SOME USEFUL ADDRESSES

Italian embassies abroad

Australia

Embassy
12 Gray St., Daken, Canberra ACT 2000, ☎ (062) 73 3333.

Consulate
6169 Macquarie St., Sydney NSW 2000, ☎ (612) 27 8442.

Canada

Embassy
275 Slater St., 11th floor, Ottawa, Ontario K1P 5H9, ☎ (613) 232 2401.

Consulate
136 Beverly St., Toronto, Ontario M5P 1Y5, ☎ (416) 977 1566.

Great Britain

Embassy
14 Three Kings Yard, London W1, ☎ (01) 629 8200.

Consulate
2 Melville Cres., Edinburgh EH3 7JA, ☎ (031) 226 3631.

United States

Embassy
1601 Fuller St. N.W., Washington, DC 20009, ☎ (202) 328 5500.

Consulates
690 Park Ave., New York, New York 10021, ☎ (212) 737 9100; 500 North Michigan Ave., Suite 1850, Chicago, Illinois 60611, ☎ (312) 467 1550; 11661 San Vincente Blvd., Suite 911, Los Angeles, California 90049, ☎ (213) 826 5998; 2590 Webster St., San Francisco, California 94115, ☎ (415) 931 4924.

Italian National Tourist Offices

Canada: Store 56, Plaza 3 Place Ville Marie, Montreal, Québec, ☎ (514) 866 7667.

Great Britain: 1 Princes St., London W1R 8AY, ☎ (01) 408 1254.

United States: 500 North Michigan Ave., Suite 1046, Chicago, Illinois 60611, ☎ (312) 644 0990; c/o Alitalia, 8350 North Central Expressway, Dallas, Texas 75206, ☎ (214) 692 8761; 630 Fifth Ave., New York, New York 10111, ☎ (212) 245 4961; 360 Post St., Suite 801, San Francisco, California 94108, ☎ (415) 392 6206.

PRACTICAL INFORMATION

ACCOMMODATION

Rome possesses a vast hotel network: there are no fewer than 53,700 hotel beds in the city, not counting the accommodation offered by religious institutions and camping sites. Nevertheless, it is essential to make reservations well in advance if you plan to visit Rome during a school holiday, at Easter, or in the months of May and June.

Hotels

Roman hotel prices have increased enormously in recent years and, as a rule, they remain the same whatever the season. Recommended hotels are listed by neighbourhood in 'Rome Addresses' at the end of the book, p. 196.

Tax and service are generally included in the bill but it is customary to leave a tip *(mancia)* for the staff (approximately 10%).

Pensiones

The Roman hotel trade has now adopted a system of classification, and in principle pensiones are now one-star hotels (for a short listing of pensiones, see p. 196). A pensione is usually a family-run affair, well-kept and comfortable, but simple.

Convents and other religious institutions

These institutions offer simple, clean and well-kept rooms at relatively low prices. However, if you plan a late night out, you will be better off staying somewhere else because convents tend to lock their doors at 10.30pm.

A list of convents that take guests can be obtained by writing to the **Centre Saint-Louis-des-Français,** Largo Tonolio 20-22, Rome 00186, ☎ 656 4869.

Convents situated in the centre of Rome include:

- **Nuns of the Immaculate Conception,** via Sistina 113, IV, D2, ☎ 46 1194.
- **Pensione Fraterna Domus,** via Monte Brianzo 62, III, E5.
- **Suore del Sacro Cuore,** piazza Trinità dei Monti 3, IV, C1, ☎ 67 9245.

Camping

All of the following camping areas are located outside Rome proper but are well served by public transportation.

Northwest of Rome

- **Camping Seven Hills,** via Cassia 1216, ☎ (06) 376 5571.

Access: Metro line A to Ottaviano (terminus), then bus n° 32 to bus terminus, then bus n° 201 and, finally, the shuttle between the bus stop and the camping site. The site closes at 11pm.

● **Harry Camping,** via Prato della Corte 1915, near Cassia bis-Suincolo, via della Giustiniana, ☎ (06) 642 2401.

Access: Metro Termini to piazzale Flaminio, change for Prima Porta. A bus shuttles regularly between Prima Porta and the camping site.

By car, take the road to Viterbo on the Cassia bis. When you reach the sign 'SS 3 via Flaminia-Prima Porta', take the road downhill following the signs for **Harry Camping.**

North of Rome

● **Camping Flaminio,** via Flaminia Nuova, 13 mi/8 km from Rome, ☎ (06) 327 9006.

Access: Metro Termini to piazzale Flaminio (line A), then bus n°s 202, 203, 204 or 205 (n° 203 runs at night). There are 600 places available.

● **Camping Tiber,** 1 mi/1.6 km from Prima Porta metro station on the road to Terni, ☎ (06) 691 2314. Beside the Tiber.

Access: By train, from the Flaminio station to Prima Porta, then take bus n° 202 or n° 204.

Northeast of Rome

● **Camping Nomentano,** via Nomentana, ☎ (06) 610 0296.

Access: Bus n° 36 from in front of the Termini station to piazza Sempione, then take bus n° 337 to the site. This camping area has 440 places and is open in summer only.

South of Rome

● **Camping Internazionale di Castel Fusano,** via Castel Fusano 45, ☎ (06) 560 2301.

Access: Metro to Cristoforo Colombo station, then take bus n° 7.

By car, take the Autostrada Rome-Lido di Roma. At Lido di Roma, take the turn for Ostia. The camping area is about 1 mi/1.6 km further. It is open all year and has 1800 places.

▄▄▄ BUSINESS HOURS

Banks

Banks are open Monday-Friday, 8.30am-1.30pm. Some banks also stay open 2.45-3.45pm.

Churches

Churches are normally open 9am-noon and 4-7pm. These times are only approximate, however, and you can never be certain if a church will be open until you try the door.

Filling stations

Filling stations are open 7am-12.30pm and 3-7pm. There is reduced service on Sundays and holidays.

Museums

Although efforts are being made to make museum hours more reasonable, most still close at 1pm. As a general rule, museums are closed on Mondays. In addition, the Vatican Museums are closed on the first three Sundays of each month, and the Forum and Palatine Museums remain closed on Tuesdays.

Post offices

Post offices are open Monday-Friday, 8am-2pm, Saturday 8am-noon. The Central Post Office and the office in the Termini railway station stay open until 8pm. See also p. 40.

Restaurants

Restaurants are normally open 12.30-3.30pm and 7.30-10.30pm. A list of restaurants that stay open after midnight can be found in 'Rome Addresses' p. 196.

Shops

Hours vary from one type of shop to another but most shops are open Monday-Saturday 9am-1pm and 5-7.30pm. Food shops close on Thursday afternoons (Saturday afternoons in summer).

CHILDREN

If you decide to visit Rome in December, take your children to see the creches of San Giacomo del Corso, San Rocco, Santa Maria in Via, San Lorenzo in Lucino, San Marcello or Santo Ignazio—all of which are near piazza del Popolo and piazza Venezia. Other fine creches may be seen at Santa Maria in Aracoeli and at the **Creche Museum,** via Tor de Conti 31a, V, A1, ☎ 678 7135.

A Toy Fair is held on piazza Navona from December 15 to January 6, featuring toys, religious statuettes and Christmas decorations.

Entertainment

There are performances by apprentice magicians every afternoon at **Curiosità e Magia,** via in Aquiro 70, III, E5, where magicians' equipment is also sold. Punch and Judy shows are held in Trastevere (**Alla Ringhiara,** via dei Riari 81, IV, A2, ☎ 656 8711), at the Villa Borghese and in the Janiculum Park. In addition, **Teatro Goldoni,** vicolo dei Soldati 3, III, F4, ☎ 656 1156, and **Teatro In,** vicolo degli Amatriciani 2, III, E4, ☎ 589 6201, sometimes put on plays for children.

Luna Park, the EUR *(Esposizione Universale di Roma)* amusement park with its huge ferris wheel, is one of the most modern complexes of its kind in Europe. It stays open all year. ☎ 591 0608.

Children will enjoy visiting the zoo at **viale Giardino Zoologico** 20, IV, A2-3 ☎ 87 2031.

Baby-sitting

Should you need a baby-sitter in Rome, your best contact will invariably be the hall porter at your hotel.

CURRENCY EXCHANGE

Nearly all banks operate an exchange counter and most will change traveller's checks. For banking hours, see p. 28.

Bureaux de change

These establishments are open during normal office hours.

- **American Service Bank,** piazza Mignanelli 5, IV, C1, ☎ 678 8874.
- **Cambio Roma,** via F. Crispi 15, IV, D2, ☎ 678 1076.
- **Società Rosati,** via Nazionale 186, IV, E2-3, ☎ 46 5498.
- **Via Viaggi,** via Due Macelli 105, IV, D1-2, ☎ 679 6580.

There is a bureau de change in the main lobby of the **Termini railway station** that stays open until 7pm on weekdays. The bureau de change at **Leonardo da Vinci Airport** is open daily until 11pm.

DO'S AND DON'TS

Romans are meticulous about their appearance but tolerant of how others look. Nonetheless, whether you are attending a service or not, you are expected to wear suitable clothing in churches and this will be vigorously pointed out to you at the door if you fail to do so. In addition, do take care

to exercise maximum discretion at all times in church, especially during services.
If you wish to take photographs in museums or in churches, you should know that tripods are usually forbidden. In some cases, you may not be allowed to use a flash. The best policy is to find out in advance what is or is not permitted.

ELECTRICITY

Almost everywhere in Rome, the electrical current is 220 volts. Bring an adapter for electrical appliances such as hairdriers and portable irons.

EMBASSIES

Embassies to Italy

Canada
Via G. de Rossi 27, IV, A6, ☎ 85 5341.
Great Britain
Via XX Settembre 800a, IV, CD3-4, ☎ 475 5441.
United States
Via Vittorio Veneto 119a, IV, C2-3, ☎ 46 741.

Embassies to the Holy See

Canada
Via della Concilizione 4d, III, E2-3, ☎ 654 7316.
Great Britain
Via Condotti 91, III, D6, ☎ 589 0479.

EMERGENCIES

Police assistance *(Pronto intervento):* ☎ 113.
Fire brigade: ☎ 44 441 or 44 444.
Central police station *(Questura):* ☎ 4686.
Police emergency service: ☎ 67 691.
Red Cross ambulance emergency service: ☎ 5100.
Road accident emergency service: ☎ 116.
Local police station emergency service: ☎ 112.
24-hour medical service: ☎ 475 6741.
Tourist emergency service: ☎ 46 2371.
Lost property: ☎ 21 6341.

ENTERTAINMENT

Rome's major daily newspapers all carry a theatre section; the most notable is *La Repubblica's Trova Roma* (Saturday supplement).

Cinema

The Italians take special pride in the quality of their dubbing, and this is something of a drawback for foreigners, since all major films are shown in Italian. However, Rome has a thriving group of cine-clubs and experimental cinemas that show plenty of retrospectives and films with their original sound-tracks. **Pasquino,** a small cinema in the Trastevere district, regularly shows films in English (vicolo del Piede 19, ☎ 580 3622).

Film clubs

Cineforum, la Eritrea, via Lucrino, II, B4.
Grauco, via Perugia 34, II, D5, ☎ 755 1785.

A charming crèche is set up every year at Christmas in the piazza di Spagna.

Labirinto, via Pompeo Magno 27, II, C4, ☎ 31 2283.
Officina, via Benaco 3, II, B4, ☎ 86 2530.
Sadoul, via Garibaldi 2a, IV, BC2, ☎ 581 6379.

Theatre

Traditional and avant-garde plays may be seen year round in Rome's 60-odd theatres. The best theatre companies tend to perform at the **Argentina** (largo Torre Argentina, III, F5, ☎ 665 4460), the **Quirino** (via M. Minghetti 1, III, E6, ☎ 679 4585), the **Valle** (via del Teatro Valle 22a, III, F5, ☎ 654 3794) and the **Teatro Ghione** (via delle Fornaci 37, III, F2, ☎ 637 2294).

Concerts and recitals

L'Accademia di Santa Cecilia, L'Accademia filarmonica and the **RAI Orchestra** may be heard, respectively, at:

● **Auditorio di Santa Cecilia,** via della Conciliazione 4, III, E3, ☎ 654 1044.
● **Teatro Olimpico,** piazza Gentile de Fabriano 17, III, B3, ☎ 396 2635.
● **Foro Italico,** piazza L. de Bosis, II, B2, ☎ 39 0713.

Apart from these, there are about 40 other institutes and associations offering a range of ancient, classical and contemporary productions, both Italian and foreign.

Local newspapers do not always advertise church concerts; look for information about these on posters around Rome. Occasionally, concerts are held in beautiful oratories such as the **Auditorio di Gonfalone,** via del Gonfalone 32a, III, F3, ☎ 65 5952, or the **Aula Borrominia dell'Oratorio di S. Filippo Neri,** piazza della Chiesa Nuova 18, III, F4, ☎ 655 9374.

Tickets are sold on the spot, both in advance and on the day of the performance. You can also reserve seats at via Vittoria 6, ☎ 679 3617.

Opera, ballet, dance

The opera season lasts from November-June at the **Teatro dell'Opera,** piazza B. Gigli 1, IV, E4, ☎ 46 3641. In summer, the **Baths of Caracalla** are the site of a number of important cultural events. The **Teatro Olimpico** mostly specializes in ballet, while musical productions can usually be found at the **Teatro Brancaccio** and the **Metateatro** (☎ 589 5807).

■■■ FESTIVALS AND PUBLIC HOLIDAYS

January

1st: New Year's Day.

5th: The Toy Fair on piazza Navona, IV, F5, closes amid tremendous fanfare.

6th: Epiphany *(Befana).*

17th: Blessing of Animals at Sant'Eusebio on piazza Vittorio, IV, F5

February

Shrove Tuesday (day before Lent begins): Children in fancy dress parade around piazza Navona, IV, F5, via Cola di Rienzo, III, C3-4, via Nazionale, IV E2-3, and the Corso, III, D6.

March

9th: Blessing of cars beside the church of Santa Francesca Romana, IV, A1

19th: Festival of St Joseph is a huge celebration that takes place in the Trionfale district, III, B1.

Holy Week: This week is marked by masses at many churches and basilicas around Rome. On Good Friday, the Pope leads a procession from the Coliseum. On Easter, the Pope delivers the benediction, *Urbi et Orbi,* from St Peter's. On Easter Monday, which is a holiday, Romans celebrate with a traditional family meal.

April

21st: Natale di Roma features ceremonies celebrating the anniversary of Rome's founding.

25th: Anniversary of the Liberation.

May

1st: Labour Day is a public holiday.

Mid-May: Antique Fair takes place on via dei Coronari, III, E4

21st-31st: International Tennis Championships, Foro Italico, II, B2-3

June

23rd: Festival of St John takes place around the porta San Giovanni, V, C5

29th: Festival of St Peter and St Paul is celebrated as a holiday.

July

Mid-July: Noantri festival is an ancient tradition, organized by the people of Trastevere in honour of the Madonna of Carmel.

August

15th: Assumption *(Ferragosto)* is a public holiday.

November

1st: All Saints' Day *(Ognissanti)* is a public holiday.

December

8th: Festival of the Immaculate Conception is celebrated by putting flowers at the feet of the statue of the Virgin on piazza di Spagna, III, D6. This is a public holiday.

25th: Christmas.

FOOD AND DRINK

Roman cuisine is a combination of several traditions, being based on the country cooking of Latium and the Abruzzi, as well as the sturdy diet of the Roman working class. There is a prevalence of fresh and dried vegetables, and meats, such as liver and kidneys are popular. Jewish cooking has also had a powerful influence. All in all, Roman cuisine is not renowned for its lightness, but it will delight anyone partial to stews and strongly aromatic herbs.

Pasta

Pasta is the obligatory prelude to any Italian meal. The variety of pasta sauces is inexhaustible, but the following are types you are likely to encounter in any Roman restaurant: *alla matriciana* (Abruzzi), a sauce based on bacon; *alla carbonara,* a mixture of bacon, eggs and cream; *alle vongole,* which is made with little clams cooked out of their shells; and the quintessentially Roman *rigatoni alla pajata,* which consists of rigatoni with a sauce of veal giblets. If you can't decide which pasta to choose, order an *assagiata* (a bit of each), or fall back on the risotto.

The pasta parade

Sorting out Roman pasta can be a challenge for the visitor to Italy. Seemingly every shape, size and configuration has been exploited. The list below provides the terms and their description.

Long
Spaghetti: thin, round strings.
Fettucine: Roman version of the flat egg noodle.
Tagliatelle: long, thin egg noodles; a speciality of Bologna.
Bucatini: a thicker, hollow version of spaghetti, also known as *perciatelli.*
Tonnarelli: square-shaped spaghetti strings, white or green (when made with spinach).
Lasagne: the broadest pasta noodle, ridged or smooth.

Short
Rigatoni: ridged, tubular macaroni.
Penne: short, tubular macaroni.
Conchiglie: macaroni in the shape of seashells, ridged or smooth.

Pasta stuffed with meat, ricotta cheese or spinach
Cannelloni: shaped like a tube when filled.
Ravioli: square, pillow-shaped dumplings.
Tortellini: small, ring-shaped dumplings.

Pasta in soups
Quadrucci: little squares of tagliatelli.
Capellini: very thin variety of flat spaghetti.
Occhi di pernice: literally means 'partridge eyes'.
Puntine: little dots.
Farfalle: shaped like a bow tie.
Maltagliati: irregular shapes.

There are also several varieties of *gnocchi* and *gnocchetti,* pasta (sometimes potato) dumplings shaped like seashells.

Meat dishes

Giblets of all kinds have traditionally formed the meat portion of the ordinary Roman's diet; formerly, the best cuts of meat were reserved for the clergy. Even the less adventurous traveller might try *trippa alla Romana* (a boiled tripe dish with a mint sauce and grated cheese) or *coda all vaccinara* (braised oxtail—a speciality of the old slaughterhouse area), or *animalle* (sweetbreads). *Abacchio* (milk-fed lamb) is another Roman speciality. *Abacchio* comes in several different forms, but is available only in winter. More than anything else, the pride of Roman cuisine is its veal. A famous Roman veal dish is *saltimbocca* (literally, 'jump-in-the-mouth'), a veal scallop rolled in ham and served with marsala sauce.

Fish

Fried fish—such as *filletti di baccala* (cod filets) and *polpe in purgatorio* (octopus)—is to be found in restaurants all over Rome. Other excellent fish dishes are *seppie con carciofi* (cuttlefish with artichokes, cooked in wine), *spigola* (sea bass), *orata* (sea bream) and *anguilla* (eel).

Contorni (vegetables and salads)

Vegetables and salads are served separately. *Carciofi alla giudia* (artichokes Jewish style) is traditionally Roman: the artichokes are crushed and fried in oil. *Carciofi alla Romana* is different; here the artichokes are fried in oil and flavoured with mint and garlic. Excellent salads are *puntarella*, tender shoots not unlike dandelions, and the strong-tasting *rughetta*. You can also try spinach served cold in the Roman style, broad beans and *cipolline in agrodolce*, bittersweet onions.

Cheeses

Cheese is one of the major products of Latium and the Abruzzi. Among the many varieties are several kinds of *pecorino*, made from sheep's milk; the famous *ricotta*, basis for a number of sauces; and *mozzarella*, made from ox or cow's milk and served with olive oil, pepper and a little lemon juice.

Drinks

Beware of badly-made local wines served in carafes and do not be taken in by picturesque, straw-covered flasks which all too often contain undrinkable brews. You will always be better off if you select a bottle with a label guaranteeing its vintage *(denominazione di origine controllata)*. The fine reputation of the *Castelli Romani* area to the southeast of Rome (Frascati, Marino, Colli Velletre, etc.) goes back to ancient times, and remains well-merited. Other regions (Emilia, Piedmont, Tuscany and Sicily) also produce excellent wines.

The traditional aperitif is red or white vermouth with a slice of lemon or, in summer, with ice. Other popular drinks include the slightly bitter tasting Campari, Punt e Mes and Aperol. A glass of *spumante*, or sparkling wine, is also popular.

The classic liqueur is *sambuca*, but sweet after-dinner drinks like *amaretto* or Strega are also worth trying.

Types of restaurant

Apart from the ordinary *ristorante*, you will find several other categories of eating houses in Rome. The *osteria* is usually a family-run affair, more modest than the *trattoria*. The *trattoria*, in turn, is usually less expensive than the *ristorante*. Oddly enough, certain *osterias* are among Rome's most fashionable establishments. The *rosticceria*, serving hot food to take away, have lately begun to be almost indistinguishable from the *tavola calda*, which offer hot meals at a counter or on the corner of a table. Pizzas may still be found at *pizzerias* and in some bakeries. *Latterias* (milk bars), snack bars and cafés offer sandwiches and cakes.

Cafés

Espresso and *cappuccino* coffee are known throughout the world. However, if you prefer your coffee less strong, ask for a *caffé lungo* (diluted coffee) or *caffé macchiato* (which has plenty of milk). You can also sample *cioccolata,* a thick, creamy hot chocolate, uniquely Italian, but before you do so try one of the delicious *tramezzini* (assorted canapés).

GETTING AROUND ROME

By car

If you tour the centre of Rome by car you will miss most of its charm. The city is ill-adapted to vehicular traffic and many areas allow only taxis, buses and vehicles belonging to residents. Traffic regulations are very severe, and the system of one-way streets can be nothing short of baffling. Even if you do finally arrive at your destination by car, you must still face the problem of finding a place to park.

Parking

There are two vast underground parking lots in the centre of Rome:

● Via Ludovisi 60, on the corner of via Crispi, IV, C2.

● Villa Borghese, entrance on piazza del Canestre and viale del Muro Torto, IV, BC2 (this is linked to the piazza di Spagna metro station by an escalator).

Attended parking lots are to be found near all major monuments, on the larger piazzas and beside the Termini railway station. Payment is by the hour and, as a rule, you will have to leave the keys of your car with the attendant. If the attendant does not specifically tell you how much you owe, give him 1000, 2000 or 3000 lire, according to your estimate of the length of time your car has been parked.

Removal of your car by the police

If you park illegally on the street, your car may be towed away, in which case you should go to the nearest policeman. He will direct you to one of Rome's two car pounds—the Villa Borghese parking lot or the Orto Botanico parking lot, V, C2 (between the Coliseum and San Gregorio).

Filling stations

Apart from the ordinary filling stations, which observe customary business hours, there are a number of self-service pumps around Rome that operate 24 hours a day (only 5000 and 10,000 lire notes are accepted).

Car rental

You may wish to rent a car for an excursion to the outskirts of Rome.

● **Avis,** piazza del Esquilino 1, IV, E4, ☎ 4701.

● **Europcar,** via Lombardia 7, IV, C2, ☎ 46 5802.

● **Hertz,** via Sallustiana 28, IV, C3-4, ☎ 51712.

● **Inter Rent,** Leonardo da Vinci Airport, Fiumicino, ☎ 601 1184; via Nizza 1546, IV, B4-5, ☎ 859 1111.

● **Mattei,** Leonardo da Vinci Airport, Fiumicino, ☎ 601 1379; via Ludovisi 60, IV, C2, ☎ 46 0920.

By taxi

Rome's yellow taxis are easily identifiable. The city's main taxi ranks are to be found at the Termini railway station, IV, E5, piazza di Spagna, III, D6, piazza Cavour, III, D4, piazza del Esquilino, IV, E4, and in front of the principal hotels. Fares are displayed on the meter. If, however, you are travelling with more than three people in a taxi, or with luggage, or at night (7-10pm), or on a Sunday or a holiday, you will have to pay a surcharge. It is customary, also, to give the driver a tip (around 10% of the total fare). Avoid unofficial taxis, which bear no sign and operate without meters.

Radiotaxis

The following taxis can be called and/or reserved in advance by telephone:

● **Cooperativa Radiotaxi Romana:** 3570.

- **Cooperativa Taxiradio Roma Sud:** 3875.
- **Radiotaxi Cosmos:** 8433.
- **Radiotaxi La Capitale:** 4994.

By bus or tram

This network, which is very comprehensive, makes up to some extent for the failings of the Roman metro. A map of the bus and tram system may be obtained at the **ATAC** office, in front of the Termini railway station, piazza dei Cinquecento, IV, D4, and in most newspaper kiosks. Cards that allow you to travel on all the various forms of public transportation are sold in **ACOTRAL** offices.

Tickets

Individual tickets and books of tickets are sold in most bars, tobacconists, newspaper kiosks and in the green kiosks of the ATAC. Half-day tickets, 24-hour tickets and weekly passes (also valid for the metro) are more economical—these are on sale at the ATAC offices, largo Montemartini, IV, D4.

How to catch a bus or tram

Stops are marked by a sign saying *fermata* (stop); this sign also shows the schedule and principal stops of the bus in question before it reaches the *capolinea* (terminus). The bus may be entered from the front or back *(entrata);* your ticket will be punched by a machine at the back. The exit door *(uscita)* is in the middle of the vehicle.

Buses and trams leave their depots at 6:30am and stop running at 9 or 10pm.

Apart from one or two privileged lines in the centre of town, the buses and trams of Rome encounter the same traffic jams as everyone else. Their average speed has been reliably calculated as being 3.5 mi/6 km per hour.

The tram

If you would like to get a good general idea of Rome and its monuments, the popular n° 30 tram offers an almost complete tour of the city.

By metro

The Roman metro system is relatively new, construction having been slowed by the subsoil's archaeological riches and distinctive geological makeup. Two lines, A and B, serve central Rome and a section of the suburbs (Cinecittà, Ostia Antica, Ostia Lido). See map II of Rome pp. 8-9.

Tickets

Metro tickets are sold in most bars, newspaper kiosks and tobacconists. All metro stations have automatic ticket distributors (coins of 50, 100, 200 and 500 lire accepted). Metro and bus tickets are not interchangeable. Ticket books and monthly passes *(tessera)* are sold in the offices of **ACOTRAL**. Cards can be purchased which allow you to travel on all the various forms of public transportation. The metro operates 6am-11pm.

By scooter

To rent a scooter, you must be 21 years old or over and possess a valid identity card, or passport, and a valid driver's license. You will also be required to put down a deposit, unless you plan to pay by credit card.

- **Motonoleggio or Scooter for Rent,** via della Purificazione 66, IV, D2, ☎ 46 5485.
- **Scoot-a-long,** via Cavour 302, IV, F3, ☎ 678 0206.

If your scooter breaks down, look in the Rome yellow pages directory under *motocicli, motoscooters, motocarri* or *riparazione* for assistance.

By bicycle

The bicycle is perhaps your best mode of transportation if you want to

Tourists, craftsmen and local artists often meet at the lovely piazza Navona.

ramble from the Villa Borghese to the Palatine, or coast down the slope of the Aventine hill.

Bicycles may be rented in the gardens of the Villa Borghese, IV, B1, in piazza del Popolo, III, C5, beside the piazza di Spagna (vicolo S. Sebastianello, III, D6), or at **Collati's Bicycle Rental,** via del Pellegrino 82, III, F4, ☎ 654 1084.

By carriage

Horse-drawn carriages *(carrozzelli)* can be rented by the hour or by the day, whichever you prefer. These vehicles are permitted to carry a maximum of five passengers, and they cover most of Rome's tourist itinerary. Settle on a price with the driver *before* you start. For information, ☎ 72 8370.

Carrozzelli for rent may be found on piazza di Spagna, III, D6, by the Trevi Fountain, IV, E1, on piazza Venezia, III, F6, and on piazza San Pietro, III, D2

On foot

Chi va piano va sano! Slowly but surely! There can be no doubt that the best way to see Rome and absorb its atmosphere is on foot. The most beautiful squares, such as piazza Navona and piazza Farnese, are open only to pedestrians, as are a number of streets around the Pantheon, the Corso and piazza di Spagna. In these areas you will be free from Rome's pervasive pollution and traffic noise. If you get tired of walking you can always catch a bus, tram or metro and, in summer, there is nothing to stop you taking a siesta in one of the city's parks or public gardens.

Before you set out, make sure you have a pair of comfortable shoes, binoculars for a close-up view of monuments, and whatever the season, some kind of protection against the rain. You should also take along plenty of change for bus tickets, tips and electric lights in dark churches.

LANGUAGE

The Italian spoken in Rome has a cadence all of its own—Northern Italians say Roman speech is 'lazy-sounding'. The *Romani di Roma* are inclined to glide over their words and drop certain consonants: for instance, *andiamo* becomes *annamo* on the lips of a Roman. The familiar *tu* form is very commonly used. People tend to talk at the tops of their voices, with lavish use of gesture. In general, the Italian you will hear in the streets of Rome is often crude, but always full of verve.

Hotel personnel and tradespeople in the centre of Rome usually speak English, and English is the predominant second language among younger people. If you can't find a common language with the person you're talking to, you can always consult the useful vocabulary section at the end of this guide (see p. 208).

MEDIA

Foreign newspapers and magazines are sold in most of the kiosks in the centre of Rome.

Press

*La Repubblica,*founded in 1976, is one of Italy's most influential newspapers. In addition to daily editions, *La Repubblica* publishes two weekly supplements, including the essential *Trova Roma*, which comes out on Saturdays and provides listings of theatre performances, concerts, cinemas, television shows and restaurants.

Le Corriere della Sera is the foremost Italian daily. It now prints a local Roman edition.

Il Tempo is a popular daily tabloid with a penchant for sensationalism.

Other dailies worthy of note are *l'Unita,* the official organ of the Italian Communist party, *Il Popolo,* the Christian Democratic organ, and *Osservatore Romano,* published by the Holy See.

Weeklies include *Panorama, L'Espresso* and *L'Europeo,* all of which contain many supplements.

Radio

The Roman airwaves are cluttered by several dozen independent radio stations and by the **RAI,** the state-founded television and radio corporation. The BBC and the Voice of America may be picked up easily.

Television

In addition to the culture-oriented state television (*Raiuno, Raidue, Raitre*), and the so-called national (but privately funded) television channels (*Retequattro, Canale 5, Italia 1*), Rome has about 20 private, regional channels. Hence, the choice of television programmes is very wide. One drawback about Italian television is that it is often hard to say whether the film is being interrupted by commercials, or vice versa.

NIGHTLIFE

On the via Veneto, little remains of the former *dolce vita* except the décor. Rome's nightlife has moved elsewhere, mostly to restaurants. Dinner is eaten late in the Italian capital—over 50 Roman establishments serve meals after midnight— and after dinner you can while away the night on the terrace of a café, in a piano bar or at an ice-cream shop (see 'Rome Addresses' p. 196).

Young people tend to gather at the Caffé della Pace or the Esprit Nouveau, while socialites prefer the Hemingway or the Cornacchie. Roman night-clubs tend to be very expensive and rather formal; the piano bars offer much better value. You may prefer to follow your fancy around the back streets and the main piazzas, where you will always find excitement and life. In summer, don't miss the various events that take place within the framework of the **Estate Romana,** an annual festival launched in the late 1970s by Niccolini, cultural advisor to the Italian government. Estate Romana has proved an unqualified success; in the 10 years since Niccolini's festivals began, tourists and Romans of every stripe have been gathering happily shoulder to shoulder in the city's great gardens and buildings, for evenings that have become famous all over the world.

ORGANIZING YOUR TIME

We have included two itineraries—a weekend and a five-day tour—which cover the essential sights.

Rome in one weekend

First day
Morning: St Peter's Basilica (see p. 104).
Afternoon: Vatican Palace and museums (see pp. 111, 183).
Evening: Dinner in the Trastevere area (see p. 203).

Second day
Morning: Coliseum, Imperial Forum, piazza Campidoglio (see pp. 78, 65, 76).
Afternoon: Piazza di Spagna, Trevi fountain, piazza Navona (see pp. 126, 127, 91).
Evening: Dinner along via Veneto (see p. 201).

Rome in five days

First day
Morning: Coliseum, Imperial Forum, piazza Campidoglio (see pp. 78, 65, 76).
Afternoon: Palatine, Ss. Luca e Martina, palazzo Venezia, colonna Traiana (see pp. 72, 67, 74, 81).
Evening: Dinner in the Trastevere area (see p. 203).

Second day
Morning: Piazza Navona, Pantheon, Pont Sant'Angelo, Castel Sant'Angelo (pp. 91, 98).
Afternoon: Piazza di Spagna, Trevi fountain, via Veneto (see pp. 126, 127, 168).
Evening: Restaurants and cafés near St Peter's Basilica (see pp. 197).

Third day
Morning: Vatican Palace and museums (see pp. 111, 183).
Afternoon: St Peter's Basilica (see p. 104).
Evening: Dinner in piazza Navona (see p. 198).

Fourth day
Morning: Trastevere Il Gianicolo (see pp. 137, 142).
Afternoon: San Clemente, Baths of Caracalla (see pp. 150, 146).
Evening: Stroll and dinner along via Veneto (see p. 201).

Fifth day
Morning: Santa Maria des Popolo, Borghese Museum (see pp. 165, 180).
Afternoon: Ostia Antica (see p. 190).
Evening: Dinner in restaurant around Trevi fountain (see p. 201).

PARKS AND PUBLIC GARDENS

The largest and most famous garden in Rome is that of the Villa Borghese. The city possesses many other green areas, mostly inherited from the great Roman families. Unfortunately, these are not always maintained to the highest standards.

Villa Ada, II, B4, extends over 370 acres/150 hectares. Roman families like to come here on Sundays to picnic on the grass. The entrance is on via Salaria 113.

Villa Borghese, IV, AB1-3, offers bicycle paths, boating and roller skating. The Pincio offers a remarkable view of the city.

Villa Celimontana, V, C2-3, is a garden on the western slope of the Coeline hill.

Villa Doria Pamphili, II, D2, lies to the west of Trastevere. This large park includes pine woods, wide lawns, and graceful statues, and is much-favoured by morning joggers. The entrance is on via S. Pancrazio.

Villa Glori, II, B3, was landscaped by De Vico in 1923.

Villa Scarria, IV, CD1-2, consists of a series of terraces covering 14.8 acres/6 hectares and overlooking Trastevere. The park commands a very fine view of the left-bank area of Rome. You'll find the entrance between via Dandolo and via Rosselli.

Villa Torlonia, IV, A4, was formerly the residence of Mussolini. The park, planted with palm trees, surrounds a neo-Classical ensemble built by Valadier in 1800. One discovers an oasis of tranquility here. The entrance is on via Salaria.

POST OFFICE AND TELECOMMUNICATIONS

Post office

The central post office on piazza S. Silvestro, IV, D1, is open Monday-Friday from 8.30am-6pm and Saturday from 8am-noon. Rome's other post offices close at 2pm during the week and at noon on Saturday. The following is a list of conveniently located post offices:

- via Taranto, V, C6, San Giovanni district, ☎ 755 4350.
- viale Beethoven, EUR district, ☎ 542 2027.
- via Andreoli II, B3, Prati district, ☎ 31 0031.
- piazza San Pietro (St Peter's Square), III, E2, Vatican Post Office.

Stamps are sold at post offices and tobacconists. Letterboxes are easily identifiable—they are bright red in colour.

Telephone

Public telephones are available on practically every corner in Rome. They work with *gettones,* which are sold in post offices, bars and tobacconists. There are still a few public telephones that accept coins. As you have probably already noticed in reading this guide, telephone numbers in Rome can include four, five, six or seven digits.

The telephone code for Rome is 06.

Useful telephone numbers include:

- time: 161
- wake-up calls: 114
- traffic: 194
- information for Italy and European countries : 184; other countries: 170
- police: 112
- emergency: 113

Telegraph

This service is open 24 hours; ☎ 679 5530 or 186.

▄▄▄ *SAFETY PRECAUTIONS*

Rome has a reputation for crime that is not, perhaps, merited. Nevertheless, tourists remain a favorite target for pickpockets on buses, in train stations and in popular tourist neighbourhoods. With a little common sense, you will avoid most problems: do not carry large amounts of cash, leave your money and valuable objects in the hotel safe, and never leave your bags unattended in a train station or car.

▄▄▄ *SHOPPING*

The more you wander around Rome, the more you will notice the astounding number and variety of shops. Many have retained their original provincial character, especially the ones in the centre. The finest clothing, leather goods, jewellery, gold and silverware all bear the mark of an ancient tradition and are famous for their refinement, excellent workmanship and overall quality. They are also extremely expensive.

Shopping areas

Rome's **luxury shops** are clustered around two principal centres. The Ludovisi district, IV, C2-3, is the Roman equivalent of Bond Street in London or Madison Avenue in New York. The most famous shops are located on the via Veneto, where you will also find all the city's best hotels and cafés. The via del Corso, III, CDE5-6, is the other major commercial centre. The piazza di Spagna and its neighbouring pedestrian precincts (vias dei Condotti, Borgognona, Frattina, Bocca di Leone, III, D6) are mainly occupied by the well-known **fashion houses.** Clothing at more moderate prices can be found on via Nazionale, IV, E2-3, on via del Tritone and near the Trevi Fountain, IV, D1-2.

Antique shops are mostly concentrated on via del Babuino, III, E4, and via Giulia, III, F3, while **art galleries** extend from via Margutta, III, C6, as far as the Tiber. Outside these traditional shopping areas, you will find less expensive stores on via Ottaviano, III, C2, and via Cola di Rienzo, III, C3-4, near the Vatican, and on via Salaria, II, B4, and via Nomentana, II, CB4-5, in northeast Rome.

Sales

Sales (*soldi*) take place in the fall (for summer items) and in spring (for winter items). Occasionally, you will stumble on promotional sales in January, February, July and August. Before you buy, however, check that the articles in question really are on sale: they should carry two price tags.

Types of shops

In Rome, the preponderance of small traders over large department stores is considerable. Popular department stores include **Upim, Standa** and **Coin.** They offer fairly reasonable prices but are some way from the centre. Addresses of major shops and department stores are listed by category in 'Rome Addresses' at the end of the guide, p. 196.

Markets

Supermarkets and grocery shops are relatively rare in Rome; thus, people do the bulk of their daily shopping at street markets. There is no better introduction to ordinary life in Rome; you can hardly fail to be charmed by the atmosphere of the markets, which are full of colour, life and good humour. The most famous Roman market is the one at **Campo dei Fiori,** VI, A3, but there are countless others. Some of the best markets are:

● **Mercati Generali,** via Ostiense, I, E3, is the central covered market of Rome. This market opens at 10am daily and offers by far the best value for money, but be prepared for jostling crowds.

● **Mercato dei Fiori,** via Trionfale, III, B1, is a flower market that is open only on Tuesdays from 10.30am-1pm. The prices are very reasonable.

- **Piazza Vittorio Emmanuele,** III, A4, contains the city's most colourful market. It offers a wide range of products at very reasonable prices. The market is open Monday-Saturday 7am-2pm.

- **Porta Portese** is the Roman flea market and is open every Sunday morning.

- **Via Alessandria,** IV, B5, is a small market that nevertheless draws a large crowd. Its prices are slightly higher than elsewhere.

- **Via Andrea Doria,** II, C1, offers everything from fresh produce to silk thread. Renowned for its high quality, this bustling market is open Tuesday-Saturday 8am-1pm.

- **Via Sannio** is a market for new and second-hand clothes. It is open Monday-Friday 8am-1pm and Saturday 8am-7pm.

SPORTS

Soccer

Rome is still a place of violent factional feuding, but nowadays the partisan instinct tends to focus on soccer, not politics. On Sunday afternoons, the fortunes of two local teams (AS Roma and Lazio) are followed with rapt attention by thousands of supporters at the Stadio Olimpico and the Foro Italico. For information, contact the following organizations:

- **Associazione Sportiva Lazio,** via Col di Lana 8, ☎ 38 5141.
- **Associazione Sportiva Roma,** via Circo Massimo 7, ☎ 574 1414.

Tennis

Every year, the international tennis championships are held in the last week of May at the Foro Italico (lungotevere Maresciallo Cadorna, II, B2). For information, either visit or telephone: via Gladiatori 31, ☎ 361 9064.

Racing

The horseracing season (steeplechase, hurdle, flat race) takes place March-June and September-December.

The events take place at the Hippodromo delle Campanelle, via Appia Nuova, II, F6, 7 mi/12 km from the city centre, ☎ 79 4359.

Trotting races are held at the Hippodromo de Tor di Vallem, via del Mare, II, F3, 5.5 mi/9 km from the city centre, ☎ 592 4205.

Horse shows

Every year in the last week of April and the first week of May, European high society may be found near the piazza di Siena, IV, A2, for Rome's International Horse Show. This is an event of major importance in the social and sporting calendar.

Horseback riding

If you are interested in horseback riding, apply to the **Società Ippica Romana,** via Monti della Farnesina, II, B2, ☎ 396 6386, or to the **Villa Borghese Sporting Association,** via del Galoppataio 23, IV, B1-2, ☎ 36 6797.

Golf

If you would like to play golf during your stay in Rome, contact the following organizations:

- **Rome Golf Club,** Acqua Santa, via Appia Nuova 716a, II, EF5-6, ☎ 78 3407 *(closed Mon, except holidays)*.

- **Golf Club Olgiata,** largo dell'Olgiata 15, on the via Cassia, 12 mi/19 km north of Rome *(closed Mon, except holidays)*.

A lively crowd supports the local soccer team.

Swimming

The **Lido di Roma** is in Ostia, 17 mi/28 km south of Rome. It can be reached by metro (Termini station) and by train (Ostiense station, IV, F5). However, you will have to travel much farther if you want to swim in crystal clear water.

Lake Bracciano is 24 mi/39 km along the via Cassia north of Rome. It can be reached by car or by ACOTRAL bus (via Lepanto, on the corner of via G. Cesare, III, B3).

The indoor swimming pool of the **Foro Italico,** lungotevere Maresciallo Cadorna, II, B2, is open November-May, ☎ 360 8591. The outdoor pool is open June-September, ☎ 396 2926.

▬ *TIME*

The time in Rome is one hour ahead of London, six hours ahead of New York, and nine hours ahead of Los Angeles.

▬ *TOILETS*

Except at the Termini railway station, Rome has few public toilets. Bars seldom have their own toilets. In a café, you may have to ask for 'the key' *(la chiave).* Some museums provide toilet facilities.

▬▬ TOURIST INFORMATION

For fuller information on any of the topics discussed in this guide, refer to the offices of the **EPT** *(Ente Provinciale per il Turismo):*

- via Parigi 5, IV, D4, ☎ 46 1851.
- Termini railway station, IV, E5, ☎ 46 5461.
- Leonardo da Vinci Airport, Fiumicino, ☎ 601 1255.

The EPT puts out a number of publications, among them a free monthly brochure entitled *Carnet di Roma e del Lazio,* published in English as well as Italian, which lists cultural events in the city.

See also p. 26 for information concerning the **Italian National Tourist Office.**

▬▬ WORSHIPPING

Catholic

- St John Lateran, V, C5
- St Peters, V, C5
- San Silvestro in Capite, III, E6
- Santa Maria Maggiore, IV, E4
- Sant'Anselmo, VI, D4
- Sant'Apollinaro, III, E5
- Trinità dei Monti, IV, C1

Papal audiences

These take place once a week on Wednesdays at 11am, either on St Peter's Square or in the Audience Room. When the Pope is at his residence of Castel Gandolfo, audiences are fixed at 10am on Wednesdays.

Seats can be booked at the sacristy of **San Luigi dei Francesi** or at the **Prefettura della Casa Pontificia** in Vatican City, ☎ 6982. Reservations must be made one week in advance.

Eastern Orthodox

- Santa Maria in Cosmedin, VI, C5, ☎ 678 1419.
- Sant'Anastasio al Babuino, III, C6, ☎ 679 5355.

Protestant

- All Saints Church of England, III, C6, ☎ 679 4357.
- S. Paolo, IV, E3, ☎ 46 3339.

Jewish

- Lungotevere Sanzio 9, IV, B3, ☎ 580 3662.
- Oratorio Ashkenazita, IV, E3, ☎ 475 9881.

Islamic

- Via Conca 6, II, B3

ROME IN THE PAST

EARLY ROME

According to legend, Rome was founded in 754 BC, when Romulus traced the perimeter of the city on the Palatine hill. The legend began with two splashes in the Tiber River, as the baby twins Romulus and Remus were tossed into the swirling waters by their usurping uncle. Instead of drowning, however, the hardy twins washed ashore at the foot of the Palatine hill. Here they were found and suckled by a she-wolf before being adopted by shepherds. When the brothers reached manhood, they successfully avenged themselves on their uncle. Afterwards they returned to found a city in the place they had known as children, marking out its sacred contours with the assistance of a flock of birds. Some time later, Remus angered the gods by crossing a furrow that Romulus had ploughed, thereby condemning himself to death at the hands of his brother—in 753 BC, according to tradition. With this mythical fratricide, the history of Rome began.

Historically speaking, the earliest nucleus of a Roman community probably consisted of a small group of Latin shepherds who may have settled on the Palatine hill because it afforded protection against the flooding Tiber; in any event, excavations have revealed vestiges of human occupation that date from the 8th century BC.

Other clans, such as the Sabines from the north, lived on other hills in the vicinity (Caelian, Quirinal and Esquiline). A degree of contact and trade was maintained between these settlements, but there was no real urban organization.

In the late 7th century BC, Etruscan kings annexed the area during their advance towards the south of Italy. They built a port on the Tiber and drained the marshy plain, providing the local communities with a place to meet, thus stimulating a variety of commercial, political and religious activities. A temple was built and dedicated to Jupiter, and with its completion, the city of Rome came into being. Subsequently, King Servius erected the first protective ramparts; some vestiges of these remain today.

In 509 BC, the 'patrician' families of Rome abolished the Etruscan kingdom and established republican institutions. The great adventure of Rome had begun.

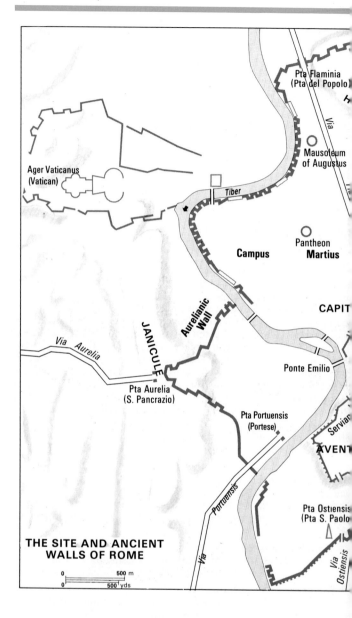

THE SITE AND ANCIENT
WALLS OF ROME

0   500 m
0   500 yds

THE ROMAN REPUBLIC

The first years of the republic were difficult and dangerous.
Rome was a small town dependent on its own resources and
surrounded by volatile neighbours. The rivalries and ambitions of
the various tribes and cities in the region were eventually settled by
force. The gods favoured Rome. The Romans gratefully acknow-

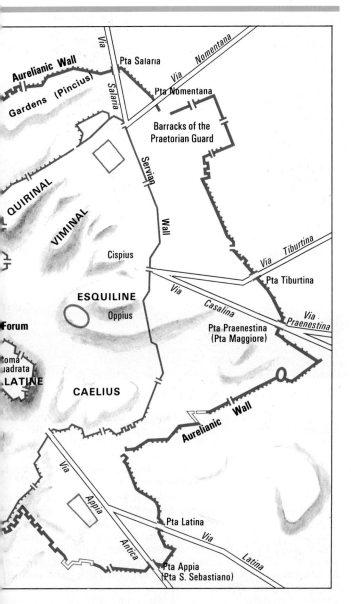

edged the gods' assistance by erecting new temples to commemorate their victories.

The succession of wars was followed by the internal social
upheavals of the 5th century BC, which pitted patricians and
plebians against each other. These conflicts were finally resolved
through the Law of the Twelve Tables, a political compromise that
proclaimed civil equality between the two social groups.

Monumental design and a sense of volume characterize the architecture of the ancient Roman Forum.

In 390 BC, Rome was sacked by the Gauls. Though devastated, the city recovered and became, by the 3rd century BC, the dominant power in southern Italy. From here, Rome embarked on the conquest of the Mediterranean world. The annexation of Greece and the obliteration in 146 BC of Rome's African rival, Carthage, secured Rome's supremacy.

Ironically, Rome's victories abroad led to a serious crisis at home. Farmers were ruined by war and by the unfair competition of products pillaged from conquered countries. The population of Rome was swollen by a flood of unemployed people. A taste for luxury gradually eroded the traditional values of the little republic and, at the same time, Rome's institutions were ill-suited to control its new empire. The result was a period of intrigue, with conflicts between private armies, political assassinations and attempted coups d'état. Julius Caesar, an ambitious and talented leader, tried to install a monarchy with himself at its head but only succeeded in provoking a final republican backlash. Caesar's assassination in 44 BC achieved nothing and led to further struggle between the aspirants to his legacy.

THE ROMAN EMPIRE

Octavius learned the lesson of Caesar's failure. Carefully avoiding any allusion to monarchy, which might recall the shameful era of the Etruscan kings, he preserved a façade of republicanism posing as the defender of traditional Roman values, and gradually accumulated real power in his own hands. Thus in 27 BC, the Senate invested him with the title of Augustus, and the Roman Empire was born.

Augustus imposed *pax romana* (Roman peace) on all the provinces of the empire and reorganized their administrations. In Rome, he joined with his friend Maecenas in patronizing the arts: Virgil, Horace, Livy and Ovid thrived under their protection, as did countless architects, painters and sculptors. The period between 27 BC and AD 14 marked the Golden Age of Roman culture.

Augustus's successors included several tyrants and madmen, namely Caligula, Nero and Domitian, as well as a number of solid strategists and efficient administrators, such as Tiberius, Vespasian and Titus. The empire attained its apogee and largest extent of territory in the 2nd century. The Antonine dynasty built up and ran a huge administrative machine. The most distinguished of the Antonines was Trajan (AD 98-117), the 'greatest of the emperors', a brilliant general and a tireless builder. His successor, Hadrian (AD 117-137), was an aesthete and lover of Greece, as well as an excellent administrator.

The imperial system was composed of many contradictions, and even the best of the emperors could only delay their inevitable effects. The absence of an irrevocable law of succession encouraged the ambitions of victorious generals and provided fertile soil for rebellion. The concentration of absolute power in the hands of a single man tended to weaken the empire whenever that man was unequal to the task. The constant threat of barbarian invasion sometimes obliged Roman emperors to spend their entire reigns campaigning with their armies. In Rome itself, luxury, moral dissolution and public and private excess bred an ever-increasing slave population. The gulf between the opulent governing class and its many dependents slowly widened. In the 5th century, the frontiers began to crumble. Rome's dominions were ravaged in AD 410 by Alaric, and the city was finally sacked in AD 455 by the Vandal chieftain, Genseric.

THE CONVERSION OF ROME

Religious cults from every corner of the empire proliferated in Rome, bringing with them their rituals, their gods and their mysteries. Such cults were tolerated, provided they posed no threat to the official religion, of which the emperor, as *pontifex maximus* (highest priest), was the titular head. The authorities were not always able to make sense of this vast cultural mosaic; thus Christianity, a small sect deriving from Judaism, was frequently confused with the parent religion.

The Roman biographer and historian Suetonius informs us that the Emperor Claudius (AD 41-54) 'banished certain Jews' from Rome who had been exhorted to rebel by one of their number named Chrestos. Jesus had been crucified in AD 30, but the apostles continued to preach in his name. The sect of Chrestos believed in a single god who had sent his own son to live among men with a message of brotherly love and the hope of life after death.

This message spread rapidly through every level of Roman society. Unlike other religions, Christianity shocked the Roman establishment by its refusal to recognize and give honour to the official gods of the empire, and the administration soon began to take discriminatory measures against the sect. Outright persecution began in AD 64, when Nero seized on Christians as victims for a campaign of demented cruelty. Subsequent emperors, among them Domitian (AD 81-96) and Diocletian (AD 284-304), sought to oppose the expansion of Christianity by administrative strictures and brutal persecution, but to no avail. In the 4th century, the empire's rulers bowed to the inevitable: after his victory over Maxentius in AD 312, Constantine granted Christians the freedom to practice their religion. Shortly thereafter Constantine himself was converted (AD 314).

After Constantine, all attempts to restore paganism failed. With Theodosius (AD 379-395), the last emperor to reign over a united Roman Empire and the first to discard the pagan title of *pontifex maximus,* paganism began to be the object of persecution by Christianity.

MEDIAEVAL ROME

From AD 330 onwards, the seat of the empire shifted from Rome to Byzantium, which was renamed Constantinople. On the death of Theodosius (AD 395), the empire was divided between his two sons, Arcadius taking the eastern regions, and Honorius the western. Honorius installed his administration in Ravenna, but the western empire proved ephemeral and was quickly overwhelmed by the barbarian hordes that entered Italy in the 5th century. Romulus Augustulus, its last emperor, was deposed in AD 476 by the German chieftain, Odoacer.

In AD 552, the Byzantine emperor took Italy from the Goths as a result, Rome became no more than another Byzantine city ruled from Constantinople. The population of Rome had been reduced to barely more than 20,000. Gradually, thereafter, the successors of Saint Peter detached themselves from Byzantine tutelage. When they turned for protection to such potentates from the west as Pépin le Bref and Charlemagne, a decisive step was taken. Charlemagne's coronation in Rome as Emperor in AD 800 by Pope Leo III assured the temporal power of the popes. The temporal security gained by the Roman popes was, however, of short duration. In AD 846, Saracen invaders sacked the basilica of Constantine. In response, Pope Leo IV, in AD 847, walled the part of Rome he occupied, so creating the Vatican.

From the 10th century onwards, Rome was dominated by powerful families who fought among themselves for control of the papacy. The King of Germania took advantage of this state of affairs to reconquer Italy and revive the old western empire, which became the Holy Roman Empire in the 14th century. In the 11th century, the Investiture Dispute (in which the pope claimed the right to crown the emperor, and the emperor countered by claiming the power to confirm or deny the election of each new pope) led to a long struggle for ascendancy between the Holy See and the German princes. This dispute served as a pretext for more invasions of Italy, and dangerous political alliances were made by the papacy. Rome paid a heavy price, undergoing constant sieges and changing hands several times during this period. The emperor had himself crowned in Rome, imposed his own nominee as anti-pope and intervened in the wars between the various aristocratic factions. As a result, the papal court was exiled, first to Viterbo, then to Orvieto and Perugia, finally coming to rest in Avignon, France, in 1309.

During this period, an independent power bloc of ordinary citizens and merchants, which had been firmly established in the capital since 1143, sought to install a Roman republic and restore the ancient influence of the Senate (1347). This adventure was brought to an abrupt end in 1354 when the Tribune, Cola di Rienzo, was assassinated.

THE ROMAN RENAISSANCE

When the papacy returned to Rome in 1377, the Middle Ages were already drawing to a close. After the Great Schism (1378-1417), which had divided the loyalties of Europe between two and sometimes three rival popes, the pontiffs set about restoring the full authority of the Holy See. They used contemporary methods: intrigue, hard bargaining, dubious alliances and the politics of prestige and princely patronage. At the same time, they took care to harness Rome itself—which emerged from the Middle Ages as one of the poorest cities in Europe—to the great movement that was transforming the other urban centres of Italy during the 15th century.

Under Pope Nicolas V (1447-1455), a blueprint was established for the city with the Vatican as the focus for a maze of convergent roads. Although this project was never completed, its existence demonstrated a renewed confidence in the city's future. Palaces were erected all over the city, replacing the old mediaeval fortresses. Among them were the Palazzo Venezia (mid 15th century) and the Palazzo della Cancelleria (late 15th century). Fountains were restored to working order. With renewed economic activity, the piazza Navona was paved, a flourishing market was set up at its centre, and shops began to open around its perimeter. Pope Paul II (1464-1471) widened the via Lata (today's via del Corso) to accommodate horse racing. Religious architecture flowered under Pope Sixtus IV (1471-1484). Santa Maria del Popolo, Sant' Agostino, San Pietro in Montorio, Santa Maria della Pace and the Sistine Chapel were all begun during this period.

When Pope Julius II took over at the beginning of the 16th century, immense building projects were undertaken—projects that matched the growth of the Holy See's political power. Europe's greatest artists flocked to Rome. Bramante was commissioned to construct St Peter's and Michelangelo to build a huge mausoleum (of which his *Moses* was only a detail), to be placed under the dome of the basilica. Raphaël was hired to paint the papal apartments.

In short, Rome had become the centre of European humanism. Architects studied her antique monuments, painters sought inspiration from the frescos of Nero's Domus Aurea, and sculptors reveled in such events as the discovery of the ancient sculpture of *Laocoon* in 1506. Pope Leo X (1513-1521), who succeeded Julius II, was a fervent admirer of antiquity who surrounded himself with artists and scholars. The Roman Renaissance appeared to have reached its zenith when suddenly disaster struck.

SPIRITUAL RECONQUEST

On May 7, 1527, the imperial footsoldiers of the Constable de Bourbon sacked Rome with the approval of Charles V, the Holy Roman Emperor. When the troops finally departed in February 1528, loaded with gold and other booty, Rome had been bled dry. There was an imminent threat of plague because the city's drinking fountains were destroyed. Significantly, on the frescos of the papal apartments painted by Raphaël, the name of Luther was scrawled. Only 10 years before, Luther had published his 95 Theses, which opposed the sale of indulgences by the Vatican to finance the building of St Peter's.

It was now up to the church to act decisively. Without repudiating the Renaissance, the papal authorities set up the Council of Trent (1545-1563) and began a comprehensive drive for spiritual regeneration, the ultimate aim of which was to reassert the pope's supreme authority and confront the challenge of Protestant-ism. This period of Catholic Counter-Reformation was spearhead-ed by the militant missionary orders, especially the Jesuits. Stringent new rules of decency in painting and sculpture completed the break with the Renaissance. Saints could no longer be depicted as handsome, scantily dressed young men; the Virgin had to be shown upright and resolute before the corpse of her son, instead of weeping on her knees; and scenes of martyrdom could no longer be idealized.

After 1585, Pope Sixtus V set the stamp of spiritual reconquest firmly on the topography of Rome itself. Broad avenues were laid through the city to connect the great basilicas and the principal points of the new network were marked by obelisks.

After the sack of the city in 1527 and the spread of Spanish hegemony in Italy, Rome as a political entity ceased to exist. All the city's energies were concentrated on the development of its power as the spiritual focus of Christendom.

THE TRIUMPH OF ROME

When Urban VIII became pope in 1624, the period of Counter-Reformation austerity came to an end. The election of this humanist pontiff, a great patron of the arts, coincided with the coming of a new sense of optimism. This optimism gave heart to the Catholic monarchies of Europe. For the next two centuries, the Roman Baroque style came to epitomize the ostentatious self-confidence of a reinvigorated Catholic church. Cortone, Bernini, Borromini and their followers, who were the principal architects of the Baroque, vied in works of marble and limestone to celebrate the certainties of the faith and the fame of the aristocratic Roman families who took turns supplying the world with popes.

ROME AGAINST ITALY

In 1814, after Napoleon's short-lived annexation of the papal states, the rights and prerogatives of the Holy See were restored. The process of Italian unification, centred on the Kingdom of Piedmont and Sardinia, was soon, however, to alter the traditional political alignments on the peninsula. Rome became a centre of the nationalist movement. A republic was proclaimed there in 1849, and the pope was forced to flee the city. The restoration of his power in 1850, under the military aegis of France, decisively lowered his stature in the eyes of the Italian patriots. As a result,

Chronology of historical events

754 BC	Rome founded by Romulus.
509 BC	Establishment of Roman republic.
390 BC	Rome is sacked by the Gauls.
146 BC	Destruction of Carthage by the Romans.
58-51 BC	Caesar's conquest of Gaul.
49 BC	Caesar assumes dictatorial powers.
44 BC	Caesar is assassinated.
27 BC	Octavius receives title of Augustus and the Roman Empire is founded.
AD 30	Jesus is crucified.
AD 64	Nero sets fire to Rome.
AD 72-80	Coliseum is constructed.
AD 312	Constantine reunifies the Empire.
AD 313	Constantine decrees religious freedom in the Edict of Milan.
AD 330	Constantine moves the capital to Byzantium.
AD 395	Empire is divided on death of Theodosius.
AD 455	Vandals sack Rome.
AD 476	End of the western empire.
AD 553	Byzantium reconquers Italy.
AD 800	Charlemagne is crowned Holy Roman Emperor in Rome.
1075-1122	Investitures Dispute.
1143	The Roman commune is established.
1309	Pope Clement V is installed at Avignon, France.
1378	The Great Schism: two rival popes.
1414	The Council of Constance brings an end to the Great Schism.
1420	The papacy returns to Rome.
1471-1484	Pope Sixtus IV. Construction of the Sistine Chapel.
1503-1513	Pope Julius II.
1527	Sack of Rome by soldiers under Charles V.
1545-1563	The Council of Trent.
1585-1590	The authority of the Holy See is re-affirmed during the pontificate of Sixtus V.
1655-1667	Pope Alexander VII.
1657	Bernini begins work on St Peter's Square.
1798	Proclamation of the Roman republic.
1809	French troops occupy Rome.
1849	The republic is proclaimed once again.
1871	Rome becomes the capital of the Kingdom of Italy.
1922	Mussolini 'marches on Rome'.
1922-1943	Fascist government.
1929	Lateran Treaties establish the Vatican City as a free state.
1946	Rome becomes the capital of the Italian Republic.
1948	First parliament elected.

the Vatican was gradually stripped of its papal states, which were subsequently absorbed into the new Kingdom of Italy. In 1870, the Italian army entered the city. The pope, deprived of every vestige of temporal power, had to retreat behind the walls of the Vatican. In 1871, Rome became the capital of Italy.

FROM FASCISM TO THE REPUBLIC

The destiny of Rome was henceforward to be linked to the nation. During the fascist interlude (1922-1943), there was much pointless destruction of the city's mediaeval, Renaissance and Baroque districts. South of Rome, an entirely new area, the EUR *(Esposizione Universale di Roma),* was erected for the 1942 Universal Exhibition (which never took place). Its functional, neo-Classical, and monumental architecture exemplifies the utopian attitude to urban planning.

After World War II, Rome became the capital of a new republic (1946) and remains the centre of Italian legislative and executive power.

ROME TODAY

TWO CAPITALS

In 1871, when Rome became the capital of a united Italy, its population was barely 200,000. Today, this figure has increased to more than 3,500,000.

Rome is not only a political capital, but is also a religious one. The Vatican, which is the headquarters of the Catholic Church and the residence of the pope, forms an integral part of the city, although it is separated from the seven hills by the Tiber River.

Among the permanent residents of Rome are the corps of foreign diplomats assigned to the Quirinale and the Holy See, along with thousands of other officials who work for the various Rome-based international organizations (notably the Food and Agriculture Organization, or FAO). In addition, there is a large population of men and women belonging to the city's many religious orders and communities.

This function as a double capital, along with an incredibly rich and varied history, gives Rome a special character.

ROME'S TOPOGRAPHY

Rome's centre is still bounded by Aurelian's wall, built in the 3rd century AD as a defense against invading barbarians. This wall still serves as an administrative boundary, defining the city's various districts, suburbs and outlying areas. It is also an example of how Rome contrives to blend the past with the present. Two of its original 10 gates, the Porta Latina and the Porta Flaminia (now known as the Porta del Popolo) are used daily by Romans on their way in and out of the busiest central areas.

The Grande Raccordo Anulare is the main road that encircles Rome. Beyond it, the commune of Rome embraces the Agro Romano, a district only recently reclaimed from marshland and still sparsely inhabited. While strolling here, you might find yourself face to face with a flock of sheep grazing peacefully just outside the city limits. Few other world capitals can offer so abrupt a transition from town to countryside.

THE EXPANSION OF ROME

In 1870, Rome was a provincial city, in no way prepared for its destiny. Over the last 100 years, however, constant building and planning have changed the shape of the city, endowing it with museums, theatres, galleries, public buildings and residences. There has also been considerable property speculation, which has led to uncontrolled development; indeed, much of the earlier, worthier Roman architecture has been effectively smothered by a riot of new construction. All the same, archaeological excavations and restoration projects have continued apace and, in general, Rome still gives a powerful impression of dignity.

Roman town planning has tended to alternate park zones, districts with villas, and areas of high population density. The more affluent citizens live in or near the centre, while the less fortunate occupy the peripheral areas.

The development of Rome has caused many problems, most of which the city has been unable to solve. The historical centre has been invaded by offices; public transportation is woefully inadequate; and the street and traffic systems remain incoherent. Nonetheless, Rome's small shopkeepers, craftsmen and artisans continue to flourish, and this adds a provincial touch which is reinforced by the many residential zones and the city's relative calm after dark.

THE ROMAN ECONOMY

The Agro Romano area has preserved its traditional economy: agriculture based upon small, family-run farms. In fact, as much as 2% of the Roman population is employed in agriculture, a record for a European capital.

Rome also holds another record for the huge number of people employed in the administrative and service sectors (75%). Industry, a sector that has only recently developed, only employs 16% of the Roman workforce. In the early 1960s, an overall plan was adopted to develop industry northwards along the Tiber, southwards along the via Pontina (as far as Acilia and Fiumicino), and westwards to Pantonograno. After 1965, a number of industries sprang up between Rome and Latina, manufacturing construction materials, machinery, printing plants, textiles, processed foods and timber products. Film studios, too, are economically important here. Economists nicknamed the area the 'Tiburtina Valley', after Tiburtina, an ancient consular thoroughfare, and California's Silicon Valley. The area has become famous as a base for small, competitive, high-tech companies.

LIVING AS THE ROMANS DO

St Peter's, the Forums, the Coliseum, the Trevi Fountain and Castel Sant'Angelo are all majestic sights in the best postcard tradition, but they should not blind you to the Eternal City's other, less obvious assets. Those who take the trouble to examine this quintessentially southern capital will discover a world of characteristic colour and sensation, and enough esoteric interest to last a lifetime. There is only one condition to this discovery: you must participate wholeheartedly in the underlying rhythm of Roman life. What follows are some basic hints on how to do this.

First, Rome is best visited on foot. The historical centre is roughly circumscribed by piazza di Spagna, piazza di Trevi, piazza Venezia, piazza Farnese, piazza Navona and piazza del Popolo. Most of this area is reserved for pedestrians, though it is also the scene of constant guerilla warfare between Roman motorists and the local authorities. The main streets of the city (vias Veneto, Nazionale, del Corso and del Tritone) all converge on the centre, although the actual heart of the city consists of a maze of mostly uneven cobbled streets, without sidewalks. Whether you are searching for imperial, mediaeval, Baroque or modern Rome, you will find that the city does not easily yield the secrets of its past. Your best policy is to set out with no particular destination and see what you can see.

You will soon discover that water is an essential feature of the Roman landscape. There are fountains round every corner and in every piazza, to delight the eye and soften the din of the traffic, and close by you will always find a café with tables set in the sun. In Rome, as elsewhere in Italy, *cappuccino* is an institution, drunk preferably in neighbourhood *caffés*. These invariably stay open until the small hours, catering to late strollers, theatregoers and revellers. The *caffés* on piazza di Panteone, piazza de Santa Maria in Trastevere and along the via Veneto are among the best spots from which to observe the endless variety of Rome's street life.

Another cherished aspect of the Roman art of living is the street market (see pp. 41-42). The market in piazza Campo dei Fiori is one of the oldest. Most Romans prefer to do their shopping in the open air. In the side alleys, you can find furniture restorers, gilders, framers, bookbinders, marble cutters and woodcarvers, the heirs of venerable Roman traditions. Some of the streets are named after the professions they once housed: *Cappelari* (hatters), *Vaccinari* (tanners), *Giubbonari* (tailors), *Coronari* (rosary-makers), and many more. The Sunday morning flea market at the Porta Portese (see p. 42) is another institution dear to the Romans. Here, you can find just about anything for sale, and can feast afterwards on *porchetta,* pieces of grilled pork that are sold in the streets.

Don't miss the piazza di Spagna, especially in April, when the steps are festooned with azaleas. The streets leading off this square are home to some of the greatest names in Italian luxury goods (Gucci, Ferragamo, Valentino, Bulgari). Of these streets, via dei Condotti is perhaps the most fashionable, because it is the site of the Caffé Greco, a fixture of Roman life for as long as anyone can remember.

Rome would not be Rome without its great gardens and villas—Villa Borghese, Villa Celimontana and Villa Doria Pamphili, among others—which not so long ago were privately owned by the city's more illustrious families. Romans seldom miss a chance to stroll among the huge parasol pines of these much-loved parks, which are somehow as naturally integrated into modern Rome as

A picturesque view of everyday life in Rome.

the great monuments of antiquity. On a typical sunny day, the gardens will be full of Romans from every walk of life, many attracted by the various horse shows, exhibitions, puppet theatres and other events that occur there throughout the year.

In the evening, the streets of the working-class Trastevere district quickly fill with people heading for their favourite trattorias. When you have sampled some Roman specialities, you still have the rest of the evening to wander through the lively backstreets where the *Romani di Roma* live. You will find them impulsive, generous, mocking, nonchalant, fatalistic, even cynical—but these are the real Romans, many of whose families have lived in this same place for generations.

Finally, at the close of a long day, you can go for a last look at the city's roofs and domes from the terrace of the Pincio. Of all Rome's views, this is indisputably the loveliest. Any Roman will tell you so.

ROME'S GREAT CREATIVE GENIUSES OF THE 16th AND 17th CENTURIES

A mong the countless artists who worked in Rome during the 16th and 17th centuries, the legacy of a few has proved vitally important in shaping the city we see today. Evidence of their work can be seen in the greatest churches, palaces and piazzas of Rome.

Donato di Angelo Bramante (1444-1514), architect

Bramante was brought to Rome by Pope Julius II to supervise the construction of St Peter's. He designed a building in the form of a Greek cross, with a great central dome and four smaller cupolas.

Bramante went on to build the Tempietto, near San Pietro in Montorio, the cloister of Santa Maria della Pace, the loggia of Julius II at Castel Sant'Angelo, and the inner courtyard and stairway of the Belvedere in Vatican City.

Bramante represents Renaissance art at its most harmonious, his work being notable for its perfect mastery of proportion.

Raffaello Sanzio, known as **Raphaël** (1483-1520), painter and architect

Raphaël spent his apprenticeship in Umbria and was a pupil of the painter Perugino. He was brought to Rome by Julius II to decorate the *stanze* of his palace at the Vatican (1508-1514). From 1514 until his death, Raphaël supervised work on St Peter's and completed the loggias at the Vatican begun by Bramante. He was also commissioned by the banker Chigi to work on the churches of La Farnesina and Santa Maria della Pace (first chapel on the right), and completed Chigi's chapel at Santa Maria del Popolo.

A number of Raphaël's paintings are exhibited at the Vatican Pinacoteca and in the Borghese and Barberini galleries.

Antonio da Sangallo the Younger (1483-1546), architect

Sangallo was indisputably the most important architect of the Renaissance, after Bramante and Michelangelo. He began as Bramante's pupil, and later worked with Raphaël at St Peter's. Santa Maria di Loreto (1507) was built according to his design and he started the work on the Palazzo Farnese in 1512.

After the death of Raphaël, Sangallo became the chief architect of St Peter's. He completed the arch spanning the central transept and added the upper stories around the courtyards of San

Damaso and the Belvedere. He later designed the tombs of Leo X and Clement VII at Santa Maria Sopra Minerva, and laid out vias Baullari, Babuino and Condotti.

Michelangelo Buonarroti, known as **Michelangelo** (1475-1564), sculptor, painter, architect and poet

Michelangelo began his career as the apprentice of Ghirlandio. Later he went to Florence to work for Lorenzo di Medici. After 1496, he divided his time between Rome and Florence and created many masterpieces in both cities.

Michelangelo's legacy to Rome includes the following:

Architecture

● Piazza del Campidoglio.

● Palazzo Farnese: central loggia, exterior cornice, top floor of the inner courtyard.

● St Peter's: the tambour of the dome, the transept and part of the nave.

● Santa Maria degli Angeli.

Painting

● Ceiling of the Sistine Chapel.

● *The Last Judgment* in the Sistine Chapel.

● The Pauline Chapel at the Vatican.

Sculpture

● *The Pietà* at St Peter's.

● *Moses* for the tomb of Julius II at San Pietro in Vincoli.

Giacomo Barozzi da Vignola (1507-1573), architect

Vignola was an architect of the period of the Counter-Reformation. He first came to Rome in 1530 and settled permanently in 1550. With Ammanati, he designed the Villa di Papa Giulio for Pope Julius III. Vignola's most important work in Rome is the church of the Gesu (1565-1573), commissioned by the Jesuits.

Giacomo della Porta (1540-1602), architect

Della Porta, a pupil of Vignola, completed most of the buildings that were left unfinished by Michelangelo. He designed the façade, the cupola and some of the chapels of the church of the Gesu and the façade of San Luigi dei Francesi (1589). He also completed San Giovanni dei Fiorentini (1589), built the courtyard of the University of La Sapienza (1587), and worked with Fontana to finish the cupola of St Peter's (1588-1590). He completed the Palazzo dei Conservatore (1563) and the façade of the senatorial palace (1582-1602). Della Porta was also responsible for some of the fountains of Rome.

Carlo Maderno (1556-1629), architect

Maderno designed the façade of the church of Santa Susanna (1603) and was responsible for the construction of the church of La Trinità dei Monti and the cupola of Sant'Andrea della Valle. At St Peter's, he lengthened the nave and installed the façade. In 1625, Maderno began work on the Palazzo Barberini.

Domenico Fontana (1543-1607), architect

Fontana was responsible for paving no fewer than 120 streets in Rome. In addition, he raised obelisks in St Peter's Square, in the piazza del Popolo, and in front of the churches of Santa Maria Maggiore and San Giovanni in Laterano.

He also built part of the Quirinale, was employed on the Lateran Palace, completed the dome of St Peter's, and built the Vatican Library building, which divided the great courtyard of Bramante's Belvedere into two.

Michelangelo Merisi, known as **Caravaggio** (1573-1610), painter

Caravaggio arrived in Rome at the age of 16, after serving a four-year apprenticeship to a painter from Bergamo. His early works celebrated the beauty and harmony of the human body.

In 1598, he received his first important commission for the church of San Luigi dei Francesi. Caravaggio's nonconformist painting seems almost provocative in the severe context of the Counter-Reformation through which he lived. His figures are spontaneous and free from convention; the models for his saints are ordinary people, and his religious scenes are drawn from everyday life.

Caravaggio had a gloomy and quarrelsome nature, and it soon involved him in difficulties. Having killed a man, he fled to Malta. Later, in 1610, Caravaggio died of fever when travelling back to Rome.

Caravaggio's paintings may be seen at the pinacotecas of the Capitol and the Vatican, in the Borghese and Barberini galleries and in the churches of San Luigi dei Francesi, Santa Maria del Popolo and Sant'Agostino.

Pietro di Cortona (1596-1669), painter and architect

Di Cortona was one of the principal masters of Roman Baroque. Among his architectural works are the church of Ss. Luca e Martina, the façade of Santa Maria della Pace (1655), Santa Maria in Via Lata (1656-1662) and the cupola of San Carlo al Corso (1668). As a painter, he was responsible for decorating the apse of La Chiesa Nuova (1633-1655), the salon of the Palazzo Barberini (1632-1639), and certain rooms in the Palazzo Pamphili and the Quirinale.

Gian Lorenzo Bernini (1598-1680), architect, painter and sculptor

Bernini, an extremely ambitious man, was an accomplished courtier. He was commissioned by several rich patrons (notably Urban VIII and Alexander VII) and had many pupils who helped him realize his projects. Rome owes many of its masterpieces to Bernini.

Churches

● St Peter's: the bronze baldachin, the decoration of the pillars in the chancel, the chair of St Peter, the tombs of Urban VIII and Alexander VII and the equestrian statue of Constantine under the portico.

● Sant'Andrea al Quirinale.

● Santa Maria del Popolo (restoration).

A 19th-century water nymph adorns a fountain in the piazza della Repubblica.

Palazzos

- Palazzo Barberini: the façade and staircase.
- The Quirinale: the loggia.
- Palazzo Propaganda di Fide: the façade.

Sculpture

- Fountain of the Triton on the piazza Barberini.
- Four Rivers Fountain and the Fountain of the Moor on the piazza Navona.

- *Apollo and Daphne* and *The Rape of Persephone* at the Borghese Gallery.
- *The Ecstasy of St Teresa* at Santa Maria della Vittoria.
- *Ludovica Albertoni* at San Francesco a Ripa.

Francesco Borromini (1599-1667), architect

Borromini was one of the greatest architects of the Roman Baroque style, although he was to some extent overshadowed by his rival Bernini.

Born in the area of Ticino (now in Switzerland), Borromini began his career as a stonecutter working on the construction of St Peter's. His principal employer was Pope Innocent X, but he also received commissions from convents and religious communities, usually for small chapels and oratories. Borromini pushed to extremes the possibilities inherent in architecture for the animation of volumes and the use of light. He was content to work with modest materials like brick, and he frequently omitted decoration. He drew most of his inspiration from antiquity—for example, the Villa Adriana at Tivoli or the Temple at Baalbec. An anxious, solitary character, Borromini eventually committed suicide.

Churches and oratories

- San Carlino (1634-1667).
- Sant'Ivo della Sapienza (1642-1662).
- Sant'Agnese in Agone (1653-1661).
- San Giovanni in Laterano (restoration).

Palazzos

- Palazzo Barberini: spiral staircase.
- Palazzo Spada: Perspective Gallery.
- Palazzo Falconieri: enlargement.
- Palazzo Propaganda di Fide: side façade and the Chapel of the Magi.

I
THE HEART OF ANCIENT ROME

The Forum, the Palatine hill

The overgrown, scattered ruins of the Forum and the Palatine hill may at first seem disconcerting. Once you get over your surprise, however, you will quickly fall under the tranquil spell of the site, with its still-magnificent reminders of republican and imperial Rome.

Access

Map VI, AB5-6. Bus: 11, 27, 81, 85, 87, 186. Metro: Colosseo (line B).

▰▰ FORO ROMANO (The Forum) VI, AB5-6

Entrance by the via dei Fori Imperiali. *Open Wed-Mon 9am (Sun 10am)-1 hour before sunset.*

Before you enter the Forum from via dei Fori Imperiali, we suggest that you take a look at the view from the terrace of the **Capitol** (access by via S. Pietro in Carcere). An unforgettable panorama extends between the via dei Fori Imperiali, on the left, the wooded Palatine hill, on the right, with the Coliseum in the background. This is well worth a visit at sunset.

When Rome was founded (754 BC), the marshy valley between the Capitol and the Palatine hill was used as a burial place by the people living on the surrounding hills. A century later, the marsh was drained by the Etruscans, who also built a dirt roadway across the area. This thoroughfare quickly became a meeting place for traders and the nucleus around which the city of Rome grew.

Under the Etruscans, considerable public works were undertaken, notably the construction of a drainage system for the marshy subsoil. The largest of the drainage systems dug at this time was known as the *cloaca maxima*. The embryonic city was then organized into working subdivisions: the **Comitia**, at the foot of the Capitol, was set apart for political activities, while the **Forum** was reserved as a place of business for merchants and traders.

In 509 BC, the Etruscan kings were driven from Rome and replaced by a republican system. The new regime gradually set its mark on the architecture of the Forum with the construction of sanctuaries dedicated to Saturn and to Castor and Pollux. The basements of these sanctuaries can still be seen today. There then followed a period of obscurity, characterized by civil wars and invasions, when little was achieved in the way of building.

The real work on the Forum was accomplished after the Punic Wars against Carthage and the subjugation of the Greek city-states. Rome, as the capital of a huge new empire, finally had to engage in serious town planning. The sanctuary to Castor and Pollux was rebuilt and four basilicas (Porcia, Aemilia, Sempronia and Opimia) were raised (2nd century BC). Later, in the

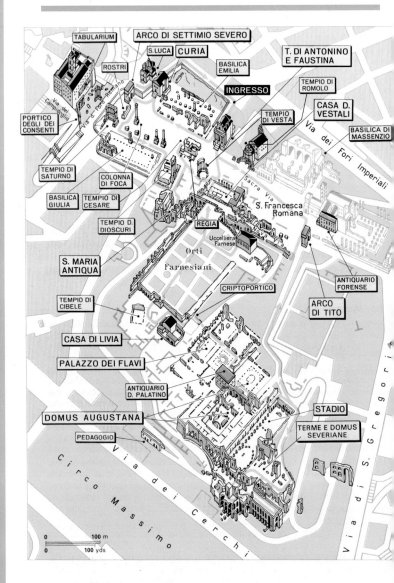

time of Sully (1st century BC), the Tabularium was built and the Capitol was reconstructed.

By the final years of the republic, the Forum no longer satisfied either the empire's administrative needs or its thirst for ostentation. Julius Caesar was the first Roman to promote a concept of town planning that skillfully reconciled Rome's new ambitions with the symbols of her republican past. At Caesar's instigation, a new Forum took the place of the old Comitia, the Curia Hostilia was moved from its original site and a number of temples were rebuilt.

Augustus and his successors altered the aspect of the Forum to suit their own individual and dynastic ambitions; the functional areas of republican political life were gradually overlaid by imperial symbols. Since then, successive catastrophes and invasions, along with the building of Christian sanctuaries and mediaeval fortresses, have slowly shaped the face of modern Rome. Over the years, the monuments have been stripped to embellish churches and palaces. In the 19th century, extensive excavations were undertaken. All these activities contributed to the random piles of broken columns, the grass-covered steps, the half-buried capitals and the heaps of masonry you will see today, haunted and infested after dark by droves of cats.

Ss. Luca e Martina** (St Luke and St Martina)

This was one of the first great churches built in the Roman Baroque style.

After his election as head of the Academy of St Luke in 1634, Pietro di Cortona (see p. 61) decided to reconstruct a small church that had been built originally in the 6th century and dedicated to St Martina. In 1588, the building was entrusted to the Academy of St Luke, which added the name of its own patron saint to the earlier dedication. At first, Cortona was unable to persuade the academy to disburse the necessary funds for the restoration but, soon after, he discovered the remains of St Martina in the crypt. The discovery coming at a time when the struggle against Protestantism ensured veneration of all relics, Cardinal Barberini was easily persuaded to finance the project. The work began in 1635 and was completed in 1650.

Bear in mind while you're looking at this church that the outer shell suffered considerably from the lowering of the ground level around it during the excavation of the Forum in the early 19th century.

The Baroque façade

In spite of its unfinished state—two more bays were planned but never built—the façade of Ss. Luca e Martina incorporates two major departures from conventional Romanesque tradition. First, the façade is not straight, but convex at its centre, a convexity that the church's two side pillars seem to hold in tension. This internal dynamic in the façade has the effect of 'detaching' it from the rest of the building. Second, the orders (columns, pilasters and entablatures) do not fulfill the traditional role of framing the bays (as in the façade of St Peter's), but are instead used to emphasize the central symmetry of the design through a lively play of opposites. Hence, the paired columns on the lower level are set into the main wall and topped by projecting pilasters, while the columns framing the window, with its triangular pediment, prolong the pilaster elements which rest on the curved pediment of the main doorway.

This contrapuntal approach is echoed by the dome of the church, which includes curved decorative motifs in direct opposition to the austere outlines of the window below.

The interior

The interior of Ss. Luca e Martina is in the general form of a Greek cross and painted white. The Ionic, formal rigor of the enclosing space contrasts strongly with the refined juxtaposition of columns, pilasters and wall facings; likewise, the architectural severity of the lower part of the church differs strongly from the decorative profusion of the upper, in which a variety of different motifs appear (e.g., the ribs and caissons of the vaulted ceiling).

Via Sacra

The via Sacra, leading into the Forum, was the most famous street in the ancient world, along which parades and triumphal state processions made their way to the temple of Jupiter Optimus Maximus on the hill of the Capitol.

Basilica Aemilia

This building, which dates from 179 BC, is the only one surviving of the four original basilicas of the republican era. It owes its name to the 'gens Aemilia', the Aemilian family, who restored it on several occasions during Rome's imperial epoch. The ruins you see today date from the restoration of the building after the sack of Rome by Alaric in 410; they give a clear idea of how such basilicas looked in their original state. Essentially, they were broad, covered areas with several distinct annexes, in which merchants and magistrates carried out their daily business. Note that the function of these buildings was in no sense religious.

Tabularium

This imposing edifice was built in 78 BC to overlook the west side of the Forum and housed the Roman state archives. Among these archives were a number of bronze tablets, upon which many of the city's most ancient laws were inscribed: hence the name 'Tabularium'. Today, nothing remains save the foundations and vestiges of the first floor, in the form of an arcaded portico. With its Doric order and peperino stone, the Tabularium is a highly representative example of republican architecture.

Tempio di Vespasiano (Temple of Vespasian)

Three elegant Corinthian columns of white marble, surmounted by an entablature, are all that remain of this temple. The original building was begun in AD 79 by the Emperor Titus and completed by his brother and successor, Domitian. It was dedicated to their father, Vespasian, who had been deified after his death by a decree of the Senate.

The Curia

This massive brick edifice (reconstructed by Diocletian after the great fire of AD 283) was raised by Julius Caesar—hence, its original name of *Curia Julia*. Caesar's building, which was faced in marble, was a replacement for an older curia attributed to the Sabine King Tullus Hostilius (672-640 BC), which burned down in 52 BC.

In the 7th century, the Curia was transformed into the church of S. Adriano. It was not until 1937 that the building reassumed its former aspect. It consists of a wide rectangular hall with a marble floor (restored), low tiers on either side of the hall which accommodated the benches of the senators, statue niches framed by columns and, at the end of the hall facing the door, a rostrum for the magistrate presiding over the session. The original bronze doors were moved to San Giovanni in Laterano by Borromini during that church's restoration; they have been replaced by copies.

The Curia contains bas-relief panels from the time of Trajan, which once adorned the speakers' rostrum. On one side, these depict creatures destined for sacrifice and, on the other, scenes illustrating imperial beneficence—a tax amnesty (left) and charity to poor children (right).

Lapis Niger (Black Stone)

The Lapis Niger is a flagstone of black marble placed opposite the Curia by Caesar to cover certain remains deemed venerable and sacred by the ancients. According to one tradition, the stone marks the tomb of Romulus. In reality, there is a little sanctuary underneath, dating from the 6th century BC and dedicated to Vulcan. Its oldest element is an inscription in archaic characters which promises to reward any profanation of the place with a virulent curse.

Arco di Settimio Severo* (Arch of Septimius Severus)

This massive structure, 69 ft/21 m high and 75 ft/23 m wide, was built in AD 203 in honour of the Emperor Septimius Severus and his two sons, Geta and Caracalla. Caracalla subsequently murdered Geta and erased his name from the arch. Four reliefs, heavily populated with figures, represent the victorious campaigns of Septimius Severus in the Orient. The arch was originally surmounted by a winged victory and a chariot, drawn by eight horses and driven by the emperor and his sons.

Piazza del Foro (The Forum)

The Forum is a rectangular piazza, paved with limestone and dating from the time of Augustus. The column which rises here (**Colonna di Foca**) was the last monument to be erected in the Forum (AD 608). It commemorates the Byzantine emperor Phoca's gift of the Pantheon to the pope and probably came from a much older building, one perhaps from the 2nd century.

Rostri (speakers' platforms)

The word *rostri* comes from the Latin *rostrum,* meaning the prow of a warship, which was usually decorated with victory trophies. The rostri, or speakers' platforms, in Rome originally stood on what is now the site of the Curia and the Lapis Niger. They were brought to their present site during Caesar's reconstruction of the Forum.

Tempio di Saturno (Temple of Saturn)

Only eight granite columns with Ionic capitals remain from the Temple of Saturn, which was built in the first years of the republic and hastily restored after the great fire of AD 283. The state treasury of ancient Rome was originally kept in the temple, and the pagan rites of the 'Saturnales' were celebrated annually on the site.

Basilica Giulia (Julian Basilica)

This building, 327 ft/100 m long and 160 ft/49 m wide, occupies the site of one of the Forum's most ancient basilicas, the Sempronia (169 BC). Begun by Caesar in 54 BC, it was completed by Augustus, destroyed by the great fire of 14 BC and then rebuilt. Destroyed once again by the fire of AD 283, it was restored by Diocletian. Progressive demolition during the Middle Ages, when many of Rome's old stones were dismantled and fed to the lime ovens, has left no trace of the basilica save its podium.

The basilica was originally covered in precious marbles, its main structural features being a great hall surrounded by two concentric porches. During the empire, this building was the headquarters of the Tribunal of the Centumvirate, a court which dealt with civil cases, notably disputes involving successions and inheritances. Ancient graffiti may still be seen on the marble floor, along with traces of *tabulae lusoriae,* or chequerboards, etched into the stone.

Tempio dei Dioscuri** (Temple of the Dioscuri, or Castor and Pollux)

Three fine Corinthian columns in fluted Parian marble are all that remain of the (reconstructed) Temple of the Dioscuri.

The cult of the Dioscuri originated in Greece and appeared in Rome in the early 5th century BC. Tradition states that two mysterious horsemen came to the aid of the Roman forces at the Battle of Lake Regillus (499 BC), at which the Latins allied to Tarquin the Proud were utterly defeated. Later, the pair, who were assumed to be Castor and Pollux, were seen watering their horses at the **Fountain of Juturnus,** close to the site where this temple was erected in their honour in 484 BC.

Santa Maria Antiqua

Santa Maria Antiqua is the oldest church in the Forum, constructed in the 6th century among the outbuildings of the Palace of Tiberius and Caligula. The frescos (6th-8th century) which cover its walls were probably the work of Greek artists driven into exile by persecution. Unfortunately, this church is not open to the public.

Tempio di Cesare (Temple of Caesar)

This temple was built in 29 BC by Augustus, Julius Caesar's heir and successor, on the site where Caesar's body was cremated after his assassination in 44 BC. Augustus's 'deifying' of his predecessor was imitated by many subsequent emperors.

Roman emperors customarily spoke to the people from the podium in front of the Temple of Caesar; this site was sometimes called Caesar's Rostrum because its walls were studded with figureheads from Cleopatra's ships, captured at the Battle of Actium.

Tempio di Vesta** (Temple of Vesta)

A circular building, rebuilt for the last time by Septimius Severus at the beginning of the 3rd century, the Temple of Vesta was a very ancient sanctuary which symbolized the religious unity of the city. A fire was kept perpetually alight here by the Vestal Virgins. Also kept on the premises were certain objects supposedly brought back by Aeneas after the sack of Troy, which were said to have bestowed good fortune on Rome: among these was the famous **Palladion,** an archaic statuette of Minerva.

Casa delle Vestali (House of the Vestals)

The cult of the goddess Vesta was celebrated in a huge two-storey building, with 50 rooms arranged around a rectangular courtyard. At the centre of this courtyard were two pools surrounded by statues of high priestesses.

At first, there were only four Vestal Virgins. Their number later increased to six. They were chosen from among the daughters of patrician families, usually when they were between six and 10 years old. For 30 years after their selection, they would be cut off from all contact with the outside world, under a vow of chastity. Any lapse from this vow was ruthlessly punished; the erring virgin was buried alive and her accomplice flogged to death. If the Vestals ever allowed the flame of the Temple of Vesta to go out—an appalling portent of catastrophe—they felt the whip of the *pontifex maximus* (high priest). In return for the services they rendered the state, the Vestal Virgins were freed from the obligation to obey their fathers, enjoyed handsome pensions and exercised a number of privileges—for example, specially reserved seats at public events and tombs within the city walls. Finally, any man condemned to death who had the good fortune to meet a Vestal Virgin on the way to his execution was always pardoned on the spot.

Regia

Nothing remains of the Regia save its foundations, which lie between the Temple of Caesar and the Temple of Antoninus and Faustina. The Regia was the official headquarters of the *pontifex maximus*, the paramount religious leader of ancient Rome. According to legend, the site was formerly occupied by the palace of Numa Pompilius (715-672 BC), who succeeded Romulus and founded the Roman religion. The archives of the pontiffs were kept in the Regia along with the calendar and annals of the city of Rome. It also housed a sanctuary dedicated to Mars, the god of war, in which the sacred shields of his cult were kept. One of these was reputed to have fallen from heaven; the others were meant to protect such a holy relic from profanation.

Tempio di Antonino e Faustina*
(Temple of Antoninus and Faustina)

The inscription on the architrave of this building dates it to AD 141 when it was built by Emperor Antoninus the Pious and dedicated to his wife, Faustina. On the emperor's death, his name was added to the dedication.

During the 8th century, the temple was converted into a church. Later, the pediment was demolished, though the columns of the façade survived. The present Baroque façade dates from 1602.

All the marble plaques of the temple's outer covering have vanished, but some fine fragments of the original frieze around the coping still remain (griffons, candelabras). The 10 monolithic columns, 56 ft/17 m high, are finished on their bases and capitals in white marble. They exhibit the tendency toward gigantism that characterized imperial architecture, and suggest what the rest of the Forum must have looked like during the late empire period—a small square surrounded by towering, rather heavyset monuments, crammed tightly together.

Restoration work underway in the Forum reveals traces of ancient Rome's grandeur.

Tempio di Romolo (Temple of Romulus)

The Emperor Maxentius raised this temple in the 4th century to honour the memory of his son Romulus, who had died young and been elevated to the divine. The building is circular and flanked by two apse-like halls. The façade is concave, with two porphyry columns and an architrave framing the original bronze door.

Basilica di Massenzio o di Constantino** (Basilica of Maxentius or Constantine)

The colossal ruins of this basilica, begun by Maxentius (AD 306-312), and completed by Constantine, form the most impressive ancient monument in the Forum. The architect seems to have set aside the traditional rules of basilica design (i.e., colonnades supporting a wooden structure) to produce something much more daring and original: a gigantic groined vault, 115 ft/35 m high, overarching a central nave. This nave was closed at its western end by an apse facing the church of Ss. Cosma e Damiano. Constantine, who modified the axis of the building by constructing the via Sacra entrance to the Forum—today's via dei Fori Imperiali—added a second, similar apse to the north wall. The central nave was quoined on each side by three transversal, buttress-like supports. The entire area of the vaulting was decorated with octagonal caissons; the roof originally consisted of plaques of gilded bronze, but these were removed by Honorius in the 7th century and used to cover the first basilica of St Peter's.

The western apse once housed a huge statue of Constantine, a few fragments of which have survived. These fragments are now exhibited in the courtyard of the Palazzo dei Conservatore at the Capitol.

Like all the other Roman basilicas, the basilica of Maxentius was habitually used as a court of justice and as a venue for the transaction of business.

Arco di Tito** (Arch of Titus)

This triumphal arch was built to commemorate the conquest of Jerusalem by Titus in AD 70, and its bas-reliefs show a triumphal procession bringing the spoils of the temple into Rome. The arch is crowned by a sculpted *Apotheosis of Titus,* with an eagle bearing the emperor's soul into heaven.

IL PALATINO (The Palatine hill) VI, B5-6

Entrance by the Clivus Palatinus to the right of the Arch of Titus.

As an archaeological site, the Palatine hill is incomparable. It is also an unforgettable place for a stroll among gigantic, tumbled vestiges of the imperial past, weird parasol pines and the aviaries and fountains of the Farnese Gardens.

History

Under the republic, the Palatine hill became a residential area for the Roman ruling class, complete with a 'House of Romulus' and a 'she-wolf's cave' for the edification of the people.

When Augustus, who was born on the Palatine, built himself a palace there, he effectively determined its history for the next three centuries: his successors Tiberius, Caligula, Claudius, Nero and the Flavians also made the Palatine their home.

Decline began in the 3rd century AD, when the emperors moved their headquarters outside Rome. In AD 330, the foundation of the 'New Rome' in Constantinople led to the final abandonment of the huge palace complex which had gradually grown up on the hill, the name of which had by then passed into every language of Europe as a simile for a royal residence.

During the Middle Ages, the Palatine was fortified, but with the coming of the Renaissance, the richer Roman families began to install their country houses, their gardens and their vineyards on the site, ruthlessly ransacking the remaining monuments for building materials.

Orti Farnesiani (Farnese Gardens)

This park was laid out by Cardinal Alessandro Farnese on the ruins of the Palace of Tiberius. In the 17th century, when it was created, it constituted the world's foremost botanical garden.

Tempio di Cibele (Temple of Cybele)

This temple was built in 204 BC to house the black stone, the phallic emblem of Cybele, a Phrygian deity. Dedicated to the *Magna Mater* (i.e., Cybele, the Great Mother), the temple constitutes the earliest evidence of Rome's penetration by oriental religious cults. The statue of the goddess, which stands under an arcade of Tiberius's palace behind the temple, dates from the imperial epoch.

South of the temple is the site of an excavated **prehistoric village,** containing vestiges of the first houses to have been built on the Palatine hill.

Casa di Livia** (Livia's House)

This house, which is supposed to have belonged to Livia (the wife of Augustus), is one of a group of buildings to the east of the Temple of Cybele. These date from the last years of the republic and somehow escaped demolition when the imperial palaces were being built. They were probably the private apartments of Livia within the residence of Augustus and, as such, offer a vivid example of an aristocratic Roman household in the 1st century BC. Two of the four rooms on the ground floor are open to the public: the **triclinium** (dining room) with trompe l'œil and still-life frescos, and the **tablinum** (reception room) which originally contained pictures of mythological subjects framed by architectural motifs (Mercury rescuing Io from Argus, and Galatea fleeing from the cyclops Polyphemus).

Criptoportico (Cryptoporticus)

This is a long, cool gallery, stuccoed and vaulted, which originally connected the residence of Augustus with the palace proper. The mad emperor Caligula was assassinated here in AD 41.

Palazzo dei Flavii e Domus Augustana* (Palace of the Flavians and House of the Augustans)

This huge complex was built by the Emperor Domitian (AD 81-96), a lover of oriental luxury. Domitian's priorities for his palace were that it should be big enough to suit his imperial dignity and that it should be equipped with sumptuous private apartments.

The resultant building was used by Roman emperors until the end of the 3rd century. Unlike Tiberius's palace, which faced the Forum, Domitian's brainchild symbolically faced the rising sun, towards Rome's eastern provinces. According to P. Grimal, this building signalled a fundamental change in attitude of Roman emperors, from that of first citizen of Rome to that of master of the world.

As you enter this palace from the Cryptoporticus, you pass through a broad peristyle courtyard with an octagonal fountain at its centre. Suetonius relates that Domitian often came here to relax, but was so afraid of assassins that he had the walls covered in shiny, mirror-like marble. In this way he was able to watch his back.

North of this peristyle are three parallel rooms. These are, from left to right:

- The **basilica,** the emperor's tribunal.

- The **throne room,** once adorned with colossal statues, in which imperial dignitaries and foreign ambassadors were received. Here, in the centre of the apse, the emperor appeared in full majesty as 'dominus et deus' (god and master of all). This was the title assumed by Domitian.

- The **lararium,** the emperor's private chapel.

On the other side of the peristyle, you'll find the dining room **(triclinium).** Here, under the polychrome marble floor, hot air was circulated to heat the area. On either side of the triclinium are **nympheas** (amenity rooms). The one on the right, which is the better preserved of the two, is overlooked by a building from the Farnese era (16th century).

The **Domus Augustana** (House of the Augustans, i.e., of the Augustan emperors) was the private wing of the palace, reserved for the emperor and his intimates. The rooms of this building were distributed around two peristyle courtyards, one on a much lower level than the other. The lower portico used to lead into a circular-shaped garden, known as the **stadio.** On his doctor's advice, the emperor used to come here for regular walks among the flowers and shrubs.

Terme Severiane, Domus Severiana (Baths and Residence of Septimius Severus)

These additions to the Domus Augustana were made by Septimius Severus (AD 193-211). Supported by a series of colossal arcades, they are, today, the best preserved feature of the entire site.

II
IMPERIAL ROME TO RENAISSANCE ROME

Palazzo Venezia, Piazza del Campidoglio, Santa Maria in Aracoeli, Imperial Forums, Ss. Cosma e Damiano, Coliseum

The anachronisms and time warps peculiar to Rome can be seen again and again along this itinerary, which leads around the edges of the Forum.

Taking the piazza Venezia as a starting point, the itinerary leads towards Il Vittoriano and then continues to two monumental staircases (one mediaeval, the other Renaissance). The first of these leads to the church of Santa Maria in Aracoeli, the second to piazza del Campidoglio, designed by Michelangelo and one of the most beautiful in Rome. From this piazza, you can look out over the entire Forum area before proceeding along the via dei Fori Imperiali, which will bring you into the heart of imperial Rome where the Coliseum, the Imperial Forums and Trajan's Markets await you.

Access

Map VI, A5. Bus: 26, 44, 46, 85, 87, 90, 90b, 92, 94, 95, 116, 118, 716, 719. Metro: Colosseo (line B).

▬▬ *PIAZZA VENEZIA* IV, F1

Several major roads converge on this square, which makes it notorious for its traffic jams. The skill shown by Roman drivers in attempting to make their way through the horn-blowing maelstrom is equalled only by the traffic policemen whose job it is to keep order. When negotiating the pedestrian crossings, your best course is to stop the oncoming cars with a vigorous gesture of the hand and a broad smile of gratitude.

▬▬ *PALAZZO VENEZIA** VI, A5

The construction of Palazzo Venezia was begun in 1455 by Cardinal Barbo, but assumed altogether different dimensions when Barbo was elected Pope Paul II in 1464. After his death, the palazzo was used as a papal residence until 1564, when it became the residence of the ambassadors of the Venetian Republic—hence its name. When Venice was absorbed by Austria, the palazzo passed to the Austro-Hungarian Empire until 1916. During the fascist era, Mussolini used the palazzo as a presidential office and frequently delivered speeches from its balcony.

With its massive tower, crenellated battlements, high-ceilinged ground floor, and narrow window embrasures, the building is a blend of mediaeval solidity and early Renaissance refinement. The severity of the ensemble is tempered by the decoration of the interior and the frame of the great entryway.

To the left of the church of San Marco (an integral part of the palazzo) is a gate through which you can glimpse the **inner courtyard** with its fine two-tiered gallery (unfinished). The lower gallery has Doric columns, the upper Ionic: this combination, reminiscent of the Coliseum, provides a foretaste of the Renaissance.

The Palazzo Venezia also functions as a museum, exhibiting a wide variety of collections.

SAN MARCO VI, A5

The church of San Marco was founded by Pope Mark I in the 4th century in honour of St Mark the Evangelist. It was later rebuilt by Pope Gregory IV in the 9th century and by Cardinal Barbo (the future Paul II) in the 15th. A further, Baroque restoration undertaken in the 18th century completed the mixture of styles, in which San Marco may be said to be typically Roman.

The double-arched façade on piazza San Marco—three arches with half-columns backing on to pilasters on the lower level and a loggia with somewhat wider arches on the upper—is one of the architectural masterpieces of Renaissance Rome.

The interior has retained the floor plan of a mediaeval basilica (three naves and no transept), along with a gilded Renaissance ceiling. The 9th-century mosaic in the apse is an imitation of the one at Ss. Cosma e Damiano (see p. 78). Here, most of the figures are immobile and isolated from one another, standing out against the gold background. The exception is St Mark, who is depicted with one hand placed on the shoulder of Pope Gregory, about to present him to Christ. Gregory wears the square halo of a living saint, and the figure of Christ bestows his blessing from a low dais after the Greek manner. Every one of these features betrays Byzantine influence.

IL VITTORIANO VI, A5

In 1878, it was decided to erect this enormous building of white limestone as a memorial to Victor Emmanuel II, the architect of Italian unity. Inaugurated in 1911, it was intended by its builders to represent the physical expression of Rome's new destiny as capital of Italy. The result is both pompous and funereal, while the siting is little short of disastrous. Italians call it 'the Typewriter'.

▬ PIAZZA DEL CAMPIDOGLIO*** (Capitoline hill) VI, A5

History

Piazza del Campidoglio sits on the smallest and probably the most famous of Rome's seven hills. The Capitoline hill was the religious centre of ancient Rome. In the Middle Ages it became the seat of government of the Roman commune, a status it has held ever since.

The area was settled well before the founding of Rome in 754 BC; Bronze Age ceramics discovered here date from the 14th century BC. According to legend, the original fortification was handed over to the Sabines by the treachery of Tarpeia, a Roman matron. Later, as a mark of their gratitude, the Sabines crushed Tarpeia to death beneath their shields.

This citadel, well-protected by the steep, rocky flanks of the hill, enters the history of Rome with the construction by the Tarquins of a large temple dedicated to Jupiter. This temple was reinaugurated at the beginning of the republic (509 BC), after the expulsion of the Etruscan dynasty. It was here, by tradition, that the famous geese raised their alarm, thus saving Rome from a band of Gauls in 390 BC.

It was customary for newly elected consuls to take their oaths on the Capitoline hill, and victorious generals came here to crown their triumphs with a sacrifice at the Temple of Jupiter. The ancient buildings on the hill were burned down and rebuilt on several occasions. They finally disappeared forever in the 15th century, when columns dating from the 1st century AD were consigned to the lime ovens.

Architecture

With its architectural unity and harmony of proportion, the piazza del Campidoglio is one of Rome's most successful Renaissance features. Set well apart from the din of the city, Michelangelo's buildings (skillfully lit by discreet floodlights) provide an extraordinary setting at nightfall.

After the sack of Rome in 1527, Pope Paul III commissioned Michelangelo to restore the abandoned hill in anticipation of Charles V's arrival in 1536. The result is universally recognized as Michelangelo's architectural masterpiece.

On the two sides of the piazza are the **Palazzo dei Conservatori** (on the right) and the **Palazzo Nuovo** (on the left), symmetrical, with majestic façades framing the **Palazzo Senatorio**. A stairway, the **Cordonata**, opens onto the piazza with colossal **statues of Castor and Pollux** at its top. These statues date from the 4th century. At the centre of the piazza, amid Michelangelo's geometrically designed paving stones, stands an equestrian **statue of Marcus Aurelius** (currently under restoration).

The three palazzos border the piazza without closing it off. They were built after Michelangelo's death, largely according to plans he had drawn, though with one or two questionable alterations such as the giant pilasters of the Palazzo Senatorio and the fountain below its steps with its heavy, disproportionate figures. The Palazzo dei Conservatore and the Palazzo Nuovo more faithfully reproduced Michelangelo's designs.

Along the via delle Tre Pile, to the right of the Palazzo dei Conservatori, runs a terrace which gives an excellent view of the **Theatre of Marcellus** (see p. 131). Lower down is the **Rock of Tarpeia,** named after the traitress. From here the Romans used to hurl criminals convicted of treachery.

▬ SANTA MARIA IN ARACOELI* IV, F1-2

A broad staircase to the right of the Palazzo Nuovo leads directly from the piazza to the church of Santa Maria in Aracoeli. If you take this route, you will avoid having to climb the 124 steps of the main staircase, built by the Romans to thank God for sparing their city from the plague of 1346.

An oratory existed here from the 6th century to the mid-13th century, at which time Franciscan monks moved to the site and began building a church. The church was completed just after 1400. The present façade, which dates from that time, is austere and formal, despite its superb Renaissance doors. The interior of the church is designed as a basilica—it is the last of its type in Rome—with three naves of monumental size separated by antique columns. The paving was laid by the Cosmati, a dynasty of Roman marble masons who did much fine work between the 12th and 14th centuries.

The church contains paintings and sculptures of widely varying styles and epochs. Its most interesting feature is the **Bufalini chapel** (to the right of the main entrance), which is decorated with **frescos** by Pinturicchio (1485). The frescos illustrate the life and death of the Siennese preacher St Bernard.

To the right of the main entrance is the 15th-century **tomb of Cardinal d'Albren** by Andrea Bregno. Against the wall is the **tombstone of Giovanni Crivelli** by Donatello, from the same period.

Before leaving the church, do look into the **chapel of the Santo Bambino** (last chapel at upper left). Its 16th-century statue of the baby Christ is supposed to have miraculous attributes.

To continue the itinerary, leave the church by the side entrance that opens on to the piazza del Campidoglio.

FROM PIAZZA DEL CAMPIDOGLIO TO THE IMPERIAL FORUMS VI, A5-6

The itinerary follows the via **San Pietro in Carcere,** which circles the entire Forum and passes alongside the church of **San Giuseppe dei Falegnami** (St Joseph of the Carpenters). Beneath this church are two dungeons in which captives of the Roman state were strangled after being led through the streets. Jugurtha (d. 104 BC) and Vercingetorix (d. 46 BC) both perished here. According to a mediaeval legend, St Peter spent some time in the dungeon, hence the name San Pietro in Carcere.

At the next major junction, the itinerary enters the **via dei Fori Imperiali.** This 98 ft/30 m wide street was opened in 1932 and named via dell'Impero (Empire Road); it cut the forums in two and destroyed an old district of Rome, but created a direct link between the Coliseum and Mussolini's palace.

FORI IMPERIALI (Imperial Forums) VI, A5-6

By the close of the republican era, the old Roman Forum was no longer large enough to accommodate all the commercial and administrative activities of a city with one million people. Concerned about the prestige of their capital, the rulers of Rome decided to remedy this defect. Caesar appropriated land for the construction of a new forum to the north of the old one; his example was followed by Augustus, Vespasian, Domitian, Nerva and Trajan. Within a century, five imperial forums had been constructed, complete with porticos, basilicas, temples and libraries.

In the Middle Ages, these monuments were gradually surrounded and overwhelmed by housing. The great forum precincts were systematically pillaged for building materials until the 18th century, by which time they had been almost entirely dismantled.

FORO GIULIO (Forum of Julius Caesar) VI, A5

If you turn right and continue down the via dei Fori Imperiali, you will come to the ruins of Caesar's Forum immediately on your right.

Three fine columns on a raised platform are all that remain of the Temple of Venus Genitrix (Venus was the mother of Aeneas and a mythical ancestor of Caesar). This sumptuous building was constructed on Caesar's orders after his victory over his rival Pompey in 48 BC.

▬▬ SS. COSMA E DAMIANO* VI, A6

In the 6th century, Pope Felix IV installed the church of Ss. Cosmi e Damiano in the former library of the Forum of Trajan (see p. 81). The first known example of a pagan edifice 'converted' to Christian use, the church was further modified in the 17th century.

The **mosaic** in the apse, which dates from the 6th century, blends the naturalism of ancient Rome (the two saints being presented by Peter and Paul), with the first signs of Byzantine influence: the stern Christ figure and St Theodore in flowing Byzantine robes. The composition is broad and sweeping and the decoration especially beautiful. Note the sky (a rich sunset colour), the pebbly greensward, the two palm trees symbolizing Old and New Jerusalem, and the phoenix which represents Christ's resurrection. Below, the Lamb of God is depicted in the company of 12 other lambs, which symbolizes the apostles.

A fine 18th-century **Neapolitan crèche** is displayed in the vestibule, which occupies the former **Temple of Romulus** (see p. 71).

▬▬ SANTA FRANCESCA ROMANA VI, B6

In the middle of the 6th century, Pope Leo IV transferred the church of Santa Maria Antica to this site, which was formerly occupied by the Temple of Venus and Rome (see below). The church was subsequently renamed, becoming first Santa Maria Nova, then Santa Francesca Romana.

The present building has an elegant Romanesque campanile (138 ft/42 m) dating from the 12th century, which is encrusted with coloured ceramic. The façade (1615) is in white limestone; the tympanum with its statues is supported by two pairs of giant flat pilasters on raised bases.

In the sacristy there is a fine painting by the French artist Subleyras entitled *Saint Benoît Ressuscitant un Enfant Mort* (St Benedict Raising a Child From the Dead).

Santa Francesca Romana is the patron saint of motorists; on her feast day, March 9, huge numbers of cars gather between the church and the Coliseum.

▬▬ TEMPIO DI VENERE E ROMA
(Temple of Venus and Rome) VI, B6

This temple was built by Hadrian and consecrated in AD 135. It stands on a broad terrace (327 ft/100 m by 476 ft/145 m) and contains two sanctuaries back to back: one for Venus and one for the goddess Rome. The original building was raised on the site of the vestibule of Nero's Domus Aurea (see p. 80), in the centre of which stood a 115 ft/35 m statue of Nero in bronze. According to tradition, the statue could be moved only by the combined strength of 24 elephants.

▬▬ COLOSSEO*** (Coliseum) V, B2

Open daily 9am-1 hr before sunset.

The **Amphitheatre of the Flavians** (i.e., of the Flavian family, which included Vespasian and his two sons Titus and Domitian) has been known as the **Coliseum** ever since the Middle Ages—either because of its proximity to the colossal statue of Nero or, more simply, because of its sheer size. It was the largest amphitheatre in the ancient world and today is still Rome's most impressive monument.

History

The construction of the Coliseum was undertaken by the Emperor Vespasian in AD 72 on the site of Nero's **Domus Aurea.** Vespasian's motives were to a certain extent demagogical; by building his amphithe-

The magnificent Coliseum, where gladiators fought and fell in ancient Rome.

atre he restored a part of the land confiscated by his hated predecessor to the people of Rome. The inauguration of Titus in AD 80 was marked by a festival that lasted for 100 days and included the killing of 5000 wild beasts and many gladiators at the Coliseum. Its decoration was finally completed by Domitian in AD 82.

A thunderbolt (AD 217), an earthquake (AD 442) and sundry other disasters necessitated several restorations of the Coliseum during imperial times. During the Middle Ages it became the fortress of a powerful Roman family, the Frangipani, and then a source of building materials for the construction of the Palazzo Venezia (see p. 74), the Palazzo della Cancelleria (see p. 87) and St Peter's (see p. 104). Pope Benedict XIV (1740-1758) saved the Coliseum from total demolition when he declared it a holy place in recognition of the martyrs' blood that is believed to have been shed within its precincts (although this belief is now contested). After 1870, the edifice was isolated from neighbouring buildings and the exploration of its foundations began.

Dimensions

The Coliseum is elliptical in shape: the distance around its perimeter is 1730 ft/527 m; its length 617 ft/188 m; its width 512 ft/156 m. The height of the façade is almost 164 ft/50 m. An astronomical amount of materials was used to build the Coliseum: originally it contained 388,465 cubic ft/11,000 cubic m of limestone. Approximately 300 tons of iron were needed for the staples to hold the blocks together. During the Middle Ages, the staples were torn out, leaving innumerable holes in the stone.

Stone corbels project from the walls at the fourth level: these originally supported 240 masts, on which a huge canopy could be stretched to shelter the stepped rows of seats. A detachment of sailors was garrisoned nearby to rig up this canopy when necessary. The Coliseum could accommodate 45,000 spectators, perhaps more: by some calculations, its capacity was as much as 73,000.

Architecture

The proportions of the Coliseum were a source of amazement to the architects of the Renaissance, who never tired of admiring this example of perfection bequeathed to them by the ancients. The outer limestone facing is composed of three levels of arcades, one on top of another, which rest on pillars with engaged columns: Doric on the first level, Ionic on the second and Corinthian on the third. A fourth row of Corinthian pilasters with flat arches regulates the coping which crowns the edifice. The same succession of architectural themes may be found in a number of Roman palaces dating from the Renaissance.

Today, vehicle exhaust fumes are the main threat to this ancient monument, but the measures required for its protection have stirred controversy. Anyone opposing them might consider the pronouncement made by the Venerable Bede (AD 673-735): 'While the Coliseum lasts, so too will Rome last; when the Coliseum falls, so will Rome fall; and when Rome falls, the whole world will fall with her'.

Spectacles at the Coliseum

Thanks to its many staircases, the amphitheatre could be filled or emptied very rapidly. Seats were numbered and reserved for spectators according to their social rank. The imperial box and that of the Prefect of Rome occupied the two extremities of the minor axis, while the senators, magistrates and Vestals sat in the front row.

The gladiators, dressed in purple and gold, entered in serried ranks through the gates at the ends of the major axis. After marching once around the arena, they would halt before the emperor and pronounce the famous salute: 'Ave Caesar, morituri te salutant!' ('Hail Caesar, we who are about to die salute thee!'). No fewer than 2000 gladiators died at the Coliseum during the 100 days following its inauguration in AD 80.

Gladiatorial combats at the Coliseum ceased in the 5th century, and staged battles between wild animals were stopped in the 6th century.

▄▄▄ *ARCO DI COSTANTINO*** *(Arch of Constantine)* V, B2

This monumental arch (82 ft/25 m high) was built in AD 315 'by the Senate and people of Rome' to commemorate Constantine's victory over his rival Maxentius at Pons Milvius.

The proportions of the Arch of Constantine are harmonious, but its decoration is uneven. The parts which date from the 4th century are generally mediocre, while certain features taken from older (2nd century) monuments are very fine, particularly the superb Athenian reliefs.

The Arch of Constantine has been undergoing restoration (or protection) work for some years and is at present sheathed in scaffolding.

▄▄▄ *DOMUS AUREA* V, A2

This sumptuous palace, which backs onto the Oppian hill, was built by Nero after the Great Fire of AD 64. It originally covered a vast area and included a lake surrounded by gardens and vineyards.

After Nero's suicide in AD 68 and the proscription of his memory by the Senate, this famous site soon went the way of its creator. Nero's lake was drained and the land was used by Vespasian for the Coliseum. Later, the upper areas of the palace were razed to make way for the Baths of Trajan, and many rooms filled in at this time remained hidden underground until the 16th century. Renaissance artists were amazed by the paintings contained in the excavated 'grottos' and made many copies of their grotesque decorative motifs. The decor of certain Renaissance palaces in

Rome (for example, Raphaël's Loggia at the Vatican) owes much to a contemporary fascination with the frescos of the Domus Aurea.

From the Domus Aurea, the itinerary continues along the via dei Fori Imperiali towards the piazza Venezia. Passing via Cavour, it follows via Alessandrina, which leads past the Imperial Forums, with the remains of the **Forum of Nerva** (of which only two fine columns remain to mark a street junction), the **Forum of Augustus** and the **Forum of Trajan.**

FORO DI AUGUSTO (Forum of Augustus)* VI, A6

The Forum, named after Caesar's adopted son, was built between 31 BC and AD 2, the result of a vow made by Caesar during the Battle of Philippi (42 BC). Caesar's sword was formerly kept as a relic in the **Temple of Mars Ultor** (Mars the Avenger), a colossal marble edifice, of which only three columns and one or two stone blocks remain today.

A massive, irregular wall once separated the Forum of Augustus from the plebeian quarter of Suburra, where there were frequent outbreaks of fire.

CASA DEI CAVALIERI DI RODI
(Lodge of the Knights of Rhodes) VI, A6

Entrance at piazza del Grillo n° 1.

The loggia that stands between the Forum of Augustus and Trajan's Markets is the old Roman priory of the order of the Knights of St John of Jerusalem (also called the Knights of Rhodes or of Malta). It was built towards the end of the 12th century and was restored during the 15th. The view from the loggia across the forums is well worth a detour.

*MERCATI TRAIANI** (Trajan's Markets)* VI, A6

Entrance by the via IV Novembre. *Open Tues-Sun 9am-1pm.*

In order to create this huge semicircle of buildings, Trajan's architect, Apollodorus of Damascus, had to make deep step-like cuts into the rocky side of the Quirinal hill to a height roughly equivalent to that of Trajan's column. The semicircular façade of his building, which was faced in brick, offered an initial level of shops set to no great depth against the solid rock. The next level consisted of an arcade with alternating triangular and curved pediments, while the third was taken up by shops facing in the other direction onto an ancient road that is still in fair condition today.

Trajan's Markets provided Rome with a huge warehouse for goods like wheat, wine, oil and fish. Here, the imperial officials took delivery of merchandise and redistributed it to retail merchants, while the imperial tax gatherers levied dues on each transaction. Thus the market precinct constituted one of the most perfect examples of utilitarian architecture in the ancient world and symbolized the imperial control of Rome's economic existence.

BASILICA ULPIA (Ulpian Basilica) VI, A5

Only one or two columns remain of this basilica, once the largest in Rome (558 ft/170 m long, 197 ft/60 m wide). Its five naves, supported by marble columns, were terminated at their northern and southern ends by two symmetrical apses. On either side of the courtyard containing Trajan's Column stood two libraries that housed the 'volumes'—rolls of parchment placed in recessed cabinets—of the imperial archives.

*COLONNA TRAIANA*** (Trajan's Column)* VI, A5

This great monument (125 ft/38 m tall) is unique in ancient Roman architecture. It originally contained the ashes of the Emperor Trajan, who was entombed within the city walls—a rare exception to the rule forbidding it.

The 17 drums of the column, all in Carrara marble, are decorated with a spiral relief, a continuous sculpted band some 656 ft/200 m long and 3 ft/1 m high. The column was made slightly broader at the top in order to correct the impression created by perspective. The relief contains nearly 2500 figures, and the image of Trajan himself appears about 60 times. It depicts Trajan's two campaigns against the Dacians, and is therefore an inestimably rich source of information on Roman military equipment and warfare.

The overall concept of Trajan's Column is doubtless attributable to a single brilliant architect, probably Apollodorus of Damascus. The representation of landscapes, the disposition of the various planes in relief and the organic continuity of the scenes depicted are all Greek-inspired. Expressive tension is somehow maintained at a constant level within this formal framework, peaking from time to time with especially important scenes (for example, the final deportation of the Dacians). All in all, Trajan's Column is one of the world's great masterpieces of sculpture.

The statue of Trajan that originally crowned the column was replaced at the close of the 16th century by that of St Peter; in the eyes of the Counter-Reformation Catholic church, this 'annexation' symbolized the triumph of Christianity over the power of paganism.

▬▬▬ *SANTA MARIA DI LORETO*

This church was begun in 1507 by Antonio da Sangallo the Younger and was finally completed in 1582 by Giacomo del Duca, who designed the skylight in the dome. The octagonal shape of this dome ensures a smooth geometrical transition between the square floorplan of the church and the hemisphere crowning its roof.

On the left-hand side of the choir is a **statue of St Suzanne,** by Fra Duquesnoy (1630), which was considered by contemporaries as a perfect synthesis between nature and the ideals of antiquity.

III
LOOP OF THE TIBER

**Il Gesù, Palazzo della Cancelleria, Palazzo Farnese,
Piazza Navona, San Luigi dei Francesi, The Pantheon.**

T his itinerary leads through the valley that was dedicated by the
ancient Romans to Mars, the god of war—hence its name of
Campo Marzio.

The district is an old one, bounded to the west by the winding
course of the Tiber River. It consists of a maze of narrow streets and
mediaeval alleys, where blacksmiths, cabinetmakers, framers and
gilders still ply their trades. These small thoroughfares link the
area's many piazzas, with their majestic churches and rich palazzos.
In all, this is a wonderful area to explore on foot.

Because of the profusion of monuments included in this
itinerary, you may wish to divide it into several different parts,
depending on how much time you have.

Access
Map III, F6. Bus: 26, 44, 46, 50, 60, 61, 64, 65, 70, 75, 81, 87, 90, 170, 710.

▬▬ IL GESU** VI, A4

The church of Il Gesù, as the principal Jesuit church in Rome, was the
model for many others built in Europe at the time of the Counter-
Reformation.

Towards the end of his life, St Ignatius Loyola (1491-1556), the founder of
the Jesuits, felt the need to build a great church in the heart of Rome; a
church large enough to accommodate the ever-growing congregations that
flocked to the Jesuits' chapel. The project threatened to be enormously
expensive. But in 1562, Cardinal Alessandro Farnese, a generous protector
of the order, donated some 40,000 écus towards the construction costs.
Work was begun in 1568 by Vignola and completed in 1584. Giacomo della
Porta, who took charge of the project after Vignola's death, was responsible for the façade and the cupola.

Façade

Della Porta's sober, monumental façade consists of two levels topped by
a broad pediment and linked laterally by mighty volutes. The basic stylistic
elements later used by Baroque architects are all present here: engaged
columns take the place of pilasters at the centre of the lower level, and
setbacks are introduced to accentuate the play of light and shade. At the
same time, a novel emphasis is laid on the central part of the structure,
where the doorway, the emblem of the Jesuit order, the double pediment,
the broad window with its balcony and the escutcheon with the Farnese
arms and the Holy Cross form a subtly articulated vertical ensemble.

Interior

Before you start to explore the church, try to imagine the walls without their ugly 19th-century covering of yellow marble. The interior of the church was planned to satisfy the pastoral and liturgical imperatives of the Counter-Reformation down to the last detail. The idea was to uplift the heart with majestic structures and imposing ceremony, touch the soul with populist sermonizing, and promote the cult of intercession by the Virgin and the saints, which the Protestants had so firmly rejected. The broad nave of the church is specially designed for preaching to large congregations; the floorplan, in the form of a Latin cross, separates the apse from the nave and underscores the distance between the priest and his flock. Above, the heavy coping which runs the length of the nave combines with the light falling from the transparent dome to draw the eye towards the altar. Here the priest celebrates mass; the sacristy is sufficiently far away from the apse to permit him a grand processional. Lastly, the side chapels, which replace the naves of the old basilica design, allow the faithful to carry out more private devotions to individual saints.

The lively **fresco** which decorates the vault of the nave was painted a century after the church was built, by Giovanni-Battista Gaulli, known as Il Baciccia. Within a framework supported by angels appear the letters of Jesus's name. From these, rays of light pour forth to illuminate a throng of cherubs and saints and to shatter the forces of evil and heresy, which are hurled into the abyss. The *trompe l'œil,* which fuses the painted surfaces and the stucco figures, creates the spectacular illusion that the world of the supernatural is bursting into the church from above.

The frescos of the dome *(Vision of Heaven)* and the choir *(Triumph of the Lamb)* were also painted by Il Baciccia.

In the left transept, the **altar of St Ignatius** (1696-1700), a sumptuous Baroque composition by the Jesuit Andrea Pozzo, contains the remains of the founder of the Jesuits. The altar features a silver statue of the saint, columns faced with lapis lazuli with green marble bases and crowns, bas-reliefs in gilded bronze depicting scenes from the life of Ignatius, and white marble sculpted groups of figures. All this creates a daring chromatic effect which made a strong impression on Pozzo's contemporaries.

Via del Gesù

To the right of the church (n° 45) is the house where St Ignatius lived and died. The walls of the corridor are entirely covered with *trompe l'œil* frescos (1675-1686) by Andrea Pozzo and Jacques Courtois.

In the Baroque courtyard of n° 62 via del Gesù there is a curious water clock (1882).

▄▄▄ *TEMPLI REPUBBLICANI (Republican Temples)* VI, A4

Excavations carried out between 1926 and 1929 uncovered vestiges of four temples from the republican era, which form an ensemble now called the **Area Sacra dell'largo Argentina.** They are among the most ancient temples in Rome.

Via San Nicola de' Cesarini offers the best vantage point from which to view these temples, which are designated by the letters A to D, from left to right.

Temple A, far right, may have been dedicated to Juturna, the Roman goddess of springs. It was built during the 3rd century and subsequently reconstructed. During the Middle Ages, the church of San Nicola dei Cesarini (of which nothing remains but the two apses and an altar) was installed within the temple's walls.

The circular **Temple B,** to the left of Temple A, was built much later, following Marius's victory over the Cimbri at Vercelli (101 BC). It was dedicated to Fortune. Behind Temple B, a few massive blocks of tufa are all that remain of the podium of Pompey's Curia, where Caesar was assassinated in 44 BC.

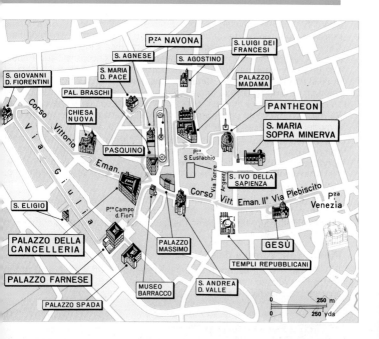

On the corner of via Santa Nicola and via Florida is a tower flanked by a portico, clumsily rebuilt in 1932. These vestiges of the old mediaeval district date from the 12th century.

Via di Torre Argentina is the site of the **Teatro Argentina,** which was built in 1731 and has a 19th-century façade. This theatre was one of the largest in papal Rome; the world première of Rossini's *Barber of Seville* was staged here in 1816.

Temple C, the oldest of the four (late 4th-early 3rd centuries BC), has foundations of tufa blocks, like those used for the wall of Servius Tullius, which encircled the city in the fourth century BC.

On the left, **Temple D** is the largest and dates from the 2nd century BC; this building was entirely faced with limestone at the end of the republican epoch.

▬ *SANT'ANDREA DELLA VALLE* III, F5

The construction of the church of Sant'Andrea was begun in 1591 by the Theatines, one of the most active religious orders of the Counter-Reformation. In 1608, Maderno was commissioned to complete the church, and to him we owe the majestic dome built in 1622-1625 (the second highest in Rome after St Peter's) and the plans for the façade*, which Girolamo Rainaldi freely interpreted during the Baroque era (1655-1665).

The façade, with its set-back planes, twin columns on both levels, variations on curved and triangular pediments and sculptures, is one of the most remarkable of the 17th century.

The **interior** is designed as a Latin cross, like the church of Il Gesù, with barrel vaulting, large inter-connecting side-chapels, a broad apse and a transparent **dome***.

The decoration of the dome

When Giovanni Lanfranco's fresco of the *Assumption* was unveiled in

February 1628, it caused a considerable stir. It consists of a single composition covering the entire inner surface of the dome, which depicts Christ descending from heaven to greet his mother. Clustered around the Son of God are cherubim bearing a garland and, in concentric cloud-circles, the heavenly court contemplating the scene to music by a concert of angels. For the first time in Rome, an artist had broken with the Mannerist tradition of dividing domes into sections. Lanfranco's fresco was inspired by Correggio's more modest works of a century earlier in the domes of Parma. For 150 years afterwards, Lanfranco's innovation was to serve as a model for European painters decorating a vault or a dome.

The pendentives of the dome show the *Four Evangelists* (1621-1628) painted by Domenichino. The same artist was responsible for the *Glorification of St Andrew* (1624-1628) on the vault overlooking the choir. The *Martyrdom of St Andrew* in the apse is the work of Mattia Preti (1650-1651).

At the top of the nave are the tombs of Pius II and Pius III. The former, on the left, is from the school of A. Brogno (1470-1475) and is a good example of late 15th-century funerary art. The latter, a virtual copy, was completed in 1503.

Piazza Sant'Andrea della Valle

In 1957, an elegant **fountain** by Carlo Maderno (1614) was moved to the piazza Sant'Andrea della Valle in front of the church. It had formerly graced another piazza which was demolished to make way for via della Conciliazione.

▰▰▰ *PALAZZO MASSIMO*★ III, F5

Open only March 16 in honour of the miracle performed on that day in 1587 when young Paolo Massimo was raised from the dead by St Filippo Neri.

This Renaissance palazzo was begun in 1532 by Baldassare Peruzzi for Pietro Massimo, on the site of an earlier one which had burned down during the sack of Rome in 1527. The smallness of the plot of land and the line of the old street (which at 15 ft/4.5 m wide was far narrower than the present corso Vittorio Emanuele) obliged the architect to adopt a convex façade, completely unique at the time.

The **interior** is both original and elegant. If you are lucky enough to be in Rome on March 16 and visit this palazzo, you will see the main courtyard, which is modelled on an antique atrium to satisfy the tastes and genealogical ambitions of the Massimo family, who claimed descent from the illustrious Roman consul Fabius Maximus (3rd century BC). There is a fine loggia of Doric and Ionic columns, one above the other. Note the peculiar rectangular openings on the lower floor, which light the vaulting and reduce the optical disproportion between its height and that of the main floor. This design is reminiscent of the architecture of the Roman cryptoportici at the Palatine or Hadrian's Villa.

▰▰▰ *MUSEO BARRACCO* III, F4

Open Sun 9am-1pm; Tues-Sat 9am-2pm; Tues and Thurs also 5pm-8pm.

This collection of antique sculpture was bequeathed to the city by Bara Barracco in 1902. It is housed in a palazzo which was built in 1523 for the French ambassador. The architect is believed to have been Antonio da Sangallo the Younger.

Because of a confusion between the French *fleur de lys* and the emblem of the Farnese family, this little palazzo acquired the name of **Piccola Farnesina**, or Farnesina dei Baullari (the via dei Baullari, literally 'bag-makers's street', runs alongside it). The façade facing the corso dates from 1901.

▬ *PALAZZO DELLA CANCELLERIA*** (Palace of the Chancellery)* III, F4

This palazzo is one of the masterpieces of the Roman Renaissance. Commissioned in 1485 by Cardinal Raffaele Riario, nephew of Pope Sixtus IV, it was completed in 1513. The architect, Andrea Bregno, was probably assisted by Bramante. The building was no sooner finished than it was confiscated from the Riario family, which was accused of plotting against Leo X. Later, it belonged to a number of different families before becoming the papal Chancellery in 1870, which endowed it with extraterritorial status under the 1929 Lateran Treaties.

The Palazzo della Cancelleria was begun only 15 years after the Palazzo Venezia, yet it seems to belong to another century altogether, so clear is the break with earlier architectural tradition. The lower basement, the many mullioned windows and the crenellations are all new features. The flat pilasters of the two upper floors lend liveliness to the façade by imposing a regular binary rhythm (blind spaces alternating with window openings). The doorway, which is heavy by comparison, was added by Fontana in 1589.

The remarkably harmonious inner courtyard is surrounded by two levels of elegant arcades, supported by simple columns which have the effect of opening up rather than enclosing the space. Only the wall of the upper floor, which is lined with windows and pilasters, reminds us that this is a closed courtyard. The granite columns came from the primitive basilica of **San Lorenzo in Damaso** which was rebuilt and integrated into the palace in 1495, then altered again in the 19th century. Entry is by the right-hand door at the front of the building.

▬ *PIAZZA CAMPO DEI FIORI** VI, A3

This charming piazza, surrounded by old houses in pale stone, was the centre of Rome in the 16th century and much famed for its lodging houses. Among these were the 'della Campana', favoured by visiting Germans, whose proprietor was known as 'Angelo' because of his blond clientele; and the 'Hostaria della Vacca', at the entrance of the vicolo del Gallo, on the right. This latter establishment belonged to Vanozza Catanei, mother of Cesare and Lucrezia Borgia, the famous offspring of Pope Alexander VI.

Every morning, except Sundays, a lively and picturesque market is held in the piazza Campo dei Fiori. The noise of the fountain is drowned out by the banter of the market vendors and their customers, at stalls laden with meat, fish, vegetables, fruit and flowers and shaded by cream-coloured parasols. If the somber statue of the monk Giordano Bruno were not there to remind us, it would be easy to forget that four centuries ago heretics were regularly burned at the stake in this piazza.

▬ *PALAZZO FARNESE**** VI, A3

This palazzo is closed to the public, but an authorization to visit may be obtained, if it is requested in writing. Group tours are scheduled every Wednesday at 4pm.

The Palazzo Farnese, begun in 1514 by Antonio da Sangallo the Younger, was the largest and most sumptuous of Rome's Renaissance mansions and the first of many built by the papal families. It was originally intended for Alessandro Farnese, the most powerful dignitary in the College of Cardinals at the beginning of the 16th century, whose retinue was said to include no less than 300 people. When Farnese was elected pope in 1534 under the name of Paul III, Sangallo was commissioned to enlarge and improve upon his original project. The work was completed up to the cornice, but this feature was not to Paul III's liking and, in 1646, he invited Rome's best architects to submit different proposals. Michelangelo won the competition, and Sangallo, cut to the quick, died a few weeks later. Michelangelo then had a free hand not only to execute the cornice, but also to complete unfinished parts of the building, such as the balcony window on the first floor and the two upper floors overlooking the courtyard. He even planned a bridge to link the palace with the Orti Farnesiani (see p. 72), but this project was never realized. The back façade (1569-1573) on the via Giulia was designed by Vignola and Giacomo della Porta, who also completed the graceful loggia on the second floor (1589).

The Palazzo Farnese has served as the **French Embassy** since 1874. Purchased by France in 1911, it was bought back by Italy in 1936 and subsequently leased to France for 99 years at a symbolic rate of one lire per year (this gesture is reciprocated: Italy rents its embassy on the rue de Varenne in Paris for one franc).

Façade

The main façade of the palazzo takes up one whole side of the piazza Farnese, which is in fact designed to set off the facade's beauty. The two fountains which complete the decor are of Egyptian granite and were taken from the site of the Baths of Caracalla. The façade is 197 ft/60 m long, longer than all the other private palaces in Rome. The bare mass of its three floors is broken at the edges by 'rustic' embossing which becomes less emphatic towards the summit; this has the effect of drawing the window alignments into strong relief, especially those of the first floor. The aedicules which frame the windows with alternating triangular and curved pediments imitate the niches in the Pantheon. The projecting cornice is the work of Michelangelo, who considered it the crowning glory of the whole edifice, not merely of the top floor. Nevertheless, in order to avoid any possibility that this cornice might overwhelm the architecture of the rest of the building, it was erected slightly higher than Sangallo had planned. The central window of the first floor, topped by the arms of the Farnese family, is also the work of Michelangelo who, by a characteristically Mannerist paradox, contrived to draw attention to it by making it smaller and embedding it in the body of the wall.

Interior

The entrance to the **inner courtyard** leads through a magnificent vestibule with three naves, the arches of which are covered in finely wrought stucco caissons. The courtyard itself is inspired by the ancient Theatre of Marcellus (see p. 131). It is surrounded by an arcaded portico which rests on pilasters with engaged Doric columns. Above this portico are two floors, the first with Ionic columns, the second with flat Corinthian pilasters. The third and final level is the work of Michelangelo, as is the frieze (revolutionary for the time) which surmounts the first floor. Instead of lightening the upper level in traditional fashion (see Palazzo della Cancelleria p. 87), the artist gave it unusual breadth, adding windows with fantastical frame-linings and pediments that seem to float above them. Unlike Sangallo, who took immense pains to respect the Classical principles of architecture, Michelangelo sought freedom through innovations that often astonished his contemporaries.

From here a fine staircase leads to the first floor **Hercules Salon,** which is filled with busts of Roman emperors and with 17th-century tapestries, and to the **Long Gallery***, covered in superb mythological frescos on the theme of Love's Victory. These frescos (1597-1606) were executed by Annibale and Agostino Carracci, along with their pupils Domenichino and Giovanni Lanfranco.

◼◼◼ *PALAZZO SPADA** VI, A3

This palazzo was built around 1540 by Cardinal Girolamo Capo di Ferro, a protégé of Cardinal Alessandro Farnese (Paul III), and bears no resemblance to the Palazzo Farnese, its exact contemporary and neighbour. There is no Classical majesty here; instead, there is a Mannerist profusion of decorative effects: walls richly covered with garlands of stucco, ornamental frames with Latin inscriptions, and statues in niches with triangular pediments. Giulio Massoni's inner courtyard, though more harmonious than the façade, is also lavishly decorated.

During alterations made after the palace's purchase by Cardinal Bernardino Spada in 1632, Borromini built the famous **perspective colonnade*** (1652), which should be viewed from a window on the left-hand side of the inner courtyard. The colonnade appears to be far longer than it really is (29.5 ft/9 m). *The custodian will produce the key on request.*

The **Galleria Spada** on the first floor is *open to the public* and contains a number of fine pieces collected by Cardinal Spada and his family. This little gallery offers something of the atmosphere of an aristocratic private collection from the 17th century. Compare the portraits of Bernardino Spada by Il Guercino and Guido Reni. Note also canvases by Gaspard Dughet, Domenichino, pupils of Caravaggio, and a preparatory sketch for the ceiling fresco at the church of Il Gesù.

Today, the Palazzo Spada is the seat of the Italian Council of State.

VIA GIULIA* VI, A2-3

The via Giulia is named after Pope Julius II, who opened it in the early 16th century. Nearly a mile long, it is Rome's first planned rectilinear thoroughfare and was built to link Trastevere with Borgo and St Peter's, and to be the site of the pontifical state's administrative buildings.

During the 16th century, the via Giulia was the widest and most fashionable street in Rome. The city's aristocratic families built palaces here, but within a century, the area had lost much of its cachet, especially after the construction of the Carceri Nuovi state prison in 1655. However, recent efforts at restoration, along with the appearance of antique shops, art galleries and an annual music festival, have revitalized the street.

Fontana del Mascherone

This fountain, which faces the gardens of Palazzo Farnese, was built in 1626. It owes its name to the grotesque marble mask that adorns it, which, like its basin, comes from an ancient building.

Arcade of Palazzo Farnese

The purpose of this arcade was to span the via Giulia and link the palazzo to the modest building on the other side of the street. The original intention was that is should be prolonged by a bridge between the palace and the Farnesina.

Just beyond the arcade stands the church of **Santa Maria dell'Orazione e Morte,** with its curious façade covered in death's heads (Baroque, Francisco Fuga, 18th century).

Palazzo Falconieri

Palazzo Falconieri, at n° 1 via Giulia, has a fine Borromini loggia (17th century) overlooking the Tiber. Borromini also restored the façade on the street side, decorating at each end with busts of women with the heads of falcons—an unequivocal allusion to the name of the palazzo's owners.

Sant'Eligio degli Orefici*

A short distance from Palazzo Falconieri, on the left, at the end of vicolo di Sant'Eligio, is the charming church of Sant'Eligio degli Orefici, built in 1509 to a design by Raphaël (dome and skylight by Baldassare Peruzzi), and later retouched in the 17th century (façade). This sanctuary would appear to be a smaller version of Bramante's early plan for St Peter's—a Greek cross covered by a cupola. At all events, the geometrical clarity of its design makes Sant'Eligio one of the purest expressions of Renaissance architecture in Rome.

Carceri Nuovi (New Prison)

A massive edifice in brick, at n° 52 via Giulia, this prison was built by Pope Innocent X in 1655.

Palazzo Sachetti

Palazzo Sachetti, at n° 66 via Giulia, is a fine Renaissance building that was begun in 1542 by Antonio da Sangallo the Younger, the architect of Palazzo Farnese. Sangallo hoped to live in the palace himself, but at his death (1546) it was still unfinished. It was subsequently sold to Cardinal Giovanni Ricci, who completed the building work in 1555.

San Giovanni dei Fiorentini*

The Florentine Pope Leo X Medici (1513-1521) intended that this church should be a 'national' sanctuary for his compatriots. He rejected plans submitted by Michelangelo, Raphaël and Peruzzi in favour of one by Jacopo Sansovino. At Sansovino's death, construction continued under Antonio da Sangallo the Younger (1520), Giacomo della Porta (1583-1602) and Maderno (1610-1614). The broad façade (1734) is the work of Alessandro Galilei, who was also responsible for the façade of San Giovanni in Laterano (see p. 116).

The Baroque decoration of the choir is by Piero di Cortona and Borromini (17th century); at the centre is the *Baptism of Jesus,* a marble group sculpted by Antonio Raggi, a pupil of Bernini (17th century). The church also contains the tomb of the architect Maderno, close to which Borromini asked to be buried (see the commemorative plaque on the third pillar to the left).

CORSO VITTORIO EMANUELE III, F4-5

The corso, which was opened in the 19th century, profoundly altered this old Roman district in the loop of the Tiber. However, the narrow mediaeval alleys, full of junkshops and craftsmen's workshops, which wind between the via Giulia and the corso (via del Pellegrino, via dei Cappellari, etc.), have preserved something of the district's former flavour.

CHIESA NUOVA (New Church)* III, F4

St Filippo Neri (1515-1595), a fervent proponent of the Counter-Reformation and one of Rome's most popular saints, founded the order of the Oratory in 1561. This informal fraternity of men of sound faith and goodwill was recognized as a congregation by Pope Gregory XIII in 1575. In addition, Gregory presented the order with the little church of Santa Maria in Vallicella, which they decided to rebuild. The new building, completed in 1605, was given the name of Chiesa Nuova (new church).

Neri had stipulated that the walls of the church should be painted white. After 1640, such austerity seemed old-fashioned, and Pietro di Cortona was commissioned to paint the magnificent series of frescos which now adorn the nave (a representation of the miraculous vision of the Virgin that appeared to St Filippo during the construction of his church), the dome and the apse. The high altar, the organ pipes and the reliefs of the ceiling vault form a splendid ensemble of Baroque ornamentation.

In the choir are three early canvases (1606-1608) by Rubens. The chapel of the Visitation (the fourth on the left) contains a *Visitation* (1594) by Barocci, which St Filippo was often to be found contemplating during his lifetime. Another of the saint's favourite works was Barocci's *Presentation of the Virgin,* in the left transept. St Filippo is buried under the altar of the chapel on the left of the apse. In the sacristy, which is one of Rome's finest, you will find a beautiful marble group by Alessandro Algardi, *St Filippo and the Angel* (1640).

ORATORIO DEI FILIPPINI* III, F4

St Filippo loved music and insisted on its prominent role in the liturgy. Around him, his friends Palestrina and Cavalieri, along with several other musicians, created a new musical form known as the 'oratorio'. In the same spirit, the oratorians commissioned Borromini to build an 'oratory' (1637) to the left of their church; this oratory was reserved for music. Its façade was built in brick so as not to clash with the church next door. At its top is a heavy pediment, which for the first time combines curvilinear and rectilinear motifs, thus resolving the Baroque ambiguity of the other features. The Borromini-style pediments over the window seem to anticipate this architectural compromise.

TOWARDS PIAZZA DI PASQUINO AND PALAZZO BRASCHI III, EF4-5

The itinerary continues along the left side of the Oratorio dei Filippini. Above piazza dell'Orologio rises the graceful **campanile** erected by Borromini, culminating in a group of cast-iron volutes which support the clocks (1647-1648). At the corner of this building is a delightful Baroque framed Madonna, like those found on street corners in older parts of Rome.

From here, the route follows the **via del Governo Vecchio,** along which papal processions used to pass. The street is narrow and picturesque as it winds its way gently up to piazza Navona. Today, it is mostly occupied by antique shops and dealers in secondhand goods.

On **piazza di Pasquino**, at the corner where Palazzo Braschi is, you will notice a small, badly damaged statue, which was placed here by Cardinal Oliviero Carafa in 1501. At one time, the people of Rome came after dark to attach pamphlets to this statue. The figure was nicknamed **'Pasquino'** and the offending pamphlets were known as 'pasquinades'. By next morning, their contents would be the talk of the town and, though the practice was punishable by death, the sentence was rarely applied.

Behind Pasquino stands **Palazzo Braschi,** which was built at the close of the 18th century by Pope Pius VI Braschi for his nephews. This was the last palazzo in Rome to be constructed for a papal family and is now the home of the Rome Museum.

PIAZZA NAVONA*** III, EF4-5

This piazza is often cited as the loveliest in the world. The warm colours of its façades, the lively architecture of the church of Sant'Agnese in Agone, the play of water and light in the fountains—all seem to perpetuate the memory of past pageants. Piazza Navona's history is full of such lavish spectacles, including firework displays, carnivals and tournaments organized by princes of the church, aristocratic Roman families and ambassadors from the various European courts.

Today, the piazza is reserved for pedestrians. There are tourists as well as Romans strolling with their families and friends. If you can, come here early in the morning, when everything is still cool and fresh and full of rich colour.

Piazza Navona owes its name and its narrow, extended shape to the Emperor Domitian. It occupies the site of a stadium built by him in AD 86 for athletic games; *in agone,* meaning 'in competition' was distorted to *n'agone,* then to *navona*. Constantine stripped the stadium of its marble in the 4th century, leaving it a waste area of tumbled masonry where builders of churches and palaces habitually foraged for cheap construction materials. At the close of the 15th century, the market of Rome (by then a city with only 25,000 inhabitants) had abandoned the Capitol for the new piazza, which was gradually paved and built up with shops.

During the Baroque era, piazza Navona was the scene of many festivities, for which its buildings were frequently hung with temporary decorations of pasteboard, painted wood and bright drapery.

Until the mid-19th century, the piazza was regularly filled with water on

A statue of Neptune adorns the lovely piazza Navona.

Saturdays and Sundays in August, a manœuvre made possible by its sloping contours, sunken at the centre. When the water was in place, various nautical diversions were arranged, in which princes and prelates as well as the common people took part.

Every year, from December 8 to January 6 (the festival of *La Befana*, the good witch who is the Roman equivalent of Santa Claus), stalls are set up in piazza Navona to sell sweets, toys and Neapolitan crèches. The *piferari* (flute-players) still come down from the Abruzzi hills for this occasion, wearing their beribboned hats and sheepskin-lined coats.

Fontana dei Fiumi***

This spectacular fountain (1651) by Bernini was commissioned by Pope Innocent X Pamphili, whose family palace was on the piazza Navona. Innocent X disliked the fountain, but recognized that no other sculptor but Bernini could give the piazza the lavish decor it deserved. Bernini succeeded in raising an Egyptian obelisk, which had been lying in fragments in the circus of Maxentius, onto a high limestone plinth. To this he added four figures representing the great rivers of each continent, sculpted by his pupils after his design: the Danube (Europe), Rio de la Plata (America), the Ganges (Asia) and the Nile (Africa). Note that the face of the Nile figure is veiled, because at that time its source was unknown. A somewhat spiteful tradition has it that the Rio de la Plata's hand is raised for protection against the imminent collapse of Borromini's church of Sant'Agnese. There is no question that Bernini and Borromini were bitter rivals; but in this case, the church was built after the fountain, so no sarcasm can have been intended.

The obelisk, soaring to the sky in defiance of the law of gravity, bears the tiara and keys of the papal insignia. At its summit is the dove of the Pamphili family, holding an olive branch.

Fontana del Moro and Fontana del Nettuno

The **Fountain of the Moor**, to the left of Palazzo Pamphili, was installed at the end of the 16th century. The group that includes the Moor (the savage of the Baroque age) locked in combat with a dolphin is the work of one of Bernini's pupils, after Bernini's original design (1654).

The **Fountain of Neptune** was set up at the other end of the piazza at the close of the 16th century; its statues were added much later, in 1873.

Sant'Agnese in Agone*

The original building on this site was a small church erected to commemorate the place of St Agnes's martyrdom. Innocent X, who wanted his 'piazza Pamphili' to be the finest in Rome, decided on a magnificent reconstruction of the sanctuary. The work was begun by Girolamo Rainaldi in 1652 and continued by Borromini from 1652 to 1657. In 1657, Innocent died and Borromini was replaced by Carlo Rainaldi, son of Girolamo, working under Bernini's supervision. The result is an architectural hybrid but, despite changes made by the younger Rainaldi and Bernini (e.g., the top levels of the towers, the skylight and the austere pediment), the façade of Sant'Agnese still bears the elegant stamp of Borromini.

SANTA MARIA DELLA PACE** III, E4

Open Sun 11am-noon; Mon-Sat apply to the caretaker of the cloister to the left of the church.

Santa Maria della Pace acquired its name from Sixtus IV, who had the church rebuilt after the Pazzi conspiracy against the Medicis, in which one of his nephews took part. It was altered in the 17th century by Pietro di Cortona on the orders of Alexander VII Chigi and, along with its piazza, forms one of the most delightful monuments in the **Campo Marzio**. The small piazza in front of the church was designed by its Baroque architect to solve a delicate traffic problem. Santa Maria della Pace was a fashionable church, at which mass was held in the afternoon—a rarity in Rome. However, the streets alongside the church were too narrow to allow the carriages of the Roman aristocracy to reach the church and turn around in front of it without causing disputes over precedence—hence, the need for a new piazza.

Façade

In harmony with the style of the piazza, the façade of Santa Maria della Pace is composed of subtle curves and counter-curves. The semicircular Doric porch achieves a successful transition, in terms of colour and shape, between the inside and the outside of the church; it was much imitated subsequently. In addition, the broad concave wings which form the façade's backdrop serve to draw the eye away from adjacent buildings like the apse of Santa Maria dell'Anima. Far from clashing with the convexity of the porch, these wings have the optical effect of shifting the façade towards the centre of the piazza.

Interior

The church has retained its highly original 15th-century floor plan, which combines a short nave and side chapels with an octagon topped by an ample cupola.

The arcade of the first chapel on the right is decorated with frescos by Raphaël, commissioned by the Siennese banker Agostino Chigi, who had the chapel built in 1513. Raphaël's figures, subtly festooned around the arch, represent the somewhat pagan theme of the four Sybils inspired by the angels. Above them, the prophets Daniel and David (on the right) and Habakkuk and Jonah (on the left) were created by one of Raphaël's pupils from a cartoon by the master.

Baldassare Peruzzi was responsible for the frescos above the altar (1516) in the first chapel on the left, which depict the Virgin, St Bridget, St Catherine and the donor, Chigi. The second chapel on the right (1530) was designed by Antonio da Sangallo the Younger and is decorated in classic Renaissance style.

The high altar (1516) is the work of Maderno. Tradition has it that blood flowed from the Virgin of Peace above the altar after she had been struck by a pebble; it was this miracle that prompted Sixtus IV to rebuild the church.

Bramante's **cloister**★★ (1500-1504) may be reached by way of a door on the left-hand side of the church—this is a sober but admirable work by the great Renaissance architect.

▬▬ *SANT'AGOSTINO*★ III, E5

Sant'Agostino (1479-1483) is one of the earliest buildings of the Roman Renaissance. Cardinal d'Estouteville, Archbishop of Rouen, paid for its construction. The simple limestone façade is similar to that of Santa Maria del Popolo, built at roughly the same time. The upper area, with its rose window, is harmoniously connected to the lower by broad lateral volutes. The interior of the church shows no such restraint, having been 'modernized' in the 18th and 19th centuries, but it does contain some extraordinary masterpieces.

To the right of the main entrance is a fine work by Jacopo Sansovino, *La Madonna del Parto*★ (Virgin of Childbirth), which is much revered, to judge by the number of ex-voto tablets it has accumulated. On the third pillar of the central nave is Raphaël's *Prophet Isaiah*★ (1512). This painting clearly shows how much Raphaël was influenced by Michelangelo's fresco in the

Sistine Chapel. Beneath the fresco is another fine piece by Sansovino, a *Virgin and Child with St Anne* (1512).

A very beautiful painting by Caravaggio, *Madonna of the Pilgrims*** (1605), hangs in the first chapel on the left. It forcefully redefines the traditional vision theme by placing the figures of the composition within a decor that has been stripped to the barest essentials. Here, the fragment of a door and threshold have an ambivalent purpose; they serve both to bring the groups together and to place an unbridgeable chasm between them. To achieve this effect, Caravaggio does not need to load his Virgin with princely clothing—the silky glimmer of her garnet-red coat, the blue-green of her right sleeve, her youth and the beauty of her body are sufficient. Despite the dirty feet and torn garments of the figures with their backs to us (probably an accurate portrayal of 17th-century pilgrims to Rome), the effect of realism is purely superficial: this work is profoundly spiritual in tone.

SAN LUIGI DEI FRANCESI* III, E5

San Luigi has been France's national church in Rome since 1589. Its majestic two-storied façade is the work of Giacomo della Porta and Domenico Fontana. The broad pediment that crowns the edifice bears a salamander, the emblem of François I. The statues, in niches, were installed in the 18th century.

Three admirable works by Caravaggio may be seen in the Cointrel (Contarelli) Chapel (fifth on the right of the nave), which was commissioned by the French Cardinal Matthieu Cointrel and dedicated to the apostle whose name he bore. Caravaggio was asked to paint three pictures of the life of the saint (1599-1602). In *The Vocation of St Matthew*** , on the left, the painter revolutionized the conventional treatment of God's appearance on earth by using a scene and figures from contemporary Rome. At left, Matthew the tax official and his companions, in brightly-coloured garments, are seen doing their daily accounts. At right, two unknown figures emerge from the darkness. St Peter, leaning on his staff, is seen from behind wearing an ancient costume; his bulk partially obscures the figure of Christ, who points a finger at the astonished Matthew. Above Christ, the beam of light which illuminates the wall and the faces of the protagonists symbolizes the supernatural, while at the same time forming a link between the two groups.

In the centre of the chapel, *St Matthew and the Angel* represents St Matthew writing his gospel while an angel dictates.

The Martyrdom of St Matthew , on the right, is a remarkable composition: the canvas is closed in on all sides by figures who watch helplessly as the event unfolds. Among them Caravaggio has depicted his own face, contorted with grief, to the left of the executioner. The deliberate impassivity of the onlookers concentrates emotion at the center of the painting, where the innocent victim and, above all, the executioner appear in full light: the latter's powerful physique and bloody sword, along with the figure of the fleeing, terrified clerk, express the savagery of the act which has just been committed. But hope is also present in the form of the martyr's crown which the angel proffers to St Matthew.

In the second chapel, on the right of the nave, are a series of frescos (1616-1617) by Domenichino illustrating the life of St Cecilia. The spirit of Raphaël and the teachings of Annibale Caracci are evident in these frescos, which are characteristic of the Classical trend in Rome at the beginning of the 17th century. The figures have the grace of ancient statues; their feelings are expressed by way of studied gestures. In contrast to Caravaggio, Domenichino uses light not to generate form, but to emphasize line and tone down colour (for iconographic details, apply at the entrance of the church). Lastly, behind the altar hangs a painting by Guido Reni entitled *St Cecilia and Four Saints*, which is copied from an original by Raphaël.

■■■ PALAZZO MADAMA* III, F5

This palazzo, on the left-hand side of San Luigi dei Francesi, was built by the Medicis in the 16th century. It owes its name to 'Madama' Margaret of Austria, the illegitimate daughter of Emperor Charles V; Margaret later married Alessandro di Medici. The fine Baroque façade facing the corso del Rinascimento is the work of Cardi and Marucelli (1649). Palazzo Madama has been the seat of the Italian Senate since 1871.

■■■ PALAZZO DELLA SAPIENZA III, F5

Until 1935, this building was the headquarters of Rome University. Its principal feature is a magnificent **courtyard*** with two levels of arcades, designed by Giacomo della Porta (1575).

At the end of the courtyard, don't miss the beautiful **chapel of Sant'Ivo****, built by Borromini between 1642 and 1660 (open Sun 10-11am). If you wish to visit at some other time, apply to the caretaker and offer a tip.

The exterior of the building is curious. The structure resembling a drum that overlooks the courtyard is in fact an envelope of masonry which absorbs the lateral thrust of the cupola. Farther up, a series of slightly convex tiers leads to a lantern-turret, which closely resembles the Roman Temple of Venus at Baalbek but which in fact is based on a 17th-century engraving of a temple at Tivoli. The turret is crowned by a spiral-shaped tower, the spiral being the traditional form of the Tower of Babel, but in this case symbolizing wisdom (sapienza).

The chapel's interior is equally strange. It is planned around two intersecting equilateral triangles, which form a six-pointed star. The points of this star are either replaced by semicircular apses or sealed by convex walls. A continuous sequence of giant pilasters supports a massive coping, the groins of which accentuate the building's complex but harmonious design.

The white walls of the chapel perfectly offset these subtleties of Borromini's architecture, and the building is flooded with light. There can be no doubt that Sant'Ivo represents a high point in Roman Baroque.

■■■ THE PANTHEON*** III, F5

Open daily 9am-5pm (6pm in summer).

The Pantheon is both the most beautiful and the best-preserved of Rome's ancient monuments. Built by Agrippa, the friend of Augustus, between 27-25 BC, the building was dedicated to all the gods. However, it was probably intended to celebrate the divinity of *gens Julia*, i.e., the family of Julius Caesar, of whom Augustus was the adopted son. The Pantheon was restored by Domitian after the fire of AD 80, then rebuilt by Hadrian (AD 125), who added its massive rotunda. Looted by the barbarian invaders of the 5th century, the Pantheon was then saved by Pope Boniface IV, who named it the church of Santa Maria Rotunda in 609. This did not deter Urban VIII from stripping the bronze trusses and girders from the portico roof in the 17th century to use in the construction of Bernini's baldachin at St Peter's. Pasquino's comment was devastating (see p. 91): *'Quod non fecerunt Barbari, fecerunt Barberini'* (what the barbarians did not do, the Barberini have done). Shortly afterwards, Bernini added two pinnacle turrets to each end of the pediment. These were instantly dubbed 'Bernini's donkey ears' by Pasquino, but were not removed until the 19th century.

Exterior

The Pantheon consists of a squat cylindrical edifice attached to an impressive portico some 108 ft/33 m wide. This portico is supported by 16 monolithic granite columns with white marble capitals. In ancient times, it stood at the top of a flight of five steps, overlooking a piazza (much larger than the present one) which was framed in turn by porticos. Thus the drum of the rotunda was invisible to anyone standing in front of the temple; nor could the spectator deduce from its exterior what its interior might be like. The inscription on the architrave, *'Marcus Agrippa Luci Filius Consul tertium fecit'* ('Marcus Agrippa, son of Lucius, Consul for the third time, made this'), dates from the time of Hadrian and is a testimony to the modesty of that emperor, who always refused to put his name on the many monuments he erected. The bronze door dates from antiquity (though it was restored in the 16th century).

Interior

The interior is covered by a hemispherical flattened dome, the largest ever built: its diameter, 142 ft/43.3 m, exceeds the diameter of the dome of St Peter's by one metre. It is also exactly equal to the height of the building. The central oculus, which opens to the sky, is 29.5 ft/9 m in diameter, and the cylindrical wall which supports the dome is 19.6 ft/6 m thick. The architects of the Renaissance, from Brunelleschi (who built the dome of Santa Maria del Fiore in Florence) to Bramante (who dreamed of 'putting the Pantheon atop the basilica of Constantine', i.e., St Peter's), often came to study the monument and attempt to unravel its secrets. They also borrowed many of its architectural motifs, such as the aedicules with curved and triangular pediments that may be seen on the façade of Palazzo Farnese.

The statues of gods which once stood in the various niches vanished long ago. Today, the Pantheon contains the tombs of Victor Emmanuel II, the first King of Italy, who died in 1878, and of his son and successor, Umberto I, who died in 1900. Raphaël is also buried here (under the niche containing a *Virgin of Lorensetto*, to the left of the high altar), along with Baldassare Peruzzi, Annibale Carracci and various other artists.

Piazza della Rotunda and piazza della Minerva

The lively piazza della Rotunda is directly in front of the Pantheon. At its centre is a splendid fountain by Giacomo della Porta (1578), which includes an obelisk from a nearby temple of Isis (erected here in 1711).

On the piazza della Minerva, the little marble elephant bearing an Egyptian obelisk was designed by Bernini in 1667.

▬ *SANTA MARIA SOPRA MINERVA* ★★ III, F6

Santa Maria, which was rebuilt around 1280, is Rome's only Gothic church. However, changes wrought in the 17th century and above all a disastrous 're-Gothification' of the 19th century have removed every vestige of its original character. Today, the church is interesting only because of its contents, and in this respect it is a veritable museum. Among other things it contains a large number of very fine mediaeval, Renaissance and Baroque tombs.

Don't miss the monumental marble arcade in the right-hand nave. The arcade opens onto the **Carafa Chapel,** which is covered with superb **frescos★** (1489) by Filippino Lippi illustrating the life of St Thomas. Above the altar is an *Annunciation,* showing St Thomas presenting Cardinal Carafa to the Virgin; on the right are more scenes from the life of St Thomas.

To the left of this chapel is the **Tomb of Guillaume Durand★,** by Giovanni Cosma. In the chapel on the right is a fine **wooden crucifix★** (15th century).

Beneath the high altar lies the body of St Catherine of Siena (1347-1380), enclosed in a sarcophagus by Isaiah da Pisa.

The chapels of the left transept also contain several very fine tombs. In the second chapel is that of Giovanni Arberini (d. 1473), which includes a panel from an antique sarcophagus of *Hercules Wrestling With a Lion★*; this is a Roman copy of a Greek bas-relief from the 5th century BC.

At the end of the left-hand nave, by the door, is the magnificent **tomb★** of Francesco Tornabuoni (d. 1480) by Mina da Fiesole.

IV
TOWARDS ST PETER'S
AND PAPAL ROME

T his itinerary covers Ponte Sant'Angelo, decorated with angels, Castel Sant'Angelo, with its sumptuous Mannerist decoration, St Peter's Square and Basilica, centre of Catholicism, and the fabulous treasures of the papal palaces. The itinerary's various stages bear witness to the high points of both Renaissance and Baroque art, and to an age in which religious fervour was matched only by the ostentation of papal power.

Access

Map III, E4. Bus: 26, 70, 81, 87, 116.

▬ *VIA DEI CORONARI* III, E4

Sixtus IV (1471-1484) constructed the first straight thoroughfare through the Campo Marzio to facilitate traffic flow in the mediaeval city. Called the via dei Coronari, it was originally crowded with stalls selling rosaries *(coronari)* and other religious objects to pilgrims on their way to St Peter's by the Ponte Sant'Angelo. Today these merchants have been replaced by antique dealers.

The church of **San Salvatore in Lauro** stands on the right side of the street. This church contains a fine *Adoration of the Shepherds* by Pietro di Cortona in the third chapel on the right. On the left of the church is a door leading to a charming Renaissance cloister, with a small courtyard and fountain.

▬ *PONTE SANT'ANGELO*★★ III, E3

Only three middle arches remain of the old bridge built between AD 133 and 134 by the Emperor Hadrian to link the Campo Marzio with his mausoleum. Statues of St Peter and St Paul were installed at the end of the bridge in 1530. Later, in 1668, Bernini and his assistants added 10 angels, which bear the instruments of Christ's passion. Their graceful postures are belied by the appalling instruments of torture they display, by their anguished expressions and by the unreal rendering of their garments.

▬ *CASTEL SANT'ANGELO*★★ III, DE3

Open Tues-Sat 9am-1pm; Sun 9am-noon.

The majestic castle of Sant'Angelo was originally conceived as a huge Etruscan-inspired mausoleum like that of Augustus (see p. 166). It was the conception of the Emperor Hadrian (AD 130-139), who intended it for himself and his successors.

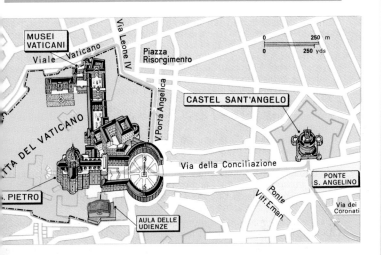

The building was constructed on a square foundation with sides 292 ft/89 m long and a height of 49 ft/15 m. This base was crowned by a cylindrical drum some 69 ft/21 m high, bristling with statues and overlaid by a mound planted with cypress trees. At the top of this mound was a square plinth bearing a bronze chariot drawn by four horses, with a statue of Hadrian driving. The funerary urns of all the Roman emperors, from Hadrian to Septimius Severus (AD 211) were placed here. In AD 271, Aurelian fortified the monument and incorporated it into an advanced bastion of his wall around the city.

The present name of the castle is linked to a vision experienced by St Gregory the Great. The vision occurred during a procession organized to stave off a plague in AD 590. Gregory saw an angel sheathing his sword on top of the mausoleum, and took this as a sign that the plague was ended.

During the turbulent Middle Ages, Castel Sant'Angelo was frequently besieged. It served as a place of refuge, as a prison and as one of the principal bastions of papal power in Rome. In 1527, Clement VII took refuge in the castle when Charles V's troops sacked the city.

Exterior

From the outside, Castel Sant'Angelo is a square, battlemented edifice, with four polygonal towers, one at each corner. In its centre stands a massive rotunda, built of ancient peperino and limestone blocks.

Interior

From the square outer courtyard, a vestibule leads into the central building, where five scale models of the castle are displayed. These show the various stages through which it has passed since its inception. An impressive Roman **spiral staircase***, 410 ft/125 m long and formerly decorated with marble and mosaic, leads to a flight of steps. In ancient times, these led to the chamber containing the imperial funerary urns; today, however, they pass above it. At the top of the steps, you enter the **Angel Courtyard,** so called because of a marble angel sculpted by Raffaello da Montelupo (16th century) which crowned the castle until the 18th century. On the right, note the guardhouse, rebuilt exactly as it was in the 16th century.

From the courtyard, you can enter the apartments of Clement VIII on the left, and then continue to the **Apollo Room,** which is decorated with 16th-century grotesques (decorative art characterized by fantastic human or animal forms distorted into absurdity or ugliness). Note in the floor tiling the mouth of a well 29.5 ft/9 m deep. At the bottom of this well is a small room, or oubliette, one of the many secret dungeons in the castle. At the end of the Apollo Room, on the right, is the chapel of Leo X ; on the left, two rooms lead to the **courtyard of Alexander VI,** with a magnificent well bearing the arms of the Borgia family. On the right, a staircase leads to the famous dungeons where Benvenuto Cellini, among others, was imprisoned in the 16th century.

From the courtyard of Alexander VI, stairs lead to the **loggia of Julius II,** by Bramante, which offers a fine view over the Ponte Sant'Angelo and the city. A further flight of steps leads to the magnificent **apartments★** of Paul III (1534-1549), set up in case he should be obliged to take refuge in the castle, as his predecessor did in 1527. From here, you can make your way through the **Council Chamber** (Mannerist decoration: grotesques, murals, *trompe l'œil*) to the **Perseus Chamber,** with its fine frieze by Perin del Vaga. The adjoining **Chamber of Venus and Psyche** is named after another frieze by the same artist.

A narrow corridor covered in grotesques leads from the Council Chamber to the **library.** This magnificent room has flattened arches decorated with frescos and stucco.

The door facing the library entrance leads through to a room known as **Hadrian's Mausoleum** which contains, among other paintings, Lorenzo Lotto's beautiful *Saint Jerome*★. The door on the right of the entrance opens into the **Secret Archive Chamber** (or Treasury), where the papacy's greatest treasures were kept in iron coffers during the 16th century; it also contained the pontifical archives in fine walnut cabinets. A small staircase leads past a small circular room (used as a prison for political offenders until 1870) to the upper terrace which offers a magnificent view★★ of St Peter's and the city.

▬▬▬ *VIA DELLA CONCILIAZIONE* III, E2-3

This arterial road was built during the fascist era to symbolize the reconciliation between the Vatican and the Italian State (Lateran Treaties, 1929). A picturesque mediaeval district, the Borgo, had to be demolished to make way for via della Conciliazione, but the result offers a fine view of St Peter's.

The church of **Santa Maria in Traspontina** (1563-1637) and **Palazzo Torlonia** (1496-1504) are on the right. The latter's façade is a small-scale reproduction of the façade of Palazzo della Cancelleria (see p. 87). On the opposite side of the road, facing Palazzo Torlonia, is the Palazzo dei Penitenzieri, dating from the late 15th century.

VATICAN CITY

The Vatican state

The Vatican is the world's smallest independent state, covering only 109 acres/44 hectares. It is also one of the most visited places on earth, made so by throngs of pilgrims and art-lovers.

On February 11, 1929, the Holy See and the kingdom of Italy signed the Lateran Treaties (the *conciliazione*). This finally settled the question which had been pending since the seizure of Rome by the army of Victor Emmanuel II in 1870. Among other things, the dispute had involved the voluntary 'interior exile' of St Peter's successors within the Vatican.

By the terms of this treaty, the Vatican became an independent state in which a sovereign—the pope—exercised full legislative,

Fortified in the Middle Ages, Hadrian's Mausoleum was used as a refuge by many popes.

executive and judicial powers. Today, the Vatican also has its own administration and services, including a bank, a railway station, a post office and a radio centre that broadcasts in approximately 40 languages. The Vatican has its own flag (the papal tiara and crossed keys against a yellow-and-white background), its own anthem (Gounod's *Papal March*), and its own currency, which is legal tender all over Italy. In 1970, Pope Paul VI dissolved three of the Vatican's four regiments, leaving only the Swiss Guards, whose uniforms were designed by Michelangelo.

The heart of the universal church

Apart from his position as a temporal leader, the pope is the Bishop of Rome, the successor of St Peter, the head of the Catholic, Apostolic and Roman Church, and the Vicar of Christ. In his mission as Pastor of the Church of Christ, he is assisted by the College of Cardinals and the Roman Curia. Popes are elected by the College of Cardinals, who meet in a conclave to cast their votes.

On the death of a pope, the **conclave** meets in the Sistine Chapel, behind locked doors, to elect the successor. Votes are cast twice a day, and the ballots are burned after each vote. The smoke from this burning is black until such time as a final decision is made; the required majority being two thirds plus one vote. When a majority is reached, the smoke of the burning ballots turns white, signalling the election of one of the cardinals. The news is then announced from the balcony of St Peter's: *'Habemus papam'* ('We have a pope'), and the new pontiff comes out to bestow his first benediction.

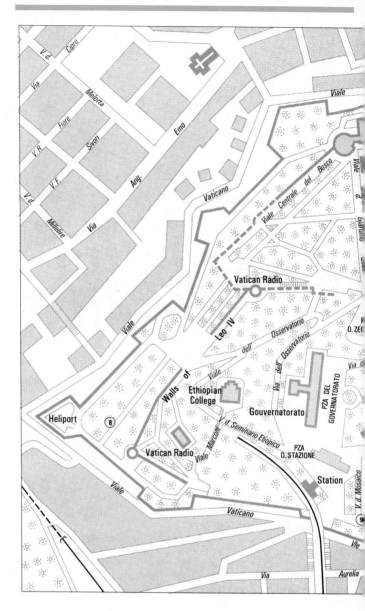

■■■ *PIAZZA SAN PIETRO**** *(St Peter's Square)* III, E2

This gigantic piazza, Bernini's major architectural achievement in Rome, cannot be considered separately from the basilica for which it was conceived. Originally commissioned by Pope Alexander VIII in 1656, the piazza had to be sufficiently large to accommodate the crowds that gathered at Easter to receive the pope's *urbi et orbi* blessing, bestowed on 'the city and the world'. At the same time, the pope had to be visible to the faithful, not only from the loggia of St Peter's, but also from one of the

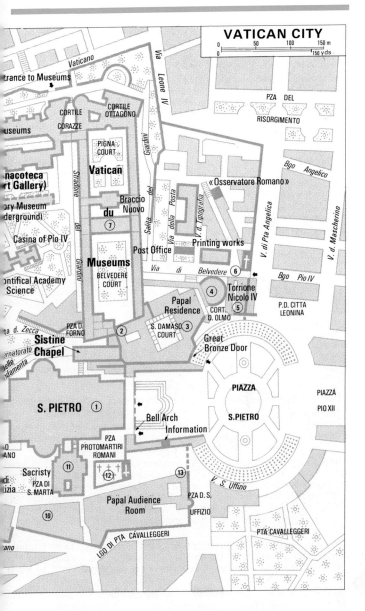

windows of his private apartments. A covered gallery was also required for processional purposes. Finally, the dimensions of the piazza had to be in keeping with the absolute pre-eminence of the new basilica above all other churches in the Christian world.

The solution adopted by Bernini was an ingenious one, incorporating all of the above-mentioned constraints while simultaneously escaping from them. His concept of a trapezoid space in front of the basilica was more or less demanded by the position of the papal palace, but he made it open on to a broad oval enclosed by the two arms of a quadruple colonnade.

Quite apart from its geometrical purity, which is based on circles with circumferences intersecting each other's centres, Bernini's elliptical design endowed the new square with optimal visibility and offset the **obelisk** placed in front of the basilica by Domenico Fontana in 1586.

The choice of **colonnades,** instead of a building with several levels, displays Bernini's talent at its greatest. Depending on the angle from which they are viewed, the colonnades reveal either a dense forest of limestone or a majestic portico. The same balance of open and closed, of stillness and movement, is found in the vertical axis of the ensemble: hence 140 lively statues of saints are opposed to a series of tranquil Doric columns beneath the coping.

Bernini also planned a third portico element which would have closed and completed the piazza. It would have created a breathtaking sight for pilgrims who had just made their way through the narrow, mediaeval streets of the Borgo. But this latter project was never realized. Today, the construction of the via della Conciliazione has eliminated the Borgo altogether, and although the area is still scenically impressive, it is totally different from the Baroque spirit in which it was originally conceived.

▬▬ *SAN PIETRO*** (St Peter's Basilica)* III, E1

Open Apr-Sept, daily 7am-7pm; Oct-Mar, daily 7am-5.30pm. Guided tours of the basilica (including Vatican City and gardens) Tues and Wed 9.30am from the Vatican Information Office (to the left of the basilica). There is no visiting during major religious ceremonies.

Papal audiences

General audiences are held on Wednesdays at 11am in the Papal Audience Room (to the left of Bernini's colonnade). Authorizations to attend are issued on Tuesdays by the Casa Pontificia from 9am-1pm (also located on the square).

(Note: Boldface numbers appearing in parentheses in the following text indicate locations as shown on the floorplan of St Peters, p. 109.)

St Peter's is the largest basilica in the world, at the heart of the capital of Catholicism. As a monument, it represents the meeting point of two great currents of history, those of the Catholic faith and of Italian art.

The first St Peter's was built by the Emperor Constantine (AD 320-322) on the site where St Peter was said to have been buried after his crucifixion (between AD 64 and 67). St Peter was one of many Christians arrested on Nero's orders following the great fire of AD 64. The original basilica had five naves, with apse and transept; the upper part of a small 2nd-century monument was visible in the choir and was supposed to mark St Peter's tomb.

On several occasions the building was looted by invaders, but each time it was quickly restored to its original state. Embellished and enriched over the centuries, the edifice eventually began to show alarming signs of wear and tear.

By the close of the 15th century, the whole basilica was in imminent peril of collapse. Utterly beyond repair, the basilica had to be replaced. Nicolas V began work on this project in 1452, but his death in 1455 interrupted the endeavour. In 1503, on the accession of Julius II, the construction of a gigantic new St Peter's was begun in earnest.

Julius II laid the first stone of the new sanctuary in 1506. His architect, Bramante, had chosen a Greek cross floorplan (i.e., four equal branches within a square) and a flattened dome like that of the ancient Pantheon. The circle and the Greek cross were considered the ideal form for a church because they mirrored divine perfection; whereas the old basilica design

Bernini's elegant colonnade encircles St Peter's Square.

was thought to be imperfect and based on pagan philosophy. Other proposals based on the Latin cross floorplan (a long nave crossed by a shorter transept) had also been considered, but despite being more suitable for liturgical ceremonies and providing a method to integrate the floorplan of the old basilica, they were rejected.

The death of Julius II in 1513, followed by that of Bramante the following year, brought the project to an early halt, with only the foundation of the pillars completed. The artists who succeeded Bramante were hesitant as to which plan they should adopt: Raphaël, who was called in to direct the work, designed a majestic edifice in the form of a Latin cross, but died in 1520 before work could begin. His successors remained divided on the question, and nothing was done.

In 1547, Pope Paul III appointed Michelangelo (then 72 years old) as chief architect for the Vatican and commissioned him to continue and complete the building of St Peter's. Michelangelo revived Bramante's original plan, but modified it to make the building grander and more majestic; in particular, he redesigned the dome to make it broader and higher.

On the death of Michelangelo in 1564, three branches of the cross had been finished and the drum of the dome had been constructed. Giacomo della Porta, his successor, raised the dome still further (1588-1590), either by altering Michelangelo's original design or by using a variant sketched out by the master.

In 1605, Paul V put an end to the long controversy by opting for the Latin cross design and commissioned the architect Carlo Maderno to prolong the nave. The Latin cross was now in fashion again, as might have been expected in the new atmosphere of the Counter-Reformation, with its emphasis on great ceremonies and spectacular processions which necessitated longer naves. Symbolically, Maderno's broad façade opening on to the naves (1614) totally obscures Michelangelo's Renaissance dome when viewed from St Peter's Square.

From 1624 until his death 56 years later, Gian Lorenzo Bernini worked to embellish St Peter's. He was originally commissioned by his friend Urban VIII Barberini, and was responsible for the baldachin over the high altar, a number of magnificent tombs, the throne of St Peter in the apse, and for St Peter's Square and colonnade. With Bernini's work, the Renaissance building became a sumptuous backdrop for the expression of Baroque piety.

Façade

At the top of Bernini's majestic staircase, the façade by Carlo Maderno (1614) is made up of giant Corinthian columns and pilasters, which carry a broad coping surmounted by an attic with windows of varying shapes. Above the attic, a balustrade runs between the giant **statues of Christ** (18.5 ft/5.65 m), **St John the Baptist** and the **Apostles.**

The façade has been violently criticized because it masks the dome from St Peter's Square. In addition, Paul V's decision (1612) to build clocktowers on either side of the façade obliged Maderno to add two outer 'wings' which enlarge it considerably, even excessively. Giuseppe Valadier installed two clocks in these towers during the 19th century.

The pope's *urbi et orbi* Easter blessing is bestowed from the balcony above the central opening (the *loggia delle benedizione*). The election of a new pope is also announced from here.

The bronze panels of the **central doorway,** beneath the portico, are those of the old basilica, cast by Filarete (1433-1445). Above these is a bas-relief by Bernini (1646). The **Holy Door,** on the right, is only opened only during Holy Years (i.e., every 25 years) though an exception was made in 1983. Above the central aperture of the portico is a heavily restored mosaic by Giotto (the *Navicella*), executed for the First Jubilee (1300). To the right of the porch, in the vestibule of the Scala Regia (closed to visitors), there is an impressive equestrian **statue of Constantine** by Bernini (1670).

Interior

The sheer quantity of works of art (e.g., there are over 400 statues on display) make it impossible to give a detailed description of each of them here. Instead, we offer a brief selection of items and an outline of their religious and aesthetic context.

The perfect harmony of the basilica's proportions may make you forget its real size. The tremendous sanctuary contains 50 chapels and, to take a single example, the baldachin above the high altar of St Peter's is the same height as the Palazzo Farnese (95 ft/29 m).

The central nave

The imposing nave added by Carlo Maderno (1614) to the original plan of St Peter's is framed by more formal Counter-Reformation architecture; its main features are the huge, flat, Corinthian pilasters set in pairs against massive pillars. Broad archways open from the spaces between these pillars, leading to the lateral naves and chapels. The coping supports an immense expanse of coffered ceiling (144 ft/44 m high), which was decorated at the close of the 18th century. In front of the entrance, a great disk of porphyry has been inserted into the pavement on the spot where Charlemagne was crowned Emperor of the Western Empire by Pope Leo III, on Christmas Eve, AD 800. On the same stretch of pavement, the lengths of the other great churches of Christendom have also been marked.

The niches between the flat pilasters of the nave and the pillars at the crossing of the transept contain statues of the founding saints of various religious orders. In the last pillar on the right stands a bronze **statue of St Peter***; note the left foot, which has been worn away by the kisses and caresses of generations of the faithful. This mediaeval statue is the work of Arnolfo di Cambio (13th century).

The baldachin**

This remarkable work was begun, at the request of Pope Urban VIII, by Bernini in 1623, when he was only 25 years old. It was a response to the structural and liturgical need to concentrate attention on the high altar, which otherwise would have been dwarfed by the immensity of the nave. The colossal proportions of the new basilica ruled out the usual mediaeval solution, which was to install a domed ciborium (similar to, but larger than, a baldachin) in the space: it was agreed that a ciborium would appear far too ponderous.

Bernini's first innovation was to reproduce, on a giant scale, the twisted columns that had stood before the altar of the original basilica (these ancient columns can still be seen among the loggias of the pillars holding up the dome). In this way he created an architectural link between the two basilicas, and expressed the difference between the simplicity of primitive Christianity and the majesty of the Counter-Reformation church, fresh from its triumph over the Protestants at the Battle of the White Mountain in 1620. Next, Bernini erected a baldachin structure over the altar, directly above the tomb of St Peter, imitating the fabric which was customarily stretched over the pontifical throne during processions within the basilica. The fragile, ephemeral, but spectacular effect thus created is sufficient to counter the heaviness of the bronze. The tightly massed flutings that begin at the base of the columns draw the eye upwards to the top of the structure, where a succession of valances seem to float in air, with no more support than garlands of flowers held by angels. Beyond are massive volutes, designed by Borromini, which meet beneath a curved coping topped by a globe and cross.

The baldachin of St Peter's had its critics, who objected to its misplaced theatricality and to the stripping of bronze plaques from the Pantheon for its construction. Nonetheless, it remains undeniably the earliest and greatest Baroque monument in Rome, and its form was so perfectly attuned to the religious sensibilities of the period that it was subsequently imitated in churches throughout Europe.

The dome***

The dome of St Peter's is one of the world's wonders. It is the highest and most majestic in Rome, resting on a building which seems to have no other purpose than to support it. The four pilings that bear the dome's weight are some 233 ft/71 m in perimeter, and the medallions with pendentives representing the four Evangelists are each 26 ft/8 m in diameter. St Mark's pen alone is 5 ft/1.5 m long. Within the dome are mosaics representing the popes and doctors of the Church; these are succeeded by Christ, the Virgin, St Paul, St John the Baptist and the Apostles; then the angels; and finally, at the apex, God the Father bestowing his benediction.

The pillars of the transept

These majestic pentagonal pillars (233 ft/71 m in circumference) were begun by Bramante, then strengthened and completed by Michelangelo. However, by Urban VIII's time, they no longer corresponded to the prevailing climate of religious feeling. In 1629, Bernini covered them in marble and cut huge niches in them to accommodate four colossal statues (16.4 ft/5 m tall) of saints whose relics are preserved in the basilica. These statues are of *St Helena* (10) by Bolgi (1639), *St Veronica* (11) by Mochi (1632), *St Andrew* (12) by Duquesnoy (1640) and, above all, Bernini's splendid rendering of *St Longinus* (9), the soldier who pierced Christ on the cross with his spear (1639). Note the effect of tumultuous movement in the saint's sculpted garment, which heightens the impression of violent emotion: here, to all appearances, is one who has just witnessed the scene of Calvary. Relics (a fragment of the True Cross, the Holy Veil, the head of St Andrew and the Holy Spear) are kept in the four little chapels above the statues.

Right-hand nave

Chapel of the Pietà*** (13)

This celebrated marble group, sculpted by Michelangelo when he was only 25, is a summation of all the progress made by 15th-century sculpture. There is an astonishing formal perfection to Michelangelo's rendering of a scene in which religious meaning is balanced by profound humanity. The artist subsequently sculpted three other *Pietàs,* but he was never again to match the deep emotion and serenity of this piece.

Chapel of the Crucifix or of the Relics (16)

This elliptical chapel was designed by Bernini to contain a fine wooden cross attributed to Pietro Cavallini (early 14th century).

Chapel of the Holy Sacrament (19)

The iron grille of this chapel was designed by Borromini, and the painting of the Holy Trinity hanging here is the work of Pietro di Cortona. The tabernacle, in gilded bronze with ecstatic angels on either side, is one of Bernini's last creations.

Monument to Gregory XIII (20)

You should stand to the left of this splendid monument (Rusconi, 1720) to appreciate its full grandeur. An allegory of courage is represented lifting a veil to contemplate a bas-relief which celebrates Pope Gregory's reform of the calendar (1582).

Monument to Clement XIII (31)

This fine neo-Classical piece by Canova (1792) is located in the passage between the right transept and the end of the right-hand side-aisle. It contrasts strongly with the monumental rhetoric of the Baroque era. The allegories of Faith, the Angel of Death and the lions form a group that is isolated from the central figure of Clement, who appears absorbed in prayer and withdrawn from the world.

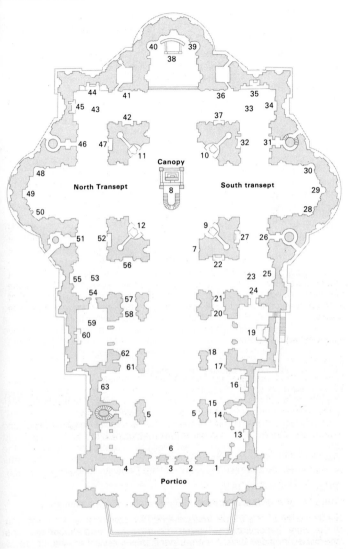

St Peter's Basilica

The apse

*The throne of St Peter** (40)*

Bernini was commissioned to create this extraordinary piece (1657-1666) by Pope Alexander VII, who wanted a majestic shrine in which to place the remains of a 4th-century episcopal seat reputedly made by St Peter himself. The decoration of the surrounding apse is in itself an extraordinary tribute to Christianity.

The throne of St Peter is composed of a massive bronze seat supported by colossal figures representing four Doctors of the Church: *St Ambrose, St Augustine, St Athanasius* and *St John Chrysostom*. Immediately above the throne are two putti, bearing the tiara and the keys of St Peter. Farther up, an immense composition in gilded stucco depicts clusters of cherubs floating amid clouds and beams of light, the ensemble surrounding an oval window which encloses a dove representing the Holy Ghost.

Monument to Paul III Farnese (40)

This monument, which sits on the left on the throne, is a small masterpiece by della Porta (1551-1575). Its composition is restrained, with no attempt at dramatic effect.

Monument to Urban VIII Barberini* (39)

This monument, on the right of the throne, was begun by Bernini during Urban VIII's lifetime (1627) and completed after this pope's death (1647). It quickly became the prototype for a definite funerary style, of which the basilica itself offers several other examples.

Altar of Leo the Great (44)

This altarpiece by Alessandro Algardi (1650) represents Leo halting Attila at the gates of Rome. It is located at the end of the left-hand side-aisle.

Tomb of Alexander VII (46)

This tomb, in the passage leading to the left transept, was designed by Bernini and executed in part by his assistants (1671-1678). The unshakable faith of Alexander at prayer can be viewed as a challenge to death, who is portrayed holding an hourglass with the sand running out.

Left-hand nave

Tomb of Innocent VIII (61)

This tomb, by Antonio del Pollaiolo (1498), is the only monument from the old basilica of St Peter's which survived the demolition. Originally, a recumbent figure representing Innocent in death was placed above Innocent on his throne, as if to remind the living of their ineluctable destiny. Note the fine bas-reliefs of the Four Cardinal Virtues.

The sacristy and treasury of St Peter

Entrance by the door of the left-hand side-aisle, before the transept (31). *Open daily 8.45am-1pm, 3-5pm (6pm in summer).*

The treasury rooms contain a number of pieces of religious gold- and silverware. Room III houses the **Monument to Sixtus IV,** a magnificent bronze ensemble by Antonio del Pollaiolo (1493), and room IX the **Sarcophagus of Junius Bassus,** dating from the 4th century. This latter is an interesting example of Lower Empire Christian funerary art.

Tour of the dome (63)

Entrance by the door in the left-hand nave, next to the baptistery. *Open daily 8am-4.45pm (6.15pm in summer).*

An elevator has now been installed to carry visitors to the broad terrace at the base of the dome: from here there is a fine view of the cupolas of the transept and nave of the basilica, as well as that of the Sistine Chapel. From the balustrade of the façade, note the sweeping view* of St Peter's Square and the city. From here a steep staircase leads between the two sides of the dome: the gallery around its inside offers a glimpse** of the whole interior. Finally, the panoramic view** from the terrace at the dome's apex is ample reward for the effort of getting there.

The Vatican caves

Entrance down a staircase within one of the main pilings that support the dome (12). *Open daily 7am-5pm (6pm in summer).*

These 'caves' stretch beneath the basilica, from Bernini's baldachin to about halfway down the nave. They occupy the space which separates the old basilica from the new and contain works of art from the demolished structure as well as tombs of various popes.

Early Christian and pagan necropolis

To visit, apply to the **Ufficio Scavi,** on the south side of St Peter's Square, or write to the **Reverenda Fabbrica di San Pietro,** 00120 Città del Vaticano, giving your address and telephone number in Rome, along with the names and nationalities of those you wish to take with you—then wait for a reply.

This fascinating tour will take you into a necropolis which was at first pagan, then wholly Christian after the 2nd century AD. It was rediscovered in 1940 and contains a tiny structure directly beneath the high altar of the basilica: this is thought to be the tomb of St Peter himself. The place was filled in sometime in the 1st century AD, and completely covered over by Constantine's basilica in the 4th century. Later, during the Renaissance, its existence was apparently unknown to the builders of the new St Peter's.

▬▬▬ *PALAZZI PONTIFICI (Pontifical Palaces)* III, D1

In the beginning there was a modest papal dwelling beside the first basilica of St Peter; Charlemagne lodged there when he came to Rome to be crowned in 800. The building was restored and enlarged in the 12th century, and after Gregory XI's return from Avignon (1377), it was the customary residence of the popes.

From the 15th century to modern times, this palace was repeatedly added to and embellished, creating a pontifical complex. Nicolas V erected a palace around the courtyard 'del Pappagallo' (1450), Sixtus IV built the famous chapel which bears his name (1473), and Innocent VIII added the belvedere (1484-1492) on the hill to the north of the basilica. Subsequently, Alexander VI Borgia constructed his apartments and tower with decoration by Pinturichio, but Julius II, unwilling to take up residence in quarters that had been occupied by the Borgias, preferred the apartments of Nicolas Benedetto Bonfigli and Andrea del Castagno. Julius had these apartments repainted by Raphaël and, at the same time, commissioned Bramante to enlarge and modernize the rest of the palace. The result was a façade with different levels of loggias (the second-floor loggia was decorated by Raphaël), and a new link between the main body of the building and Innocent VIII's Belvedere. After this, Paul III built the Pauline Chapel and the Sala Regia, and Sixtus V added the library which divides the courtyard of the belvedere into two.

Successive popes contributed to what soon became an enormous architectural complex, with 1400 rooms and chapels and no less than 20 courtyards. These constant changes made it possible for generations of artists and craftsmen (especially during the Renaissance) to display their talents and turn the papal residence into one of the world's most magnificent repositories of art (for a description of the treasures contained here, see p. 183).

V

ROME OF THE MIDDLE AGES

Santa Maria Maggiore, San Giovanni in Laterano, San Lorenzo fuori le Mura.

At the close of the 16th century, Pope Sixtus V decided to refashion Rome to better suit its role as the spiritual capital of Christendom. An ambitious project was carried out, focussed on Santa Maria Maggiore; from which the ways to the city's most venerated sanctuaries fanned out like the spokes of a wheel. Among these sanctuaries were the great mediaeval and early Christian basilicas of San Giovanni in Laterano, Santa Croce in Gerusalemme and San Lorenzo fuori le Mura.

The itinerary detailed here is broadly based on the links between Rome's major shrines created for the use of pilgrims by Sixtus V. It also includes the beautiful mosaics of Santa Prassede and Santa Pudenziana, as well as Michelangelo's famous *Moses* at the church of San Pietro in Vincoli.

Access Bus: 11, 27, 81, 85, 87, 186, Metro: Colosseo. Map IV, F2.

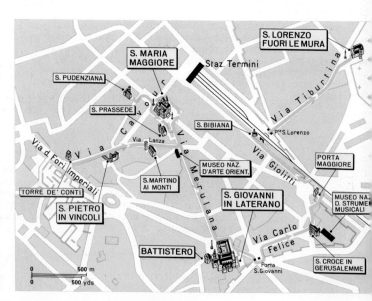

▬ *TORRE DEI CONTI* IV, F2

Built in the early 13th century by Lotario dei Conti di Segni (otherwise known as Innocent III), this tower was one of the splendours of mediaeval Rome. However, it was seriously damaged by an earthquake in 1348, and today only its lower floors remain. These were partially rebuilt at the beginning of the 17th century.

▬ *SAN PIETRO IN VINCOLI*★ IV, F3

This church was built—or rebuilt—in the 5th century by Eudoxia, wife of the Emperor Valentinian III, to house St Peter's prison shackles. The shrine was subsequently restored in the 8th and 11th centuries, before being remodelled in the 15th century by Cardinal Giuliano della Rovere, the future Julius II. There was a final, completely disastrous alteration to the roof of the nave during the 18th century, which radically altered the church's proportions.

The façade has an elegant 15th-century portico, consisting of five arches on octagonal pilings. A second level was added to this portico during the 16th century.

Inside, 20 finely fluted columns with Doric capitals divide the three naves and lend an atmosphere of austere majesty. These Doric columns, which Eudoxia took from an ancient temple, are unique in Rome. On the 18th-century ceiling is Parodi's *Miracle of the Shackles* (1706). According to mediaeval legend, there were originally two chains, one used to fetter St Peter in Jerusalem, the other in Rome. By a miracle, the two became fused together, and are now exhibited beneath the high altar in a fine 15th-century reliquary.

Mausoleum of Julius II★

Moses is only a small part of the huge tomb planned for posterity by Julius II as a reminder of his magnificent reign. The tomb, a marble sculpture on three levels including 40 colossal statues and many bronze bas-reliefs, was to have been placed directly beneath the dome of St Peter's. Michelangelo was commissioned for the project in 1513, but Julius's eccentricities and subsequent death prevented the monument's completion. At least Michelangelo was able to sculpt his *Slaves* (today in Florence and Paris) and *Moses*. The statues of *Leah* and *Rachel*, symbolizing the active as opposed to the contemplative life, were begun by the master and completed by his pupils.

Michelangelo's *Moses*★★★

There is an incomparable expressive vigour about this statue, blended with a formal perfection which has rarely been matched. Traditionally, it is supposed to represent Moses about to punish the children of Israel for their sin in worshipping the Golden Calf. However, Sigmund Freud, who was fascinated by the figure, held that it was meant to express superhuman self-mastery, or an ability to control the fiercest rage. No doubt, Freud added, Michelangelo transferred to the marble something of the inner conflict provoked by his own stormy relationship with Pope Julius II.

Closer inspection of *Moses* reveals a certain ambiguity. The right arm pressed to the chest is that of a contemplative man, but the legs, the eyes and the tension visible in the torso suggest action and physical force. Seen in this light, the statue has the same broad characteristics as the series of prophets in the Sistine Chapel (see p. 187), who are similarly poised between action and contemplation.

▬ *SAN MARTINO AI MONTI* IV, F4

A basilica was built on this site at the beginning of the 6th century and dedicated to St Martin of Tours, who converted the Gauls. It covers a 3rd-century *titulus,* or private house used as a meeting place by the early Christians, and this may be visited (apply to sacristan). The church itself was restored in the 8th century, rebuilt in the 9th century, then completely altered in the 17th century.

The three naves (built along standard basilical lines) are divided from the original church by 24 marble columns. The side-naves are covered in 17th-century frescos. On the left are some Roman landscapes by Gaspard Dughet, the brother-in-law of Poussin, along with frescos by Gagliardi representing the pre-Borromini basilicas of St Peter and St John.

SANTA PRASSEDE** IV, F4

This church was built by Pope Pascal I in 822, again on the site of a *titulus.* It has been much restored over the centuries. Santa Prassede, the sister of Santa Pudenziana (see p. 116), was present at the executions of Christians she had earlier protected; legend has it that the porphyry disk in the pavement covers a well, into which Prassede poured the blood of the martyrs.

The choir contains some magnificent 9th-century **mosaics****, the iconography of which is borrowed from the mosaic of Ss. Cosme e Damiano (see p. 78). Christ the Redeemer is shown surrounded by St Peter and St Paul (who present Prassede and Pudenziana), along with St Zenon and Pope Pascal I (note that Pascal's halo is square, indicating that he was still alive when the mosaic was laid). The Old and New Testaments and the risen Christ are respectively symbolized by two palm trees and a phoenix; the first triumphal arch shows the Heavenly Jerusalem which awaits the elect, and the second depicts the Sages of the Apocalypse (restored), the Lamb of God, four archangels, the seven lamps and the various symbols of the Evangelists.

Chapel of St Zenon***

The glorious mosaics of this chapel, built by Pascal I in the 9th century and located in the right-hand side-aisle, make it Rome's finest Byzantine monument.

Two columns of black granite taken from a pagan building frame the chapel door and support a fine antique cornice. Inside, the walls and ceiling are entirely covered by mosaics on a gold background. Depicted in the mosaics are (on the ceiling) Christ borne aloft by four angels; the Apostles Peter and Paul (over the entrance); and the Virgin, two saints and Theodora, mother of Pascal I (at left). The latter two figures both wear the square halos of the living. Note, in a small niche behind the altar, a *Virgin and Child with Saints Prassede and Pudenziana* (late 11th century). The fine polychrome marble floor is one of the oldest of its kind in Rome. The wall on the right of the chapel was mutilated in the 13th century to make way for an oratory containing the jasper column to which Jesus is said to have been tied during his flagellation.

SANTA MARIA MAGGIORE*** IV, EF4

Santa Maria Maggiore, with its noble proportions, mosaics and fine polychrome chapels, is a microcosm of the great eras of Christian art in Rome.

The original building was raised by Sixtus III (AD 432-440) shortly after the Council of Ephesus (AD 431), which endowed the Virgin with the title of Mother of God. With San Giovanni in Laterano, San Paolo fuori le Mura and St Peter's, Santa Maria Maggiore is one of the four patriarchal basilicas of Rome. It is sometimes called the **Basilica Liberiana**, or **Santa Maria della Neve** (Our Lady of the Snows), in memory of a church built on the Esquiline hill by Pope Liberius (4th century), after he had a vision, subsequently confirmed, of the Virgin sending down a fall of snow in midsummer to mark the site of her new sanctuary.

The apse was altered in the 13th century; the Romanesque campanile (the tallest in the city, 246 ft/75 m high) dates from the 14th century. During the Counter-Reformation, two broad chapels (Sixtus V's 'Sistina' on the right, and Paul V's 'Paolina' on the left) were added to create a kind of transept within the early Christian basilica. During the Baroque era Rainaldi's new outer covering for the apse was installed (1670); a main façade with portico and triple-arched loggia (by the architect Fuga, 1741) was also added. The fine Classical arrangement of colonnades dividing the naves was also completed at this time by replacing the bases and capitals of the original columns.

The naves

The magnificent interior of the basilica is divided by two fine sets of Ionic columns in Parian marble, which Fuga installed according to the ancients' laws of harmony. The ceiling is coffered and gilded, reputedly with gold from the first treasure ship to return from the New World in the 16th century; the paving on the floor is a skillful reconstruction of a fine 12th-century pattern.

Along the side walls of the central nave, above the coping with its frieze of intricate tracery, run 36 panels of 5th-century **mosaic****. The images are fresh and beautiful, illustrating scenes from the Old Testament. Among the oldest in Rome, they represent a priceless memorial of Christian art during the early empire period.

Triumphal arch**

The mosaics on the triumphal arch were done slightly later than those of the nave, and can be distinguished by their colouring, which is more Byzantine than Roman. As they were laid just after the Council of Ephesus (which repudiated Nestorius's contention that the infant Jesus was not yet the Son of God), it is hardly surprising that these mosaics celebrate the dogma of the Divine Birth. The Virgin, at top left, is depicted wearing the costume of the Eastern Empresses; the Magi bring their gifts and the Child Jesus welcomes them from a magnificent gem-encrusted throne guarded by angels. He is not a babe in arms, but a fully formed child monarch. Note also the *Presentation at the Temple* and the *Flight to Egypt,* on the right.

The apse*

The mosaic in the apse was executed by the Franciscan monk, Torriti, at the close of the 13th century, but includes decorative elements from another mosaic that adorned the apse of the early Christian basilica (5th century). Torriti's mosaic depicts the *Crowning of the Virgin,* attended by groups of angels and saints. Pope Nicolas IV, who commissioned the work, is shown kneeling in the lower part of the composition alongside Cardinal Colonna. Note the ornamental extravagance (foliage, birds and a rendering of the Jordan River with boats and swans), a feature borrowed from early mosaics.

The Chapel of Sixtus V*

This chapel (on the right) was added at the end of the 16th century by Sixtus V, a tireless builder of sanctuaries. The architect, Domenico Fontana, submitted a plan that employed the form of a Greek cross, which included a magnificent tall dome. The result is probably the earliest example of a large chapel wholly decorated with coloured marble. This started a vogue which continued for three centuries.

These colours usually offend modern taste, which tends to be less attracted to religious pomp. But this is more than an exercise in Baroque magnificence. The marbles in the chapel were mostly taken from ancient buildings, and their removal was part of Sixtus V's overall plan for the city; his aim was to express the spirit of the Counter-Reformation by 'Christian-izing' all the monuments of ancient Rome. Failing that, he was determined to 'Christianize' their materials and provide the faithful with a foretaste of the next world.

Note, above the altar, the lavishly gilded ciborium in the form of a temple supported by four angels (late 16th century).

Elsewhere in the chapel are the tombs of Popes Pius V (1566-1572) and Sixtus V (1585-1590), with bas-reliefs of the main events that took place during their pontificates.

The Pauline Chapel*

The Pauline Chapel (on the left) was constructed at the beginning of the 17th century by Flaminio Ponzio, at the request of Paul V. The pope wished to endow the left-hand side of the basilica with a chapel to match that of Sixtus V. Coloured marbles, precious stones, gilt—nothing was spared in the attempt to dazzle the faithful. The massive tombs of Clement VIII (1592-1605) and Paul V himself (1605-1621) also display a growing concern with decoration, despite the flaws in the sculpture of the bas-reliefs.

The frescos of the chapel celebrate the virtues of the Virgin and the victories of the church over paganism and heresy; they also exalt some of the more outstanding Christian saints. In short, they represent the dogmas of the Catholic Counter-Reformation.

The cupola, clumsily executed by Cigoli in 1612, is nonetheless Rome's first example of a dome entirely painted on the inside. It is interesting to compare it with Lanfranco's brilliant dome of Sant'Andrea della Valle (see p. 85), painted 10 years later.

The high altar, which is richly adorned with lapis lazuli, agates and amethysts, bears a 12th-century Byzantine painting representing the Virgin, after a 9th-century original. Tradition still attributes this work to St Luke.

Sforza Chapel*

Built by della Porta (1564-1573) from a design by Michelangelo, the architecture of this chapel (the second on the left) is unusual for its time. The colonnades are 'bent' at 45-degree angles, the pillars are set on the diagonals of the transept crossing, and the apses lack the traditional semicircular curve: in short, Michelangelo anticipated the Baroque age by an astonishing 60 years.

▮▮▮ *SANTA PUDENZIANA* IV, E4

This is one of the oldest churches in Rome. It was built at the close of the 4th century on the site of a *titulus* (see 'Glossary' p. 212) and a 2nd-century bath-house. According to legend, the residence of the Roman senator Pudens stood here; Pudens was the father of Prassede and Pudenziana, and a protector of St Peter.

The main interest of the church, which has been restored and altered many times, lies in the **mosaic**** of its **apse**. One of the oldest mosaics in Rome (late 4th century), it represents Christ surrounded by the Apostles. Behind Christ are the Cross of Calvary, the City of Jerusalem and two female figures symbolizing the Old and the New Order.

This work is suffused with the atmosphere of ancient Greece and Rome; note especially the face of Christ, full of humanity, without a trace of the stiffness which was to appear in later, Byzantine mosaics.

▮▮▮ *SAN GIOVANNI IN LATERANO*** V, C5

Open daily 7am-6pm.

San Giovanni in Laterano is the cathedral of Rome and the pope is its bishop. As Christianity's first church, it has survived both natural catastrophe and human conflict. Restored and enlarged many times, it offers a rich panorama of the spiritual and aesthetic history of Christianity.

The **basilica,** which is the oldest in Rome, was founded by Constantine between AD 314 and 318, on a site he had given to Pope Melchiades (AD 311-314). This site had formerly belonged to a powerful Roman family, the

The harmonious proportions and rich decoration make Santa Maria Maggiore the most grandiose of the four patriarchal basilicas of Rome.

Laterani, before being confiscated by Nero in the 1st century. Constantine's building was set on the foundations of a barracks, that of the imperial mounted guard (late 2nd century), which in turn had been erected on a section of the house of the Laterani (1st century).

The basilica was sacked by the Vandals in the 5th century, shaken by earthquakes in the 4th and 9th centuries and burned down twice in the 14th century; but after each disaster it was patiently rebuilt and embellished. In the mid-17th century, Innocent X commissioned Borromini to undertake a complete restoration. Clement XII altered the façade in the 18th century and, finally, Leo XIII transformed the apse at the close of the 19th century.

The main façade[*]

The façade, which was built by Alessandro Galilei in 1735, is a successful blend of Baroque treatment and rigorously Classical design.

Its main feature is a single giant series of half-columns and flat pilasters on tall pedestals; this decorates the portico, which is surmounted by a vaulted loggia. A projecting construction at centre, with a triangular pediment, brings the main entrance of the church into relief along with the balcony from which the pope blesses the people of Rome on Ascension Day.

Galilei's work here owes much to Carlo Maderno's façade for St Peter's (see p. 104), though the bays are opened more widely to stress the effect of light and shade and emphasize the orderly precision of columns and pilasters.

On the balustrade above the attic stand 15 colossal statues, each one 23 ft/7 m tall; these serve as a reminder of the certitudes of the Catholic faith. Christ, at centre, is set on a curious pedestal which appears heightened by the pediment. On either side of him stand St John the Baptist (left), St John the Evangelist (right), and the Doctors of the Church. The animated gestures and theatrical poses of these statues give them an entirely human dimension.

Beneath the portico, the bronze panels on the central door are those that originally hung at the entrance to the Curia of ancient Rome (see p. 68). On the left stands a large statue of Constantine, which was unearthed on the Quirinale. On the right is the Holy Door, which is only opened during Jubilee years (roughly every quarter-century).

The naves*

Nothing remains of the original 4th-century basilica save its grandiose five-nave floorplan and the antique green marble columns which once marked the divisions between the various side-aisles. These were shortened in the 17th century and placed in the pillar niches of the central nave.

The statues of the Apostles in the niches (1703-1718) are typical of Bernini, though in fact they were executed by a group of sculptors directed by Fontana, after drawings by Maratta. The 17th-century bas-reliefs above the niches represent scenes from the Old and New Testaments.

The naves also contain a number of works dating from the Middle Ages: notably, on the far left, a fine Gothic recumbent figure attributed to Arnolfo di Cambio (1276); on the far right, on the right-hand wall after the chapels, the tomb of Cardinal Casati by the Cosme brothers (1287); and nearby, the tomb of Cardinal de Chaves by Isaiah da Pisa (1447).

The transepts

The decoration of this area (circa 1595) is characteristic of the militant, highly charged style of the late Counter-Reformation. The façade of the right transept, with two levels of arches, is the work of Domenico Fontana. The two bell-towers which rise above it date from 1360.

The choir

The 19th-century papal altar—the pope is the only priest who says mass from here—overlays a smaller wooden table at which the first pontiffs (including St Peter and St Sylvester) are said to have officiated. Below the altar, in the magnificent confessional, is the **tomb of Pope Martin V** by Sebastiano Ghini (15th century). The 14th-century Gothic ciborium, which was repainted during the Renaissance, is said to contain the skulls of St Peter and St Paul, each preserved in a silver reliquary.

The apse

The apse was reconstructed during the 19th century, at which time Torriti's mosaic was very clumsily placed on a new mounting. A much better example of Torriti's work is the mosaic in the apse of Santa Maria Maggiore (see p. 114).

The cloister*

Entrance by the left-hand side-aisle. *Open daily 9am-1pm, 3-6pm.*

This masterpiece is the work of Jacopo and Pietro Vassaletto (1215-1232). Twin columns with highly varied shapes and capitals support the small arches that make up the four sides of the cloister portico; above, a rich frieze of mosaic runs along the coping, along with a finely sculpted cornice. The cloister still preserves many vestiges of the original church (notably some fine bas-reliefs from the tomb of Cardinal Annibaldi, executed by Arnolfo di Cambio in the 12th century).

Borromini and San Giovanni in Laterano

Borromini's Baroque restoration has often been described as cold and solemn, but to say this does the architect an injustice. He was commissioned to restore the cathedral by Pope Innocent X, at a time (1646) when it threatened to fall down at any moment. Two conditions were made: first, that Borromini should (as far as possible) respect the early Christian basilica, and second, that the work should be completed in time for the Holy Year of 1650.

These conditions weighed heavily on Borromini. He finally met the challenge by lending subtlety and rhythm to the central nave; this was achieved through the opposition of high arches to much smaller aedicules in coloured marble, and by emphasizing the contrast between these same arches and the gigantic pilasters that soar to the windows above.

The side naves, with floral decorations, putti, cherubim and Baroque tombs of popes and cardinals (especially in the right-hand nave), bear ample witness to Borromini's abundant decorative talent. Note also the remarkable balusters (rail support) at the entrance to the Orsini Chapel (first on the right).

BATTISTERO* (The Baptistry) V, C4

This building was founded by Constantine in the 4th century, then reconstructed by Sixtus III in the 5th century and restored by Urban VIII in the 17th century. At its centre, eight porphyry columns from the 5th century support an octagonal pediment, which in turn supports a second rack of smaller columns in white marble (17th century). The 5th-century baptismal font, which is of green basalt, has a 17th-century bronze lid. The pictures and frescos covering the walls also date from the 17th century.

The chapels and the narthex

For admission, apply to the warden.

The narthex contains a fine 5th-century ornamental **mosaic*** (foliage decorated with Christian symbols). An elegant portico, made from ancient materials, embellishes the original entrance opposite the present one (ask the warden to open this for you).

The Chapel of St John the Baptist, to the right of the present entrance, still has its original 5th-century doors. The ceiling of the Chapel of St John the Evangelist, to the left of the entrance, is decorated like the narthex with 5th-century **mosaics*** (animal and vegetable motifs), the style of which recalls the art of the catacombs. The Chapel of St Venance, to the left of the Chapel of St John the Evangelist, contains important examples of 7th-century Byzantine mosaics.

PALAZZO DEL LATERANO (Lateran Palace) V, C5

The Palazzo del Laterano was the residence of the popes during the Middle Ages, until their departure for Avignon in 1305. When Gregory XI returned to Rome in 1377, he found it gutted by fire and was obliged to move into the Vatican (see p. 100). The present building was designed by Domenico Fontana during the reign of Sixtus V (1586). The Lateran Treaties, which settled the 'Roman Question' that had for so long paralyzed relations between the Holy See and the Italian state, were signed here in 1929.

THE OBELISK OF THE PIAZZA SAN GIOVANNI IN LATERANO V, C5

The red granite obelisk adorning piazza San Giovanni in Laterano is the oldest and tallest in Rome. It dates from the 15th century BC and is 121 ft/37 m high. The Emperor Constantine had it transported from Egypt in AD 357 and erected in the Circus Maximus. It was unearthed in three pieces in 1587 and subsequently re-erected in its present position by Sixtus V in 1588.

SCALA SANTA V, C5

This edifice, which stands in front of the Palazzo del Laterano, was built by Domenico Fontana in 1585-1590 to shelter the *Sancta Sanctorum,* the former private chapel of the popes, and the *Scala Santa,* the staircase of the original papal palace. These objects are deeply venerated: according to tradition, the 28 steps of the *Scala Santa* were those which Christ climbed on his way to the hall of Pontius Pilate the day of his trial.

TRICLINIUM OF LEO III V, C5

Beside the Scala Santa is the Triclinium, which is the apse of the dining room of the old papal palace built by Leo III (795-816). It was partially reconstructed in the 18th century and contains a clumsily restored mosaic celebrating the alliance between Leo III and Charlemagne, in which the former is seen crowning the latter.

SANTA CROCE IN GERUSALEMME* V, B6

According to tradition, this church was set up by Constantine during the 4th century in one of the rooms of the Sessoriano Palace, the residence of Helena, Constantine's mother. Its purpose was to provide a sanctuary for the relics of the Holy Cross brought by Helena from Jerusalem. In the 12th century, the church was rebuilt by Lucius II, and a fine Romanesque campanile added. It was also heavily restored in the 18th century by Benedict XIV, who contributed a lively façade and a new Baroque interior.

Santa Croce contains two very fine works of art: a fresco in the apse, Antoniazzo Romano's *Discovery of the Cross** (late 15th century); and a **mosaic*** in the Chapel of St Helena (access at the end of the right-hand nave). This mosaic was designed by Melozzo da Forli and completed by Baldassare Peruzzi (late 15th-early 16th century).

The reliquary chapel (stairway on the left of the left side-nave) contains important relics of Christ's passion.

PORTA MAGGIORE** V, B6

An ornamental gate was built in AD 52 by the Emperor Claudius, on the site where the Aqua Claudia and Anio Novus aqueducts crossed the Labicana and Prenestina ways. It became a true gateway 200 years later, when it was incorporated into Aurelian's wall (AD 270-282).

Against the gate, on the outside, is the **tomb of Eurysaces** (late republican era), the frieze of which proclaims the profession of its occupant: Eurysaces seems to have been the state baker.

TEMPIO DI MINERVA MEDICA (Temple of Minerva Medica) V, A6

Renaissance architects' speculations on ideal forms of church architecture were sometimes based on mistaken assumptions. This was certainly true of the building in the via Giolitti, which they assumed to have religious significance and called the 'Temple of Minerva Medica'. In fact, this fine decagonal building, which dates from the 4th century BC, was a decorative feature of the gardens of Licinius, which formerly covered this area. The building used to be capped by a dome, which collapsed during the 19th century.

SANTA BIBIANA IV, F6

This little church (currently closed for restoration) was restored in 1624 by Bernini; indeed, it was Bernini's first architectural undertaking. In the façade, which protrudes in the centre, the central bay of the upper floor appears in high relief. This bay is still used for the display of relics during certain religious festivals.

The left-hand wall of the central nave is covered with frescos by Pietro di Cortona, depicting the life of St Bibiana, a young Christian woman who was flogged to death in AD 363, during the reign of Julian the Apostate. By the altar there is a statue of this same St Bibiana, by Bernini.

SAN LORENZO FUORI LE MURA** II, CD4

St Lawrence was martyred in AD 258 during the reign of Valerian; according to legend, he was slowly roasted to death, and his corpse buried in a catacomb near the via Tiburtina. The growing numbers of pilgrims to the saint's tomb caused Constantine to build a basilica on its site (330), and this was subsequently rebuilt in the 6th century by Pope Pelagius II. A second church, dedicated to the Virgin, was raised alongside San Lorenzo in the 5th century. Though it faced in a different direction, the two apses touched one another. In 1216, Pope Honorius III united these churches by demolishing the apses and adding a portico by Pietro and Jacopo Vassalletto. The resultant basilica was altered in the 15th and 17th centuries, before its complete restoration following the bombardments of 1943.

Exterior

The façade of the basilica has an elegant Romanesque portico, with marble columns from an earlier (probably ancient) structure. These columns are topped by fine Ionic capitals and support a pediment decorated with a frieze of mosaic, porphyry and serpentine. The cornice is delicately sculpted, with acanthus leaves, flowers, fruits and lions' heads doing duty as gargoyles (early 13th century).

The fine Romanesque campanile was built at the end of the 12th century. Under the portico, 13th-century frescos show scenes from the lives of St Lawrence and St Stephen. By the door, a 4th-century sarcophagus is sculpted with biblical scenes surrounding a medallion portrait of the tomb's occupant. To one side stands an aedicule in the form of a small temple (11th century) which probably indicates the presence of a tomb inside the church. Also note the beautiful 5th-century sarcophagus decorated with bas-reliefs representing cupids at a wine-harvest. Two Romanesque lions stand at each side of the main entrance.

Interior

The interior of San Lorenzo is made up of three naves separated by 22 ancient granite columns, leading to a triumphal arch. The columns have Ionic capitals, sculpted in the Middle Ages. This nave area is in fact the former Church of the Virgin; its sumptuous 12th- to 13th-century decor includes magnificent **paving**, **ambos***, the **Easter candelabra*** resting on two lions, and the **ciborium*** on its quartet of porphyry columns (one of the earliest of its kind in Rome, 1148). Note also the **papal throne**** and the **screen*** at the back of the choir. To the right of the entrance, the **tomb of Cardinal Fieschi*** (13th century) incorporates a 3rd-century sarcophagus decorated with scenes of nuptial rites and gods.

Beneath the high altar, a confessional crypt contains relics of the martyrs St Lawrence, St Stephen and St Justin.

At the side of the **triumphal arch*** facing the altar is a 6th-century mosaic which looks Roman, to judge by the costumes of its figures, but is Byzantine in terms of composition. Christ, bestowing his blessing, appears seated on an azure globe against a golden background; on his right, St Peter and St Lawrence present Pope Pelagius, who offers the basilica of St Lawrence to the King of Kings; to his left stand St Paul, St Stephen and St Hippolitus.

The high altar is in the 6th-century church of Pelagius; its apse stood between the triumphal arch and the two curving steps you can see today. This area was partially filled in during the 13th century to make way for a new choir: it was composed of a main nave and two side-naves separated by fine Corinthian columns, which supported an architrave of antique workmanship. The smaller marble columns above support the arches of the galleries reserved for women.

Cloister*

Entrance from the rear of the right-hand side-aisle, via the sacristy.

This beautiful Romanesque cloister (12th century), with its sober lines, is one of Rome's most ancient.

Behind the church of San Lorenzo stretches the **Campo Verano,** the city's main cemetery.

VI
AROUND THE CORSO

Piazza di Spagna, Trevi Fountain

T his itinerary, around the via del Corso and its immediate neighbourhood, will take you back into the mainstream of city life—to Rome's business district in the broadest sense of the term. At the beginning of the Corso are the great banking institutions with their dingy façades, the headquarters of the politicians and the press and the cafés of the Galleria Colonna. Just around the corner stands the Italian Parliament in Palazzo Montecitorio. Next, the Corso leads past the luxury shops, which are concentrated around the pedestrian streets linking the main thoroughfare to the piazza di Spagna (vias Frattina, Borgognona and Condotti).

The itinerary also takes in a number of important monuments, principally the Spanish Steps, a famous meeting place for people from all over the world, and the incomparable Trevi Fountain.

Access

Map III, F6. Bus: 26, 44, 46, 75, 85, 87, 90, 90b, 92, 94, 116, 118, 716, 719.

▬▬ VIA DEL CORSO (The Corso)

The via del Corso is a straight thoroughfare (1 mi/1.6 km long) linking piazza Venezia to piazza del Popolo. It is the main street of central Rome, and its many shops and cafés attract large crowds.

In the late 15th century, Pope Paul II broadened and straightened the Corso (then the via Lata) for horse racing. Alexander VII continued this project in the 17th century, and during this time a number of palaces were built on the Corso.

In papal Rome, an annual masked Carnival was held on the Corso. It lasted for eight days and everyone in the city attended. One hour before nightfall, the horses would be released to race riderless along the Corso. After this contest, everyone was expected to remove his mask and return home within the hour.

▬▬ PALAZZO BONAPARTE III, F6

The palace on the corner of the via del Plebiscito was the home of Madame Mère, the mother of Napoleon. She lived here, in exile, from 1815 until her death in 1836.

▬▬ PALAZZO DORIA-PAMPHILI* III, F6

The fine Rococo façade of Palazzo Doria-Pamphili was designed by Valvassori (1734); the curves of its window pediments and balconies are

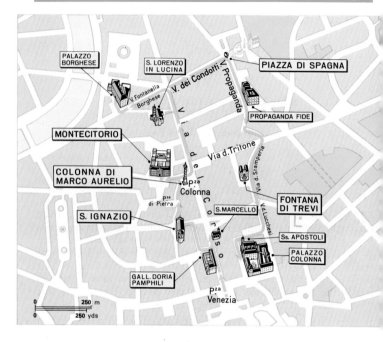

particularly elegant. Inside, note the magnificent 16th-century courtyard, and the **Galleria Doria-Pamphili****, one of Rome's most remarkable private art collections (see p. 179).

SANTA MARIA IN VIA LATA III, F6

This church owes its fine façade to Pietro di Cortona (1660). As one can see, it is badly in need of restoration.

SAN MARCELLO III, F6

This church was built in the 16th century, after a fire in 1519 destroyed the mediaeval church that formerly stood on the site. The **façade*** was added in 1682-1683 by Carlo Fontana, who borrowed the idea of the curved façade from Borromini and Cortona. Fontana's simple, concave design was an immense success and was frequently imitated thereafter. The stone frame of the central pediment was originally planned to contain a bas-relief, but this was never executed.

The interior consists of a single nave with side chapels, designed by Jacopo Sansovino and Antonio da Sangallo the Younger (16th century). Note the richly ornamented coffered ceiling (late 16th century).

PIAZZA DI SANT'IGNAZIO** III, EF6

Piazza di Sant'Ignazio, designed to resemble a stage set, is one of the most charming examples of 18th-century Rococo architecture in Rome. Raguzzini, the architect, followed in the footsteps of his Baroque predecessors (Bernini and Cortona among others), who favoured the type of closed piazza which one comes upon suddenly—a piazza that surprises. The ingeniously curved façades of the buildings are a delightful sight.

SANT'IGNAZIO* III, F6

The imposing exterior of this church contrasts sharply with the delicate charm of the piazza in which it stands. The church was built between 1626 and 1650 by the Jesuits. The solemn façade is essentially the work of Fra Orazio Grassi, the Jesuit architect, but Alessandro Algardi also made a contribution.

The interior consists of a single nave with a semicircular vaulted ceiling and communicating side chapels. The broad arches of the nave rest on columns of Sicilian jasper which combine with high, white, fluted pilasters to create a graceful effect. The vault of the nave is decorated with an impressive *trompe l'œil* composition*, completed in 1694 by Pozzo, a Jesuit mathematician and painter. This composition is a grandiose rendering of the Father, Son and Holy Ghost bursting into view past clusters of clouds and angels.

The best view of the **dome** over the transept is from the nave. The cupola was painted by Pozzo, and the fresco of the apse is also his work. In the right-hand transept is a **chapel*** dedicated to St Luigi di Gonzaga, which contains a superb marble relief by Legros (late 17th century) between fine twisted columns of green marble with fronds of gilded bronze. The chapel in the left transept is adorned by a delicate relief of the *Annunciation** by Filippo Valle (1750).

From in front of the church, take one of the small streets to the piazza di Pietra, which in ancient times was the site of the Temple of Hadrian the Divine (AD 145), built after Hadrian's death. Traces of this temple still remain, notably 11 Corinthian columns in white marble set on a high podium. The site of the main part of the former temple is now occupied by the Rome Stock Exchange.

PIAZZA COLONNA III, E6

Rome's political, commercial and cultural interests intersect at the piazza Colonna. The Corso passes through it. On one side is the 17th-century Palazzo Chigi (headquarters of the President of the Council), and in its centre is the **column of Marcus Aurelius,** executed after his death in AD 180. The shaft of this column is decorated with a spiral relief illustrating Marcus Aurelius's military victories over the Germans and the Sarmatians. In 1589, the column was restored by Domenico Fontana at the request of Sixtus V, and Marcus Aurelius's statue was replaced by that of St Paul.

PIAZZA DI MONTECITORIO, PALAZZO DI MONTECITORIO* III, E6

In the centre of the piazza di Montecitorio stands an Egyptian obelisk dating from the 6th century BC. It was brought from Heliopolis by Augustus and raised on this site.

Palazzo di Montecitorio was begun by Bernini in 1650 at the request of Innocent X, who wished to present it to the Ludovisi family. When the pope quarrelled with Cardinal Ludovisi, further work was suspended until Fontana finally completed the palace in 1694. In 1871, it was enlarged at the rear and restructured on the inside to accommodate the Chamber of Deputies.

All that remains of Bernini's original project is the polygonal design of the façade and the massive limestone blocks at ground level.

PALAZZO CHIGI III, E6

This palazzo sits to the right of Palazzo di Montecitorio and was designed for the Aldobrandini family by Giacomo della Porta. In the mid-17th century, it passed to the Chigi family, who completed the construction work. Francísco della Greca's façade giving on the piazza Colonna dates from this time. The top floor is a later addition.

Today, Palazzo Chigi is the headquarters of the President of the Council and is not open to the public.

GALLERIA COLONNA III, E6

The Galleria Colonna, a pleasant arcade built in 1923, leads from the far side of the Corso to via Santa Maria in Via.

SAN LORENZO IN LUCINA★ III, DE6

This church, founded in the 4th century, was rebuilt at the beginning of the 12th century by Pascal II, who added the portico, the two lions on either side of the door and the campanile. Heavy restoration work was carried out in the mid-17th century.

The interior is composed of a single nave, which was redecorated in 1650 by Carlo Fanzago, the Neapolitan master of the Baroque. It has not been improved by subsequent attempts at embellishment. In 1829, the French writer Chateaubriand arranged for a tomb (near the second pillar on the right) to be built here in honour of the painter Nicolas Poussin (1594-1665), who lived in Rome for many years.

The fourth chapel on the right is the Fonseca Chapel; it was designed by Bernini and completed between 1668 and 1675. The **bust of Gabriele Fonseca★★**, Innocent X's physician, is one of Bernini's last works and one of his most successful in this genre.

PALAZZO BORGHESE★★ III, D5

This palazzo was begun in 1560. The name of its architect is uncertain, although some suggest Giacomo Barozzi da Vignola. Unfinished, it was purchased by Cardinal Camillo Borghese, the future Paul V, in 1604, and further work was entrusted to F. Ponzo. When Cardinal Scipio Borghese, Paul V's nephew, moved into the palace on his uncle's death (1621), the task of completing it was given to Vasanzio and Maderno.

The result is a majestic, austere building, whose shape has earned it the nickname *cembalo,* 'harpsichord'. The palace encloses a beautiful courtyard surrounded by two tiers of galleries. An open loggia at the end of the courtyard links the two wings of the palace with the galleries and overlooks a charming **Bath of Venus,** or lily pond with fountains, which backs onto the garden wall. This ensemble was designed in 1665 by Carlo Rainaldi. The decorative exuberance of this architecture is a vivid reminder of the lavish entertainments which took place here during the 17th century. Today, Palazzo Borghese serves as the Spanish Embassy.

On **Piazza Borghese,** you will find book vendors selling old volumes and engravings, which may or may not be genuine. Proceed with caution if you are not an expert in these fields.

VIA DEI CONDOTTI III, D6

Via della Fontanella di Borghese, after crossing the Corso, becomes via dei Condotti, a street filled with luxury shops. At n° 85 is the world-famous **Caffé Greco,** founded in 1760, where Goethe, Stendhal, Baudelaire, Berlioz, Liszt and Wagner came to converse and drink coffee. In the distance, at the top of the steps leading from the piazza di Spagna, stands the church of Trinità dei Monti, with its faded ochre-and-red tones and its two campaniles.

PIAZZA DI SPAGNA★★★ III, D6

Piazza di Spagna is known the world over; it stretches from the via del Babuino to the Palazzo di Propaganda Fide and owes its names to the Palazzo di Spagna, which was built in the 17th century for the Spanish ambassador. This virtual occupation of the area by the Spaniards was an affront to the French, who possessed land nearby, and clashes between representatives of the two nations were frequent. The piazza was also the scene of lavish festivities, which served the interests of the rival monarchies: celebrations of births, anniversaries and weddings took place here, along with more dramatic events such as the Revocation of the Edict of Nantes (1685) and the healing of Louis XIV (1687). The centre of the piazza is occupied by a fountain in the form of a barge, know as the **Barcaccia***, which bears the emblem of the Barberini family. The fountain was commissioned by Pope Urban VIII; Pietro Bernini, father of the great architect, was chosen to carry out the project. The elder Bernini, had the ingenious idea of placing his barge below street level, which resolved the technical problem posed by the low water pressure supplied by the Acqua Vergine.

Until 1723, a steep alley led from here to the church of Trinità dei Monti. In that year, de Sanctis began building a monumental limestone **stair-case****, working from a design by Specchi. It soon became recognized as one of the most spectacular achievements of 18th-century Roman urban planning. The graceful play of curves and counter-curves in the steps and landings becomes more and more apparent the higher you climb, constantly reinforcing the sensation of height and grandeur.

Today, these **Spanish steps** are a meeting place for people of all nations. In May, the steps are festooned with azaleas. In the corner at the foot of the steps, on the right, stands the house in which the poet John Keats lived and died. Today, the house is a small **museum** *(open Mon-Fri 9am-noon, 4-6pm)* dedicated to Keats and Shelley.

PALAZZO DI PROPAGANDA FIDE* IV, D1

This imposing palace, the property of the Holy See, dates from the 16th century. The Congregation for the Propagation of the Faith, founded in 1622 to promote the missionary activities of the various orders, adopted it as their headquarters in the 17th century. In 1642-1644, Bernini was called in to design a new façade giving on to piazza di Spagna, but nothing concrete was achieved until Borromini took over in 1646. He reconstructed the chapel and built a Baroque-style façade on via di Propaganda.

SANT'ANDREA DELLE FRATTE* IV, D1

Sant'Andrea delle Fratte was constructed in the 12th century and rebuilt in the 17th century. Borromini contributed a design for a brick dome, which was not built, and a strange and graceful three-tiered campanile, which was. Note the busts of angels with folded wings that support the coping. Inside, there is little of interest save Bernini's two angels, on the left and right of the choir, originally intended for the Ponte Sant'Angelo. These angels were such a success that when they were completed it was decided that their places on the bridge should be taken by reproductions. From here, the itinerary crosses the noisy via del Tritone and takes the via della Stamperia. This leads to the celebrated Trevi Fountain, where Anita Ekberg took her legendary dip in Fellini's *Dolce Vita* (1959).

FONTANA DI TREVI*** *(Trevi Fountain)* IV, DE1

In 1732, Niccolo Salvi was commissioned to replace the modest pool built here by Pope Nicolas V; however the Trevi Fountain was not completed until 1762. It is a monumental structure in the form of a triumphal arch, which backs onto the adjacent Palazzo Poli. It owes its name to the *tre vie*, three streets, which meet in front of it.

The composition is an astonishing blend of Classical architecture and group sculpture in the style of Bernini. In the middle of the arch, a statue of Ocean is seen driving an exuberant team of sea-horses and tritons through a grandiose scene. Niches contain allegories of Health, on the right, and

Abundance, on the left. The left-hand bas relief represents Agrippa approving the construction of an aqueduct connecting the spring with the centre of the city (19 BC). The right-hand bas relief depicts the legend which gave the Acqua Vergine spring its name: a young girl leading a troop of Roman soldiers to water. If you are superstitious and wish to return to Rome one day, you might perform the traditional rite of standing with your back to the fountain and tossing a coin over your shoulder into the water. This is supposed to guarantee your return.

SS. VINCENZO E ANASTASIO IV, DE1

The church of Ss. Vincenzo e Anastasio sits at one of the corners of the piazza. Its Baroque façade is the work of M. Longhi the Younger and it was financed by the French Cardinal Mazarin. The columns (which stand clear of the wall), the enclosed pediment, and the set-backs in the entablature create remarkable chiaroscuro effects.

From here, the itinerary follows the via di San Vicenzo to piazza della Pilotta and the Gregorian University on the left-hand side of the piazza. In front of the university is the arcaded via della Pilotta, which links Palazzo Colonna to its gardens. The name of this street is derived from a ball-game, which was played against its walls by aristocratic youths. The itinerary then leads along the via del Vaccaro to piazza Santi Apostoli.

SANTI APOSTOLI★ IV, E1

This church was founded in the 6th century, restored on several occasions during the 15th and 16th centuries, and reconstructed by Francesco Fontana, the son of Carlo Fontana, during the 18th century. Its neo-Classical façade, designed by Giuseppe Valadier in 1827, is fronted with a broad portico set on polygonal pillars (by Baccio Pontelli, late 15th century). The loggia above this portico was fitted with windows during the Baroque era, and the balustrade with its statues of Christ and the Apostles dates from the same period (1681).

Inside the portico are a fine antique bas relief (2nd century) and two lions which once framed the doorway of the mediaeval church.

On the ceiling of the central nave is Baciccia's *Triumph of the Order of St Francis*, painted in 1707. Two years later, Giovanni Odazzi decorated the ceiling of the choir with his magnificent *Fall of the Rebel Angels*★. Also in the choir, on the left, is the **tomb of Cardinal Pietro Riario**★ by Andrea Bregno, Fiesole and Giovanni Dalmata (late 15th century). On the right stand the monuments of Count Giraud d'Ansedun and Cardinal Raffaele Riario (early 16th century). At the end of the left-hand nave is the monument to Clement XIV (1789), the earliest work by Canova in Rome.

PALAZZO ODESCALCHI★ IV, E1

Palazzo Odescalchi stands directly opposite the church of Santi Apostoli. The building's right-hand side is the work of Bernini (1664) : his façade here achieved the first break with Roman tradition since Michelangelo's Palazzo dei Conservatore (see p. 76). His idea was to replace the conventional regularity with a system that separated the upper windows with high, flat Corinthian pilasters. Sadly, Bernini's façade was doubled in width during the 18th century, and this radically diminished the initial harmony of its proportions.

PALAZZO COLONNA IV, E2

Palazzo Colonna, to the right of the church of Santi Apostoli, stands on the site of a mediaeval fortress that formerly belonged to the Colonna family.

The Trevi fountain is a popular meeting place in Rome.

The palazzo was begun in the early 15th century by Pope Martin V Colonna, but dates for the most part from the 17th and 18th centuries.

The **Galleria Colonna**⋆ is one of the most sumptuous Baroque galleries in Rome (see p. 179).

The Aventine hill

In the early years of the Republic, the Aventine hill was mainly occupied by non-Romans attracted by the commercial activities of the port area. These people became the nucleus of the plebeian class. The subsequent struggle between the patricians and plebeians came to a head with the 'Secession of the Aventine', and was finally brought to an end by a political compromise between the two social groups.

Under the empire, the Aventine was transformed into a fashionable aristocratic area. The poor emigrated to Trastevere, and their houses were demolished to make way for the villas of the rich. When Alaric's Visigoths entered Rome in 410, their first objective was the Aventine, which they pillaged ruthlessly.

During the Middle Ages, monasteries were established all over the hill, many of them built on paleochristian sites.

Today the Aventine is one of Rome's greenest and most peaceful residential areas.

VII
ANCIENT AND MEDIAEVAL ROME

The Tiber, the Aventine hill

Another facet of Rome, a blend of the ancient and the mediaeval, is to be found between the Capitoline hill, the Tiber River and the rising ground of the Aventine hill. It includes the Theatre of Marcellus, Octavia's Portico in the heart of the old Jewish ghetto, and the Isola Tiberina, an island that was formerly a place of quarantine where Aesculapius, the god of medicine, is said to have taken refuge during a plague. This itinerary also includes a walk through the piazza Bocca della Verità, past the two best-preserved temples in Rome and a pair of mediaeval sanctuaries, terminating at the monumental Porta San Paolo and the pyramid-shaped tomb of Caio Cestio.

Access

Map VI, A5. Bus: 46, 57, 90, 90b, 92, 94, 95, 116, 716, 718, 719.

▬ *PIAZZA VENEZIA TO PIAZZA CAMPITELLI*

This itinerary starts at piazza Venezia and leads down via di Teatro di Marcello, with the Capitoline hill on the left. On the right-hand side of the street, n° 32 is the **monastery of Tor de'Specchi,** founded in the 15th century by St Francesca Romana. On March 9, St Francesca's feast day, the monastery is open to the public. If you are in Rome on this day, it's worth visiting to see the charming 15th-century frescos. Still on the right, after the monastery, is the peaceful piazza Campitelli, with its rows of late 16th-century palazzos and the lovely church of Santa Maria in Campitelli.

▬ *SANTA MARIA IN CAMPITELLI** VI, A4

This church was commissioned by Pope Alexander VII and built by Carlo Rainaldi (1662-1667). He reconstructed an existing, smaller building and created a sanctuary for the *Madonna del Portico* (13th-century enamel) who was reputed to have put a miraculous end to the plague of 1656.

The limestone façade is a variation on the theme of the portico—i.e., a pediment supported by two columns. As you approach this church, you will see that the columns seem to detach themselves from the wall, creating a remarkable chiaroscuro effect. The interior of the church is also something of an optical tour de force, the narrowness of the choir being offset by an illusion of perspective due to the prominent columns and pools of light shed from the dome. This latter is purposely built over the choir rather than the transept.

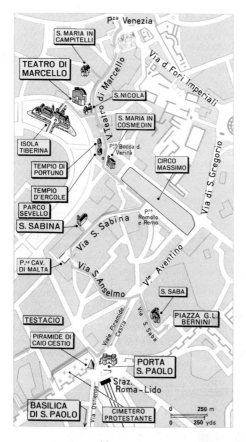

■■■ *TEATRO DI MARCELLO*** (Theatre of Marcellus)* VI, B4

The construction of this theatre was begun by Caesar and involved the demolition of a temple of Piety—an act for which his enemies never forgave him. It was completed by Augustus, who, in 13 BC, dedicated it to Marcellus, the son of his sister, Octavia.

Like all its ancient Roman counterparts, this theatre was of semicircular design. The stage, which faced the Tiber, has long since disappeared, along with the tiers of seats. The formal architecture of the theatre, with two superimposed levels (one Doric, the other Ionic), anticipated the Coliseum, for which the same building material—Tivoli limestone—was later to be used. The two levels of blind arcades which surrounded the tiers were originally surmounted by a wall with Corinthian pilasters.

In its heyday, the theatre could accommodate 15,000 spectators, and was the largest arena in Rome after the Theatre of Pompey. Most of the Christian martyrdoms actually took place here, although tradition attributes them to the Coliseum.

During the 12th century, the Theatre of Marcellus was converted into a fortress and for this reason escaped destruction. About 1530, the architect Baldassare Peruzzi erected two floors of a palace within this fortress, which can still be seen above the ancient arches. At the same time, the tiers of seats were converted into a garden.

In front of the theatre stand the three columns of the **Temple of Apollo**, which was built in the 5th century BC.

▬▬ SAN NICOLA IN CARCERE VI, B4

This small church originally occupied one of the three pre-Augustan temples that stood on the site. It was rebuilt in the 9th century, then restored in the 16th century by Giacomo della Porta. Its name comes from a mediaeval prison that stood nearby.

▬▬ PORTICO D'OTTAVIA★ (Octavia's Portico) VI, B4

Emperor Augustus was responsible for this portico (23 BC), which he named after his sister. Measuring 387 ft/118 m by 443 ft/135 m, it extended to the site of the present piazza Campitelli and contained two public libraries and a conference hall. Today, nothing remains except a few traces of an entrance pavilion facing the Tiber, which date from a cursory restoration during the reign of Septimius Severus (AD 193-211).

In the Middle Ages, a small church was built on the site, named **Sant' Angelo in Pescheria** after the fishmarket which used to be held nearby.

The portico and the synagogue that was built in 1904 mark the boundary of the former ghetto, which extended from here to the Largo Argentina. There was a large Jewish community in Rome almost from its beginning, established on the other side of the Tiber, but from the 13th century onwards, the Jewish quarter shifted to the area around the Theatre of Marcellus. In 1555, Pope Paul IV built ramparts around the ghetto and forbade anyone to enter or leave its confines during the hours of darkness. The ghetto was finally abolished in 1848, the ramparts being razed in 1888; nonetheless, the most tragic moment in the history of Rome's Jewish community was still to come, when the Nazis deported thousands of its members to the death-camps in 1943.

Today, the ancient ghetto remains a lively and picturesque area, well worth a visit.

▬▬ ISOLA TIBERINA★ VI, B4

This peaceful, boat-shaped island, which the ancient Romans equipped with a limestone 'prow' and a tall mast-like obelisk, was associated with Aesculapius, the god of medicine, who was supposed to have come here from his home in Epidaurus. The site of Aesculapius's temple is now occupied by a small church with a Baroque façade (1624) and Roman-esque campanile, **San Bartolomeo.** The **Fatebenefratelli Hospital** perpetuates the island's traditional association with medicine.

The **Ponte Fabricio** (62 BC), which has retained its primitive aspect despite successive restorations, connects the island with the right bank of the Tiber and the Theatre of Marcellus. From the **Ponte Cestio,** which leads to the Trastevere area, there is a splendid view of the **Ponte Rotto** (literally, 'broken bridge'), which fell down for the last time in 1598. The Ponte Rotto was formerly the Pons Aemilius, built in 179 BC.

▬▬ CASA DEI CRESCENZI VI, B5

If you double back to the left bank by the Ponte Fabricio, you will come to the Casa dei Crescenzi, at the corner of via dei Teatro di Marcello and via Ponte Rotto.

Part of a 12th-century watchtower is all that remains of this extensive building, which in the 10th century belonged to Rome's most powerful family, the Crescenzi. Elements of the watchtower's design are clearly borrowed from ancient Roman originals.

▬▬ PIAZZA BOCCA DELLA VERITÀ VI, B5

From the earliest times, the strip of land between the Tiber and the

The Ponte Rotto, *or broken bridge, offers a splendid view of the Tiber.*

Capitoline, Palatine and Aventine hills was a meeting place for central Italy's principal lines of communication. These were, respectively, the Tiber and the north-south route from Etruria to Campania, which forded the river just upstream of the Isola Tiberina. Well before Rome was founded, there was probably a flourishing market on this site: a number of geometrical Greek ceramics have been discovered here, which date from the 8th century BC. This ancient market may well have been the first population centre on the Palatine hill.

The port of Rome was continuously in use from the era of the Etruscan kings. There was no town planning or large-scale construction until the 2nd century BC, when the republic's conquest of the Mediterranean opened up new horizons. Later, a succession of natural disasters (notably fires and flooding) precipitated considerable alterations, in line with the city's changing needs.

The old port occupied the area between the church of San Nicola in Carcere and the Temple of Portunus. To the north of the port area stood the *forum boarium,* or cattle market.

Tempio di Portuno** (Temple of Portunus)

This rectangular temple was dedicated to Portunus, tutelary deity of the port of Rome and protector of the sailors who ferried Mediterranean goods upriver from Ostia. It dates from the 1st century BC, with various later additions. In the 9th century it was converted into a church, which probably saved it from destruction.

The round temple of the *forum boarium***

This circular building is sometimes referred to as the 'Temple of Vesta', although the name has no basis in fact. The temple, built during the reign of Augustus, was probably dedicated to Hercules, since ancient legend says that the Greek hero came here to kill Cacus, a three-headed, fire-breathing giant.

In any event, this is the oldest marble temple in Rome. Its 20 fluted columns, topped by Corinthian capitals, surround a marble *cella* faced with limestone. Sadly, the entablature and the ancient roof of this small, elegantly proportioned sanctuary have vanished. In common with many other pagan temples, it owes its survival to Christian use during the Middle Ages.

Arco di Giano* (Arch of Janus)

This arch was a *janus* (the god Janus was the traditional protector of crossroads), meaning it was a public gateway by which the various roads leading from the Forum arrived at the marketplace. It resembles a huge cube of marble, with openings on all four sides, and was built in the 4th century BC using materials salvaged from other monuments. The niches were originally framed by colonnettes and contained statues.

The upper section of the gate resisted the ravages of time until 1830, when it was mistaken for a mediaeval addition and demolished.

Arco degli Argentari* (Moneychangers' Arch)

This arch backs onto the church of San Giorgio in Velabro. It was built in the early 3rd century by the Moneychangers' Corporation in honour of Septimius Severus and his wife: a relief is visible on the arch, representing the couple making a sacrifice.

San Giorgio in Velabro*

This little church, founded in the 7th century, was reconstructed and enlarged in the 9th century with a basilical, three-naved structure. The façade, porch and campanile are Romanesque (12th-13th centuries). In general, the asymmetrical floorplan (designed to make maximum use of existing foundations), along with the wide assortment of columns and capitals, indicates the extent of Rome's poverty during the Middle Ages. The heavily restored frescos in the apse are probably by Pïetro Cavallini (1295).

Santa Maria in Cosmedin**

This church was founded in the 6th century on the ruins of a huge imperial building. A number of original columns were integrated into the church. In the 8th century, it was enlarged and turned into a place of worship for Greeks who had come to Rome to escape the persecutions of Byzantine emperors. Hence the name 'Cosmedin', which in Greek means 'ornament'. The church's porch and its fine campanile were added in the 12th century.

Under the left-hand portico, you will notice tourists taking turns putting their hands into a drainage hole. This is the fabled 'Bocca della Verità', Mouth of Truth, which is supposed to bite the fingers of anyone who has a falsehood on their conscience.

The interior of the church has recovered its original 8th-century aspect. The beautiful marble floor was laid by the Cosmatis (the Roman marbleworkers' corporation, 12th-13th centuries), which was also responsible for the pulpits, the chandelier, the ciborium over the altar, and the throne in the apse. There is a beautiful mosaic from the early 8th century in the sacristy, *Adoration of the Magi*. The crypt, which is open to the public, consists of three small naves separated by colonnettes, a rarity in Rome.

In front of the church is an elegant Baroque **fountain** by Bizzaccheri (1715).

▰▰▰ CIRCO MASSIMO (Circus Maximus) VI, C5-6

From the time of the Etruscan kings, the valley separating the Palatine hill from the Aventine hill was taken up by the Circus Maximus, an immense arena used for chariot races. It was enlarged and rebuilt on several occasions and, by the 1st century AD, it was big enough to accommodate 250,000 spectators in tiers on either side of the course. At the north-east end of the *forum boarium* were the 'boxes' from which the chariots burst at the start of the race. A raised platform (the *spina*) ran down the middle of the course and, during the reign of Augustus, an obelisk (75 ft/23 m) was raised here. This obelisk now graces the piazza del Popolo. Another taller obelisk (106 ft/32 m) appeared on the same site in the 4th century, only to be moved in 1585 to piazza San Giovanni.

SANTA SABINA** VI, C4

Santa Sabina is an almost perfect example of an early Christian basilica. Founded in the 5th century on the site of a *titulus* (see Glossary p. 212), it was restored many times in succeeding centuries. In 1222, the church was given to St Dominick for his newly created Dominican order. During the Counter-Reformation, it was heavily altered and did not regain its original aspect until 1938.

The vestibule, on the left, leads to a fine 5th-century wooden door with panels bearing scenes from the Old and New Testaments. *The Crucifixion,* at upper left, is one of the oldest renderings of this scene known to man; *Elijah Ascending Into Heaven,* below right, is equally magnificent.

The three naves of Santa Sabina are divided by fluted Corinthian columns of Parian marble, probably taken from a nearby temple. Their arrangement respects the 'perfect' proportions laid down by the ancients—that is, the diameter of the area between the columns is five times the diameter of the columns themselves. The general impression is one of great age and great nobility.

Light streams in through the many windows. During the Counter-Reformation, because of the belief that half-light favoured contemplation, many of these windows were walled up but, today, the embrasures have all been reopened.

On the inside of the façade, an inscription in gold letters commemorates the year of the basilica's construction (AD 430) and on either side the figures of two women symbolize the church stemming from Judaism and the church stemming from paganism.

Within the convent *(apply to the sacristan for permission to enter this area),* there is a fine 13th-century cloister.

From the **Savello Gardens,** adjacent to Santa Sabina, there is a fine view across the city.

PIAZZA DEI CAVALIERI DI MALTA VI, D4

This is a charming piazza laid out during the 18th century by the engraver Piranesi. At n° 3, the villa that houses the **Priory of Malta,** take a moment to look out through the keyhole in the door — it offers a unique view of the dome of St Peter's. In the gardens, which are private and very difficult to enter, Piranesi built a charming little neo-Classical church, **Santa Maria del Priorato.**

SAN SABA VI, E5

The church of San Saba was founded by Eastern Orthodox monks in the 7th century. Built on the site of an older religious building, it has been enlarged and altered on several occasions. The most recent restoration dates from 1943.

The Romanesque façade is fronted by a 13th-century portico with a 15th-century loggia. Under the portico, to the left, is a large Roman sarcophagus depicting Juno, the goddess of marriage, and two husbands. The door is by Giovanni Cosma (1205).

Inside, the three main naves are separated by 14 ancient columns. There is also a fourth nave, resting on three columns, which may have been the original church. The paved floor and the backrest of the pontifical chair are 13th-century marble. Above the apse is a fine 15th-century *Annunciation.* The vestibule close to the sacristy contains a succession of painted frescos (7th-12th centuries).

▬▬ *PORTA SAN PAOLO (St Paul's Gate)* VI, E5

St Paul's Gate, or Porta Ostiensis as it was known in ancient times, is a fortified breach in the wall built by the Emperor Aurelian (3rd century). The side facing towards the city is original, but the side facing away from Rome was rebuilt in the 5th century.

▬▬ *PIRAMIDE DI CAIO CESTIO*★ VI, EF4

This marble pyramid was built in 12 BC by the moneylender, Caius Cestio, who intended to use it as his tomb. If nothing else, the structure demonstrates the wealth of the ruling class during the reign of Augustus and its taste for Egyptian architecture.

Behind the pyramid, on via Caius Cestio, is the entrance to the **English cemetery,** which for the last 200 years has been reserved for 'anti-Catholics', i.e., Protestants and admitted atheists. Keats, Shelley, the son of Goethe, and A. Gramsci (who founded the Italian Communist Party) lie buried here among the romantic pines and cypresses.

After the cemetery, the itinerary continues along via Nicola Zabaglia (to the right), which is overlooked by **Monte Testaccio,** a mound of shards of antique pottery and amphorae. This mound demonstrates, in its own way, the sheer volume of the commercial traffic that plied the Tiber between Rome and Ostia.

▬▬ *SAN PAOLO FUORI LE MURA*★★ II, E3

St Paul was beheaded 2 mi/3 km from the site of this basilica in AD 67. His corpse was subsequently handed over to a woman, Lucina, who brought it to her own family burial ground on via Ostiense. Later, the monument *(martyrium)* erected on the tomb became a popular place of pilgrimage. In AD 313, Constantine built a church on the site, which was replaced by Valentinian (AD 386) and Theodosius. The result, an immense basilica of five naves, was the same size as Trajan's Basilica Ulpia (see p. 81). Subsequently decorated with sumptuous 5th-century mosaics and frescos by Pietro Cavallini (13th century), it was recognized as the most beautiful church in Rome. In 1823, it was gutted by fire, but instead of restoring the considerable portions of the building that remained undamaged, the authorities decided to rebuild from scratch. The many fine frescos by Pietro Cavallini were lost forever.

Despite its ugliness, the reconstruction adheres to the original basilical design of the 4th-5th centuries, and the five naves, divided by 80 monolithic granite columns, are impressive. Unfortunately, the mosaics were heavily retouched in the 19th century. The Byzantine mosaic in the apse, executed by Venetian artists in 1220, is especially noteworthy.

The high altar is surmounted with a fine Gothic **ciborium**★ by Arnolfo di Cambio (1285), which rests on elegant porphyry columns with gilded marble capitals. The altar is placed directly above the tomb of the Apostle.

A magnificent **candelabrum**★★, a masterpiece of Romanesque sculpture, is at the entrance to the right transept. The base of this 12th-century candelabrum is composed of four pairs of monstrous animals, and its stem is covered with vegetable motifs and scenes from the life of Jesus.

Access to the **baptistry,** with its ancient columns, can be gained from the rear of the right transept. Nearby is a room where the remains of 15th-century frescos and 13th-century mosaics are exhibited. These once adorned the apse of the old basilica. Finally, there is a charming **Romanesque cloister** (12th-13th centuries) encrusted with gilt and mosaic. The cloister galleries also contain numerous vestiges of the ancient basilica.

VIII
THE RIGHT BANK OF THE TIBER

From Trastevere to Janiculum

T rastevere—'beyond the Tiber'—has been a working-class neighbourhood from the earliest times. The narrow, winding streets, the weathered houses with laundry hanging from their windows, the winesellers, the small shops of craftsmen and the unique Trastevere dialect have all survived. Unfortunately, there has been a recent tendency to overdo the folklore of Trastevere: foreigners are beginning to pay large sums for apartments in the area, and trattorias are starting to trade heavily on dubious authenticity. Nevertheless, Trastevere is still a wonderful place to wander. This itinerary takes you through the maze of ancient streets to several very beautiful churches, as well as to La Farnesina, one of the greatest masterpieces of the Roman Renaissance.

More Renaissance buildings, notably San Pietro in Montorio and Bramante's lovely Tempietto, await you at the Janiculum. If you arrive at this hill at the close of day, you may be lucky enough to see the domes and roofs of the city blazing below you in the last rays of sunshine.

Access

Map VI, A4. Bus: 26, 44, 46, 55, 61, 64, 65, 70, 75, 81, 87, 90, 170, 710.

▬▬▬ *TRASTEVERE* VI, A4

In ancient times, Trastevere was inhabited entirely by the working poor; its population consisted mostly of stevedores, craftsmen and shopkeepers, attracted to the right bank of the Tiber by the proximity of the quays.

Sailors and merchants of various nationalities and religions settled here, establishing a Jewish synagogue and the city's first Christian church. Over the centuries, Trastevere changed little: its inhabitants pride themselves on being the 'real Romans', whatever their origin. The *Trasteverini* tend to be robust, brawling, kindly folk, proud of their reputation for unruliness.

San Carlo ai Catinari VI, A4

This church, which is outside Trastevere proper, was built between 1611 and 1646 by the Barnabite order and dedicated to St Carlo Borromeo, a fervent proponent of the Counter-Reformation. Its somewhat dreary façade is by Soria (1635-1638).

The interior has suffered badly from an ill-conceived 19th-century restoration but contains some interesting paintings. The pendentives of the dome, which represent the Cardinal Virtues, are the work of Domenichino (1630). *The Procession of St Carlo Borromeo* (1650), a fine composition by Pietro di Cortona, hangs beside the high altar. The Baroque chapel of St Cecilia (1692-1700) with decoration by Antonio Gherardi is to the left of the altar.

San Crisogono VI, B3

The church of San Crisogono was built in the 12th century on the site of a 5th-century sanctuary. In the 17th century, it was renovated by Giovanni-Battista Soria for Cardinal Scipio Borghese, incorporating a new façade, a coffered ceiling, broad windows, stucco capitals and a baldachin. The Romanesque campanile was retained (its spire dates from the 16th century), along with the basilical floorplan, the ancient columns and the Cosmati paving (13th century). In the apse, you can see a 13th-century mosaic by the school of Pietro Cavallini, *Virgin and Child Between St James and St Chrysogon*.

It is possible to gain access to the original church through the sacristy; this building, which stands on foundations dating from the imperial epoch, contains frescos from the 8th and 10th centuries.

Santa Cecilia* VI, C4

The entrance to this church opens onto a charming garden, with a large ancient marble urn at its centre. The church was built in the 4th century on the site of a townhouse said to have belonged to St Valerian, the husband of St Cecilia. The latter, who came from a patrician family, was martyred with her husband during the reign of Marcus Aurelius (2nd century). The original building was enlarged under Pope Pascal I (9th century) and given a portico and a campanile in the 12th century. Unfortunately, restorations carried out in the 16th and 18th centuries have destroyed its original mediaeval aspect—the columns have been embedded in masonry and Baroque decoration has superseded the ancient interior.

Beneath the altar is Stefano Maderno's **statue of St Cecilia*** (1600), representing her as seen by the artist when her sarcophagus was opened in 1599. It was the discovery of this intact corpse that determined Cardinal Sfondrati to restore the church and to commission Maderno's statue, a work of touching simplicity that has often been imitated by other sculptors portraying martyrs.

The altar is surmounted by a fine marble ciborium (1283) by Arnolfo di Cambio. There is a 9th-century **mosaic*** in the apse which reiterates the theme of Ss. Cosma and Damiano (see p. 78). Christ, bestowing his benediction in the Greek style, is represented with St Paul, St Agatha, Pascal I (on the right), St Peter, St Valerian and St Cecilia (on the left). St Cecilia's hand rests on Pascal's shoulder, guiding him towards heaven; Pascal wears the square halo of the living.

In the church's basement, there are important vestiges of Roman buildings on display (admission fee). This was the site of the original sanctuary of St Cecilia.

The convent adjoining the church *(open Tues and Thurs 10am-noon, Sun after mass)* possesses one of Rome's oldest cloisters (12th century), as well as a magnificent fresco by Pietro Cavallini, *The Last Judgment*** (1293). Christ appears surrounded by angels, the Virgin, John the Baptist and the Apostles.

San Francesco a Ripa VI, C3

The original church on this site was built in the 13th century to replace the San Biagio hospice, where St Francis of Assisi stayed in 1210. In the 17th century, it was disastrously reconstructed. Today, its main interest lies in a magnificent statue by Bernini, *The Blessed Ludovica Albertoni**** (1674), which may be found in the fourth chapel on the right.

Before you leave, take a moment to look at Simon Vouet's *Birth of the Virgin* (17th century) in the last chapel on the right.

Piazza Santa Maria in Trastevere* VI, B3

Narrow, picturesque streets converge on piazza Santa Maria in Trastevere, the oldest piazza in this neighbourhood. The fountain here was designed by Bernini, modified by Carlo Fontana and again altered during the 19th century. The cool air and lively atmosphere it generates more than make up for its ponderous form.

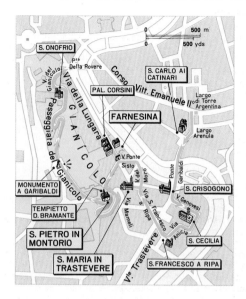

Santa Maria in Trastevere**VI, B2-3

Traditionally, this basilica is supposed to have been the first church in Christendom dedicated to the Virgin. It was founded by Pope Callistus in the 3rd century; the original building was replaced by a basilica by Pope Julius I in the 4th century and this basilica was transformed in the 9th century. The present structure dates from the pontificate of Innocent II (1130-1143). Later changes, between the 17th and 19th centuries, did little to alter its mediaeval aspect.

The principal features of the exterior are a fine Romanesque campanile (12th century) and the façade, which is decorated with 12th- and 13th-century mosaics. The porch (1702), by Carlo Fontana, contains two frescos of the Annunciation and some early Christian stone fragments.

The interior has retained its 12th-century basilical floorplan, with three naves divided by ancient columns. The coffered ceiling (17th century) was designed by Domenichino, who was also responsible for the painting of the Assumption at its centre. The walls of the apse are covered with magnificent mosaics. In the upper area, Christ and the Virgin can be seen occupying the same throne. This masterpiece is one of the earliest (1140) known representations of the Triumph of the Virgin. The lower area was executed at the close of the 13th century by Pietro Cavallini, Rome's great mediaeval artist. His six panels illustrate the Life of the Virgin.

Before you leave the church, take a moment to view the two delicate ancient mosaics in the vestibule of the sacristy (left of the choir), and also to see Gherardi's Baroque chapel (on the right as you come out of the vestibule), with its Borromini-style perspectives (1680).

Porta Settimiana VI, B2

The Porta Settimiana, a gate in Aurelian's wall, was rebuilt during the pontificate of Alexander VI (1492-1503). The house on its right is said to have been the residence of La Fornarina, who was painted by Raphaël (today it is the restaurant Romolo). Not far from here is the entrance to Julius II's **via della Lungara**; the longest of the streets built through Rome during the Renaissance.

The rooftops of Trastevere offer a panoramic view of Rome.

La Farnesina** VI, A2

Open Mon-Sat 10am-1pm.

La Farnesina was built between 1509 and 1512 by Baldassare Peruzzi for the wealthy Siennese banker, Agostino Chigi, who wanted a country villa beside the Tiber, not far from the city and his bank in via dei Banchi. Chigi, known to his contemporaries as 'the Magnificent', entertained on a sumptuous scale: to inaugurate the villa's stables, he gave a formal banquet to which his friend Pope Leo X Medici and 14 cardinals were invited, along with a bevy of ambassadors and other dignitaries. Chigi died

in 1520 and the villa was subsequently purchased by Alessandro Farnese, from whom it got its name.

La Farnesina was the prototype for many other aristocratic residences built outside the centre of Rome between the 16th and 18th centuries. Its basic architectural feature is a ground-floor loggia, enclosed between two wings and giving onto a garden. This loggia has recently been glassed in to protect the frescos, a measure which has unfortunately altered the effect of the villa's exterior. The façade, formerly covered by frescos in counterpoint to the pretty frieze of cherubs and garlands under the eaves, is now completely bare.

The interior decoration of the villa was entrusted to the greatest artists of the time. Raphaël and his assistants (Giulio Romano, Francesco Penni and Giovanni da Udine) covered the vault of the loggia with a composition entitled *Legend of Eros and Psyche**. In the adjacent salon, you can see Raphaël's rendering of *Galatea*★★, driving her sea-chariot, a shell drawn by dolphins. The ceiling in this room was painted by Peruzzi, and the *Polyphemus**, to the left of Raphaël's fresco, is by Sebastiano del Piombo.

The salon on the second floor is decorated with *trompe l'œil* frescos of Roman landscapes seen through painted columns. Some of these are disfigured by graffiti which dates from the sack of Rome in 1527. The master bedroom contains one of Sodoma's most voluptuous works, *The Nuptials of Alexander and Roxana*. On its right is another work by the same artist, *The Family of Darius at the Feet of Alexander*.

Today, La Farnesina houses the national collection of engravings and also hosts frequent temporary exhibitions.

Palazzo Corsini VI, A2

This palazzo, which stands opposite La Farnesina, was built by Francesco Fuga in the 18th century. It replaced a 15th-century palace that had been occupied by Queen Christina of Sweden after her conversion to Catholicism and abdication of the throne in 1684. It was here that Christina founded Arcadia, a famous academy of letters which remained in existence until 1925.

In 1797, General Duphot, the ambassador of the French government, was lodged in the Palazzo Corsini; his death in a riot nearby led to the occupation of Rome by General Berthier, the expulsion of Pope Pius VI and the proclamation of the short-lived Roman republic.

In 1884, this palazzo passed into state ownership and today it houses a section of the Galleria Nazionale di Arte Antica (see p. 180) and the Accademia dei Lincei, a cultural institution founded in 1603.

▄▄▄ IL GIANICOLO (The Janiculum) VI, AB1-2

The best way to reach the Janiculum is to go back to the Porta Settimiana, turn right into via Garibaldi, and follow it to the top of the hill.

The Janiculum is not one of the official seven hills of Rome. It was not included in the city limits until the 17th century, when Urban VIII built a defensive wall around the neighbourhood. It owes its name to the god Janus, who is supposed to have founded a city on its summit.

This area offers magnificent views of the city, as well as a store of monuments and works of art.

San Pietro in Montorio* VI, B2

This church was built in the 9th century on the spot where St Peter was believed (erroneously) to have been crucified. In the late 18th century it was rebuilt with the aid of Ferdinand and Isabella of Spain and given a sober Renaissance façade with a rose window and pediment.

Inside, the first chapel on the right is decorated with frescos by Sebastiano del Piombo (1518): the *Flagellation*★★, in the centre, is based on a drawing by Raphaël. The inner dome contains a *Transfiguration; St Matthew and the Prophet Isaiah* adorns an arcade, with *St Peter* and *St Francis* on either side. The *Crowning of the Virgin*, on the vault of the second chapel on the right, is the work of Peruzzi. The fifth chapel on the right was designed by Vasari and contains fine tombs (1550-1553) by Ammanati, with allegorical statues of Justice and Religion and four pairs of *putti* (children) on the balustrade.

Opposite, in the fifth chapel on the left, is a *Baptism of Christ* by Daniele da Volterra. The second chapel on the left was designed by Bernini (1640).

Tempietto**

On leaving San Pietro in Montorio, you will come upon Bramante's Tempietto ('little temple') to the left in the convent courtyard. Built in 1502, this minor masterpiece was much admired by Bramante's contemporaries for its purity and proportions. The drawings made of the Tempietto by the architects Serlio and Palladio were known all over Europe and made it almost as famous as the Pantheon and the Arch of Constantine.

The Tempietto was built to commemorate the martyrdom of St Peter. According to Bramante's original plan, it was to stand in the middle of a circular cloister with a colonnade of 16 columns similar to its own, but one-and-a-half times larger. Thus, when viewed from any point in the cloister, the building would be seen against a background of columns just like those in its main structure and would tend to look larger than it actually was. The fact that this project was never completed does not detract from the geometrical effect of the concentric volumes which regulate the architecture of the Tempietto. Note also the harmony of its proportions: the diameter of the colonnade is equal to the height of the sanctuary, not including the dome, and the height of the cylindrical structure bearing the dome is equal to its radius.

In terms of Classical purity, Bramante's design appears to be a faithful reconstruction of a Roman temple. However, while its architectural syntax was undoubtedly borrowed from the ancients, it is nonetheless a prototype, not a copy—in effect, it served as a manifesto for Renaissance architecture.

Fontana Paola* VI, B2

This monumental fountain (1612), built in the form of a triumphal arch, is the work of Flaminio Ponzio. It was commissioned by Pope Paul V (hence its name) and was supposed to be an 'improved' version of Sixtus V's Fontana dell'Acqua Felice. The openings of its central arches offer a view of the gardens behind it.

Passeggiata del Gianicolo (Janiculum promenade) VI, AB1

To the right of the Fontana Paola is the Passeggiata del Gianicolo, a panoramic promenade laid out in 1870, lined with a series of marble busts commemorating Garibaldi's more prominent comrades. The promenade leads to piazza Garibaldi, which is dominated by a monument to this great Italian patriot. The view from this site is magnificent. A bit further on, on the right, there is a narrow flight of steps which can serve as a shortcut to the church of Sant'Onofrio, described below.

Sant'Onofrio III, F2

This church was founded in the 15th century by a member of the order of the Hermits of St Jerome. Despite successive restorations, it has retained its original charm. The arched portico fronting the church is decorated with frescos (1605) by Domenichino, and inside there are delicate frescos in the apse, painted by Peruzzi (early 16th century).

To the right of the church is a graceful 15th-century cloister with frescos illustrating the life of St Onofrio, a 4th-century hermit. An adjacent cloister is associated with the great Italian poet, Tasso (1544-1595), who spent his final years here.

IX
VERDANT ROME

Around the Baths of Caracalla and the Caelian hill

T he area between the Coliseum, the Palatine hill, Aurelian's wall and the Vatican includes much undeveloped green space, most of which harbours major vestiges of antiquity and revered Christian sanctuaries.

The district around the Baths of Caracalla was known for summer-evening licentiousness during the days of the early empire, and the passage of time has done little to alter this reputation. By contrast, places on the Caelian hill recall the sufferings of Christians during the reign of Julius the Apostate. While the entire itinerary abounds with remarkable churches and monuments to early and mediaeval Christian fervour, the greatest of these are San Stefano Rotondo, one of Italy's first circular basilicas, Santa Maria in Domnica, with fine mosaics, Santi Quattro Coronati, a fortified monastery, and the magnificent complex of San Clemente.

Access

Map V, B2. Bus: 11, 15, 27, 118, 673. Metro: Colosseo.

▬▬ *SAN GREGORIO* V, C2

The church of San Gregorio can be reached from via di San Gregorio, which follows the ancient via Triumphalis between the Caelian and Palatine hills. The via Triumphalis was used by victorious Roman generals in their processions to the Forum and the Capitol.

According to tradition, this church was founded by St Gregory, the scion of a wealthy Roman family. Before his election as pope, he is supposed to have transformed his home on this site into a monastery (6th century). In the 8th century, the oratory of the monastery, which was originally dedicated to St Andrew, was rebuilt and dedicated as a church to Gregory. Today, no trace of this construction remains.

The present façade stands at the top of a flight of steps which date from the heavy restoration work undertaken by Soria, at the expense of Cardinal Scipio Borghese, in the 17th century. Note the Borghese eagle over the arches of the portico that leads into the atrium.

The interior was converted to the Baroque style in the 18th century, incorporating ancient columns and mosaic fragments. At the end of the right-hand nave is a chapel with a fine late 15th-century altarpiece. The little room on the right of this chapel is reputed to have been St Gregory's monastic cell.

The chapels of St Barba, Sant'Andrea and St Silvia

As you leave the church, you will see a little door on the right of the steps.

This leads to three charming small chapels (closed for restoration at time of writing).

The first of these, on the left, is the Chapel of St Barba. It is decorated with a fresco illustrating an episode in the life of St Gregory. Gregory used to feed 12 poor people every day, and the fresco shows a scene when a 13th guest appeared—and turned out to be an angel.

The Chapel of Sant'Andrea, in the centre, was decorated by Domenichino *(Flagellation of St Andrew)* and by Guido Reni *(Angels in Chorus)*.

The Chapel of St Silvia, on the right, was dedicated to St Gregory's mother and is decorated with a beautiful fresco by Guido Reni (1608).

Leaving San Gregorio, the itinerary turns right along the Clivo de Scauro and continues to the piazza Ss. Giovanni e Paolo.

SS. GIOVANNI E PAOLO★ V, C2

This 12th-century basilica has a heavily restored Romanesque portico. Its fine campanile, also Romanesque, rests on the remains of the Temple of Claudius, which was built by Agrippina to commemorate the husband she had just assassinated (AD 54). This temple was promptly demolished by Agrippina's son-in-law, Nero.

The importance of this basilica resides in the houses that lay concealed under it since the 4th century. At that time, the original church was built and dedicated to two Roman officers said to have lived on the site before being martyred by Julius the Apostate in AD 362. This **basement level★★** can be visited *(open Mon-Sat 8.30-11.30am, 4-6.30pm).*

From the right-hand nave of the church, a staircase leads down to about 20 rooms which were originally part of two large houses. These rooms are decorated with ancient frescos from the 2nd, 3rd and 4th centuries. At the foot of the staircase is a niche that once contained fountains and a source of water. It is adorned with 3rd-century frescos and a mosaic pavement.

There follows a succession of rooms, decorated with frescos and *trompe l'œil* marble inlays. In one of these, you can see the outline of a praying figure, which shows that this was a Christian place of worship. Another flight of stairs leads to a tiny chapel or confessional. Here, the walls are covered with late 4th-century frescos depicting the martyrdom of St Crispus, St Crispinian and St Benedicta during the reign of Julian the Apostate (relics of these three saints were placed in a trench which can be seen through a small window at the back of the chapel). The two mutilated figures are probably St John and St Paul. Beneath the window is a figure in prayer (either Christ or one of the martyrs); two other figures prostrate themselves before him. The walls on either side are covered with frescos depicting the arrest and martyrdom of the three saints.

PIAZZA DI PORTA CAPENA V, C2

On the left side of this piazza is the headquarters of the Food and Agriculture Organization (FAO). On the right is the site of the old Circus Maximus (see p. 134), next to a small 16th-century arcaded villa. The obelisk in the piazza's centre, from Aksoum in Ethiopia, dates from the 4th century and was brought to Rome in 1937.

SANTA BALBINA V, D2

Thanks to modern restoration, the church of Santa Balbina has recovered its mediaeval aspect. There has probably been a Christian place of worship on this site since the 4th century. The present building consists of a single nave with a timber-supported roof and paving recovered from ancient villas. On the right of the entrance, note the tomb (1303) of Cardinal Surdi by Giovanni Cosma; behind the altarpiece is a 13th-century episcopal throne in the same style. The side chapels contain vestiges of frescos from the 9th to the 14th centuries.

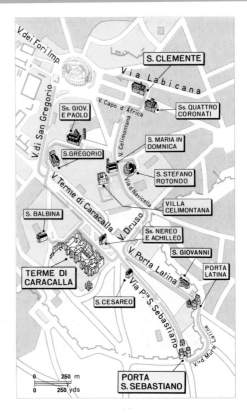

◼◼◼ *SS. NEREO E ACHILLEO* V, D3

This church, like so many others in Rome, began as a *titulus* (see Glossary, p. 212) in the 4th century. It was rebuilt in the 9th and 15th centuries, then restored and covered in frescos at the expense of Cardinal Baronius in the late 16th century. The same cardinal was subsequently responsible for moving the relics of the martyrs Nereo and Achilleo from their former sanctuary in the catacomb of Domitillus.

The church's mediaeval features include some reconstructed 13th-century furniture and the mosaic on its triumphal arch, which represents the Transfiguration, the Annunciation and the Virgin with an angel. Other points of interest are some strident paintings of martyrs in the style that was current during the Counter-Reformation.

◼◼◼ *TERME DI CARACALLA** (Baths of Caracalla)* V, DE2

Open Tues-Sun 9am-one hour before sunset.

The Baths of Caracalla (officially, the Antonine Baths) constitute the largest and best-preserved complex of such buildings to have survived from the empire. Begun by Caracalla in AD 212, the baths were completed in AD 222-235 by emperors Heliogabalus and Alexander Severus. Originally they covered an area of 27 acres/11 hectares. Restored under Aurelian, Diocletian, and Theodoric, the baths ceased to function in AD 537 when the aqueducts were wrecked by the Goths.

The baths comprised a central area (374 × 722 ft/114 × 220 m) and a broad surrounding precinct, which were raised about 19.6 ft/6 m above ground level. Underneath the baths were furnaces and fuel, and above them was a garden concealing 64 reservoirs, which were fed by an aqueduct. The east and west walls of the precinct (on the right of today's entrance) backed onto gymnasiums.

The baths were located in the central building and could accommodate up to 1600 bathers. They also contained a number of rooms sumptuously decorated with polychrome marble, frescos, mosaics and statues. The main building's central area consisted of the *frigidarium*, a coldwater swimming pool flanked on either side by cloakrooms paved with mosaic, and a larger hall (190 × 78 ft /58 × 24 m wide) with three groined vaults and many granite columns. This was probably a walkway connected to the other rooms by broad arcades. Beyond the *frigidarium* was the *tepidarium* (warm baths), small and rectangular, and the broad, circular *caldarium* (hot baths). On either side of the latter, further rooms led to the *laconicum* (steam bath), with its concave walls, which gives onto the *palestre*, a wide courtyard used for exercise.

A habitué of the baths began by warming up with gymnastics and exercise, then took a steam bath in the *laconicum* to accelerate perspiration. Next came a hot bath in the *caldarium* and a warm bath in the *tepidarium*. The cycle ended with a plunge in the cold water of the *frigidarium,* followed by a stroll in the gardens outside.

Excavations undertaken during the 16th and 17th centuries unearthed a number of beautiful objects on the site. The most famous of these, the Farnese *Bull* group and the Farnese *Hercules,* are now in the National Museum at Naples. The two urns in the piazza Farnese were discovered at the same excavation, along with an underground sanctuary dedicated to the god Mithras.

SAN CESAREO V, E3

This small, ancient church with its single nave was built on the foundations of a 2nd-century bath complex. After restoration in 1600, it gained a fine ceiling coffered with the arms of Clement VIII. The marble grill closing off the choir, the marble pulpit and the episcopal throne (17th century) incorporate fine elements of 13th-century mosaic.

On the left, a stairway leads to three rooms which were part of the old Roman baths. These are paved with black mosaics on a white background, and the motifs are exclusively nautical.

Beside the church, at n° 8, is the **house of Cardinal Bessarion,** a fine 15th-century villa (closed for restoration). Cardinal Bessarion (1400-1472) was a humanist and skilled diplomat, who translated Aristotle, befriended the painter Piero della Francesca, and championed the union of the Greek and Roman churches.

SEPOLCRO DEGLI SCIPIONI* (Tomb of the Scipios) V, E4

Open Tues-Sun 9am-1.30pm; Apr-Sept, also Tues, Thurs and Sat 4-7pm.

The Scipios were one of Rome's most famous patrician clans during the republican era. This was their family burial ground during the 3rd and 2nd centuries BC. As was customary, the site was outside the city walls. The mausoleum still contains sarcophagi from the period, along with a number of funerary inscriptions.

On request, the warden will also guide you through the public garden next door. This was formerly the property of the Scipio family and contains the **Columbarium of Pomponius Hylas** (1st century), a niche decorated with mosaics. It was discovered, perfectly preserved, in the 19th century. Originally it contained the funerary urn of the owner and his wife. In addition, a small underground room covered with stucco and paintings housed the funerary urns of slaves freed under Augustus and Tiberius.

■■■ ARCO DI DRUSO AND PORTA SAN SEBASTIANO*
(Arch of Drusus and San Sebastian's Gate) V, F4

The Arch of Drusus (3rd century) is a monumental structure spanning the Appian Way. The arch originally carried the aqueduct that fed the Baths of Caracalla. Behind it stands the Porta San Sebastiano, one of Rome's most beautiful gates, flanked by crenellated semicylindrical towers on massive foundations of white marble. These towers are connected by a gallery above the gate, which was formerly closed by great wooden doors and a portcullis.

It was through the Porta San Sebastiano that the Emperor Charles V entered Rome in 1536, nine years after his troops had sacked the city.

To the right of the gate is a small **museum** devoted to the Aurelian wall *(open Tues-Sun 9am-2pm).*

Beyond the gate, the **via Appia Antica,** lined with tombs of every form and of every period, continues.

■■■ PORTA LATINA V, E3-4

This fine crenellated gate, which is faced on the outside with blocks of travertine limestone and flanked by round towers, dates from the construction of the Aurelian wall in the 3rd century. Altered in the 5th and 6th centuries, it at one time had two swinging doors and a portcullis which could be raised or lowered from a guardroom overlooking the entry.

■■■ SAN GIOVANNI IN OLEO V, E4

This small, octagonal building was built in 1506 by the French prelate Benoît Adam, on the site where St John the Evangelist is reputed to have emerged unharmed from a cauldron of boiling oil. The founder's motto, 'As God wills', is inscribed on the door of the oratory. The frieze and roof were added by Borromini in the 17th century.

■■■ SAN GIOVANNI A PORTA LATINA* V, E4

Founded in the 5th century, San Giovanni a Porta Latina was rebuilt in the 8th century and then altered during the 12th century and again in the Baroque era. Recent work has finally restored it to its original mediaeval simplicity.

The church is fronted by a five-arched portico resting on ancient Ionic columns, with an elegant five-storey campanile towering above. The basilical interior consists of three 12th-century naves divided by marble columns of various designs, all with Ionic capitals. The central nave is decorated with three tiers of 12th-century frescos that illustrate scenes from the Old and New Testaments. Other frescos in the apse represent the throne of God the Father, angels, the symbols of the Evangelists and the 24 Sages of the Apocalypse. Note also the fine pavement of different coloured marbles in the apse, which dates from before the 12th century.

■■■ PIAZZA DELLA NAVICELLA V, C3

This charming piazza is freshened by a marble fountain in the form of a boat (1513), which is a copy of an ancient ex-voto. To the left of the church stands **Villa Celimontana,** which was built for the Mattei family in the 16th century on the western slope of the Caelian hill. Today its garden is considered one of Rome's most beautiful and verdant parks.

■■■ SANTA MARIA IN DOMNICA V, C3

Santa Maria in Domnica was built in the 9th century during the pontificate of Pascal I. Its name probably derives from a distortion of the early Christian word *dominicum,* meaning 'holy place'. The church was restored in the early 16th century by Leo X, who commissioned Andrea Sansovino's elegant portico (1513).

The interior is basilical in design and separated into three naves by 18 ancient granite columns with Corinthian marble capitals. The coffered ceiling, like the heraldic frieze which runs around the walls, dates from the 16th century.

At the back of the nave is a superb **mosaic**** from the time of Pascal I (contemporary with the mosaics of Santa Prassede and Santa Cecilia, see pp. 114, 138). In this composition, the Virgin is given a predominant place in the divine hierarchy, probably for the first time in Roman iconography. She is accompanied by angels dressed in white tunics, whose superimposed halos imply that they are a guard of honour. Pope Pascal I (with the square halo of the living) can be seen kneeling humbly at the feet of the Virgin.

A frieze over the triumphal arch shows Christ between two angels, with the Apostles striding towards him in flowing robes. The figures carry sacred texts, and their covered hands betoken respect.

This mosaic, which was executed at the height of the crisis caused by the secession of the Eastern Church, has the dual significance of a prayer for pardon addressed to the Virgin and a challenge to the Byzantine emperors. Its creators were probably exiled Greek monks.

SAN STEFANO ROTONDO* V, C3

This broad circular church, with its double colonnade, was founded in the 5th century shortly after the sack of Rome by the Vandals (AD 455). It has the same structure and dimensions as the church of the Holy Sepulchre in Jerusalem, on which it was modelled. Its columns were taken from ancient pagan buildings. Over the centuries, its originally undecorated walls were gradually covered with marble—which has now vanished.

In the 12th century, a porch was added, along with the three great supporting arches that carry the inside colonnade. These arches rest on two tall ancient granite columns with fine Corinthian capitals. In the 15th century, the exterior colonnade was walled in and the outer ring of masonry demolished, thus reducing the diameter of the building from 213 ft/65 m to 131 ft/40 m. The walls were then covered with gruesome frescos of martyrdoms, in the accepted style of the Counter-Reformation.

One of the chapels contains a 7th-century mosaic (damaged and restored) which depicts St Primus and St Felicianus, two martyrs put to death during the reign of Diocletian. The pair can be seen beside a golden, gem-encrusted cross surmounted by a head of Christ. This mosaic celebrates the carrying of the relics of the two saints from the catacombs to the church, the first time such a transfer occurred in Rome.

SANTI QUATTRO CORONATI** V, B3

During the Middle Ages, this massive, fortified ensemble was one of the largest monasteries in Rome. Founded in the 4th century, it was altered in the 7th and 9th centuries and then burned down by the Norman troops of Robert Guiscard in 1084. A smaller church (half the width and one third the length of the original huge structure) was built on the site in the 13th century and was restored in the early 1900s.

Today the church still looks austerely mediaeval. Indeed, in its time it served as a defense for the nearby Lateran basilica and papal palace against the incursions of the aristocratic families entrenched in the Coliseum and the fortified monuments of the Palatine hill.

The name of the church commemorates the martyrdom of four Roman soldiers who refused to prostrate themselves before a statue of Aesculapius, a pagan god.

The interior

The church is entered via a passage beneath a squat tower, which served as a campanile in the 9th century. This leads to an outer courtyard, of which the back wall is the façade of the original basilica. A second courtyard occupies the site of the lower naves of the early church (see the columns and arches set into the wall on the right).

The present church's interior is composed of three naves, separated by antique columns of different shapes with Corinthian and other composite capitals. The floor is covered with very fine Cosmati paving, while the galleries above the side-aisles probably reflect the structure of the original basilica. The coffered ceiling dates from the 16th century, and there is a fine 15th-century tabernacle in front of the last pillar on the left of the central nave.

The apse, from the original basilica, is disproportionate in comparison with the present three naves, all of which correspond to the dimensions of the original central nave. It is covered with frescos by Giovanni da Giovanni (1630), which illustrate the martyrdom of the four saints after whom the church is named (Severus, Severianus, Carpophorus and Victorianus), and a general view of saints in glory.

The Cloister**

The cloister can be entered from the left-hand nave (ring at the door). The work of 13th-century marbleworkers, it is one of the most charming in Rome. Its little arches rest on twinned columns with capitals sculpted in the shapes of leaves of water lilies. There is a fine 12th-century fountain in the centre of the little garden enclosed by the cloister walk. The setting is peaceful and refreshing.

On one side of the cloister, to the left of the entrance, there is a small square chapel with fine ancient entablatures and miniature apses. This chapel is a vestige of the 9th-century church.

Chapel of San Sylvestro*

As you leave the church, stop in the vestibule to the left of the first courtyard, ring the bell and request the key of the chapel (door at right). It is advisable to leave some kind of offering in the alms box.

This chapel, built in the 13th century, is covered with naive and beautifully preserved Romanesque frescos. The subject matter is the legendary 'Donation of Constantine'. The emperor, afflicted with leprosy, has been advised by his seers to kill some children and wash his sores with their innocent blood (see the wall by the door) but St Peter and St Paul appear to him in a dream and tell him to consult St Sylvester. Messengers go to fetch the hermit from his cave (wall at left). St Sylvester tells Constantine to venerate the effigies of Peter and Paul. The emperor is cured and kneels before St Sylvester to offer him a tiara, the symbol of temporal power over the city of Rome. Next, Sylvester is seen entering Rome in state, accompanied by the emperor (now his vassal) who leads the saint's horse by the bridle.

On the right-hand wall are scenes depicting the discovery of the True Cross in Jerusalem by St Helena, the mother of Constantine.

▬ SAN CLEMENTE*** V, B3

The complex of San Clemente reveals several layers of Rome's history and, for this reason, it is among the city's most intriguing monuments.

A first basilica, dedicated to St Clement, was built on this site towards the end of the 4th century, replacing a *titulus* (see Glossary p. 212). The *titulus*, in turn, had been part of a more ancient building dating from the first century. According to tradition, Clement, the third successor to St Peter, lived in this house before his martyrdom. The basilica was restored in the 9th century when the saint's relics were brought to Rome, then devastated in 1084 by Robert Guiscard's Norman troops.

The Roman baths

Public and private baths were vitally important to Roman civilization during the imperial era. It was common for all classes of society to bathe once a day, usually in the afternoon, and for this rite the rich were distinguished from the poor only by the number of slaves attending them. In the later years of the empire, there were no fewer than 11 large public baths and 830 private ones in Rome; entry was either free or exceedingly inexpensive. Baths and physical exercise were considered essential for good physical health, yet the bath house also served as a hotbed of intrigue and debauchery. The early church had difficulty in controlling this propensity, for even the clergy were addicted to baths. When Sisinnius, a bishop of Constantinople in the 4th century, was asked why he took two baths a day, he replied: 'Because I don't have time to take three'.

In 1108, Pascal II built a smaller church on the same site but on a higher level, broadly incorporating the decorative elements of the original basilica. The stuccos, frescos and heavy wooden ceiling date from an 18th-century restoration.

Upper church

The main entrance, below piazza di San Clemente, is fronted by a small 12th-century porch built on four ancient granite columns with Ionic and Corinthian capitals. The entrance leads through to a porticoed courtyard. This entrance is often closed, in which case you should use the side door on the lower left-hand side.

Despite the 18th-century alterations, the interior of the church has retained its original structure, that of a basilica divided into three naves by two rows of ancient marble-and-granite columns.

The rearrangement of the choir in the 12th century incorporated a number of elements from the former basilica, such as the side walls of the *schola cantorum* (where the choristers stand) and the marble screen in front of the presbytery (reserved for the clergy), which bears the monogram of Pope John II (532-535). By contrast, the front of the *schola*, the ambos and the twisted Paschal candelabrum are all from the 12th century, like the paving and the episcopal throne in the apse. In the centre of the presbytery a four-columned ciborium hangs over the crypt, which contains the relics of St Clement.

The **mosaic***** in the apse, with its harmonious colours and thematic diversity, includes a number of decorative motifs from the apse of the old basilica. It is recognized as one of the masterpieces of the Romanesque school that flourished in the first half of the 12th century.

The triumphal arch, which is Byzantine in style, shows Christ in an attitude of benediction, surrounded by stars symbolizing the Evangelists. On the left are St Paul, St Lawrence, the prophet Isaiah and the village of Bethlehem. On the right stand St Peter and St Clement; the latter is shown with a boat because he was thrown into the Black Sea with an anchor tied round his neck. The prophet Jeremiah and the city of Jerusalem are also depicted (Jerusalem and Bethlehem respectively symbolize the Old and New Testaments).

The central subject matter of the flattened dome is the Cross of Christ as the symbol of all life—animal or human, material or spiritual. The Virgin and St John are represented on either side of the cross; 12 doves perch on it, symbolizing the 12 Apostles who nurture their faith in the Passion of Christ. On the parasol of the dome is a multicoloured rendering of the region inhabited by God the Father, whose hand proffers a crown to the Son.

Beneath the cross—at mankind's level—deer are shown drinking from the streams that flow from its foot, an image of the souls of men slaking their thirst with the Word of God. A little stag threatened by a snake denotes the torment of the soul menaced by temptation. Between the green foliated scrolls with their gold background, symbolizing the fecundity of Union in God, are featured from bottom (the Terrestrial Regions) to top (the Divine Regions), the Material Activities, the Doctors of the Church, little winged spirits (souls that have been delivered) and finally birds (symbolizing the Virtues).

In the lower frieze of the apse, 12 lambs (the Apostles) are seen emerging from Bethlehem and Jerusalem to adore the Agnus Dei.

The **Chapel of St Catherine*** is decorated with frescos (c. 1430) by the Florentine painter Masolino. Note the artist's attempt to place his figures in some kind of perspective. Above the archway is a charming *Annunciation;* on the left inside the chapel are heavily restored scenes from the life of St Catherine of Alexandria, with the wheel on which she was martyred. At the back of the chapel is a fine *Crucifixion;* on the right are scenes from the life of St Ambrose; and, on the vault, a rendering of the *Evangelists and Fathers of the Church* can be seen.

Lower basilica

Open daily 9am-noon, 3.30-6.30pm. Admission charge.

Entrance to the lower basilica is by the sacristy. A staircase leads to the narthex of the old 4th-century basilica, which contains Romanesque frescos executed after the restoration that followed the fire of 1084. One of these frescos evokes *The Miracle of St Clement*. According to legend, a chapel appeared on the bed of the Black Sea to shelter the remains of the martyred pope. Once a year the waters receded to allow people to enter. The legend further says that one year, a woman forgot her baby in the chapel. When she realized her mistake, the waters had returned; thus the baby was presumed dead. Yet 12 months later when the waters had receded again, the baby was found in the chapel alive and well. Another fresco depicts the transportation of the body of St Cyril (who died in Rome in 869) to the church of San Clemente.

The vestibule leads through to the three naves of the great primitive basilica. Thick supporting walls fill the spaces between the columns and divide the central nave in two, thus reinforcing the upper basilica. These walls partially obscure the broad basilical floorplan, which nonetheless re-asserts itself throughout the naves.

The walls are covered by two series of frescos. The oldest of these dates from the 9th century: in a niche in the right-hand nave, a Byzantine *Virgin and Child;* on the side walls, two Byzantine heads of saints with bejewelled diadems; in the central nave, on the wall that divides it from the narthex, *The Wedding of Cana*, a *Crucifixion* and *The Descent of Jesus into Limbo*. The other series of frescos are Romanesque and date from the 11th and 12th centuries. Towards the back of the central nave, on the left, is *The Legend of Sisinius*. The legend goes as follows: The wife of the Prefect Sisinius was a Christian and went to attend a mass celebrated by St Clement. Sisinius, seeking to catch her at it, burst in on the service and was instantly struck blind.

There are many ancient Roman elements that remain in this church. Under the lower basilica are two constructions separated by a narrow passageway. These were probably public buildings from the late 1st century. The first, situated under the naves of the 4th-century church, had thick walls of tufa—it may have been a state bank. The second, slightly to the west of the church, was built a few years later and may have been an annex for the Flavian Amphiteatre nearby. Some time towards the beginning of the 3rd century, a sanctuary was installed in one of its rooms.

X
FROM THE QUIRINAL HILL
TO THE MAUSOLEUM
OF ST CONSTANCE

Piazza del Quirinale, Sant'Andrea, San Carlo alle Quattro Fontane, Santa Maria della Vittoria, Porta Pia, Sant'Agnese, Baths of Diocletian

This itinerary leads along via XX Settembre and via Nomentana, taking in the north-eastern part of the city. The architecture in this area mostly derives from the post-1870 period when the Piedmontese monarchy took up residence in the Quirinal Palace and transformed Rome into the capital of the newly founded Kingdom of Italy.

After a brief halt to admire the piazza del Quirinale, which offers a view of the ancient roofs of the *Campo Marzio* and the dome of St Peter's, the itinerary follows via del Quirinale (which turns into via XX Settembre). This street is lined with churches built by Rome's greatest 17th-century architects: Sant'Andrea (Bernini), San Carlo (Borromini), Santa Susanna (Carlo Maderno) and Santa Maria della Vittoria, which contains Bernini's stunning *Ecstasy of St Teresa*.

Beyond the Porta Pia, via Nomentana leads through various residential districts to the old church of Sant'Agnese fuori le Mura and the mausoleum of St Constance, with its beautiful 4th-century mosaics. These mosaics are among the oldest in Rome.

The last phase of the itinerary will bring you to the Baths of Diocletian, once the most extensive complex of baths in the city and today the site of Michelangelo's 16th-century church of Santa Maria degli Angeli. It then ends at piazza della Repubblica and the shopping area centred on via Nazionale.

Access

Map IV, F2. Bus: 46, 92, 94, 716, 718, 719.

▬▬ *TORRE DELLE MILIZIE (Tower of the Militia)* IV, F2

This tower, which overlooks Trajan's Markets (see p. 81), was the keep of a 13th-century stronghold built by Pope Gregory IX. It was successively occupied by several great Roman families, which testifies to its strategic importance in their rivalries. In the mid-14th century, an earthquake destroyed its upper works and left the remainder of the building with a distinct tilt.

▬ *PALAZZO ROSPIGLIOSI-PALLAVICINI* IV, E2

The itinerary follows via XXIV Maggio to piazza del Quirinale, passing between the gardens of Palazzo Colonna, on the left, and Palazzo Rospigliosi-Pallavicini, on the right. The latter, commissioned in 1611 by Cardinal Scipio Borghese, occupies the site of the ruined Baths of Constantine; its architects were Giovanni Vasanzio and Carlo Maderno. The palace subsequently passed through the hands of several wealthy men, including Cardinal Mazarin, before becoming the property of the Rospigliosi-Pallavicini family.

The central salon, the **Casino della Aurora,** is open on the first day of each month. Its ceiling is decorated with a **fresco*** (1614) by Guido Reni which is full of charm and beauty. In its time it was thought comparable to Raphaël's frescos in the Palazzo Farnesina (see p. 140). Aurora (Dawn) is shown preceding the chariot of Phoebus (Sun); Phoebus is accompanied by beautiful dancing girls, whose shapes conform to the ideals of ancient sculpture.

The **Galleria Pallavicini** contains works by Botticelli, Signorelli, Lorenzo Lotto, Annibale Carrache, Rubens and Poussin *(special permission required for visits).*

▬ *PIAZZA DEL QUIRINALE*** IV, E2

Piazza del Quirinale, which occupies the summit of Rome's highest hill (200 ft/61 m), is perhaps the finest surviving example of papal architecture in the capital. Around it stand palaces dating from the 16th-18th centuries, the great era of the papacy. At its centre are colossal statues of the **Dioscuri*,** placed there by Sixtus V at the end of the 16th century, and (since 1787) one of the obelisks which framed the entrance to the mausoleum of Augustus. The left-hand side of the square opens onto a broad terrace, overlooking the rooftops of the *Campo Marzio* and the dome of St Peter's.

The great **granite basin*,** fed by the waters of the Acqua Felice spring, was moved here in 1818 from the Forum, where it served as an ordinary drinking fountain in its position beside the ruins of the Temple of the Dioscuri. The monumental statues of Castor and Pollux are Roman copies (found in the nearby Baths of Constantine) of two Greek equestrian groups from the 5th century BC.

The ancient name 'Quirinale' is derived from the god Quirinus, who was none other than Romulus after his apotheosis. At the close of the 16th century, the Quirinal hill became the site of the popes' summer residence and remained so until 1870. The air, even at this low altitude, was infinitely fresher than the malarial air of the Vatican, which hastened so many popes to their graves.

▬ *PALAZZO DEL QUIRINALE** IV, E2

Visits by special appointment: write to the Servizio Intendenza, Palazzo del Quirinale, for details.

The construction of this palace was begun in 1574 for Gregory XIII by Mascarino. Originally, it was a small summer residence, with a five-arched loggia and two short wings along the same lines as Peruzzi's Villa Farnesina (see p. 140). The floors are connected by a fine double-columned oval staircase, the first of its type in the world. Fifty years later, the staircase was Borromini's inspiration for the staircase of the Palazzo Barberini (see p. 160). Gregory XIII had a tower added 'for a view to the sea', as a gazette of the period recounts. Poor Gregory did not benefit long from his view: he died in 1585, the year after the tower was completed. His successor, Sixtus V, decided to continue the construction work and commissioned Domenico Fontana to build the wing of the palace which today fronts the piazza. Fontana also arranged, at great expense, for water to be diverted from the Acqua Felice.

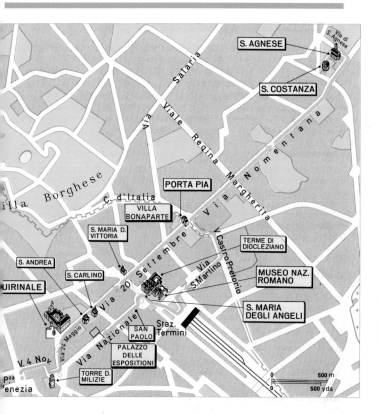

In 1590, Sixtus V died during a heatwave. The next pope, who was already ailing on the day of his election, never had time to fill his lungs with the air of the Quirinal: he died of malaria shortly after his coronation. Thereafter, a series of popes pursued the work with understandable urgency. The palace grew until the 18th century, steadily accruing more buildings, higher floors and broader wings, while Carlo Maderno added a monumental entrance, crowned by statues of St Peter and St Paul (1615).

From 1592 to 1870, all the popes without exception used the Quirinale as a summer palace. Between 1870 and 1946, it was the residence of the kings of Italy and, since 1946, it has been the seat of the president of the republic.

The fine courtyard inside has porticos by Domenico Fontana. On the main staircase, there is a fine fresco by Melozzo da Forli of *Christ in Glory Among His Angels,* transferred from the apse of the church of Santi Apostoli. In the throne room, there are noteworthy frescos by Giovanni Lanfranco and Saraceni. Carlo Maderno was the architect responsible for the Paoline Chapel, the vault of which is coffered with gilded stucco (17th century). The Chapel of the Annunciation was decorated by Guido Reni (17th century).

PALAZZO DELLA CONSULTA* IV, E2

Today, this palazzo is used for the Italian Constitutional Court. Built by Clement XII (1732-1734), it was designed to house the *Sacra Consulta* tribunal, and its façade, by Fuga, represents one of the architect's greatest achievements.

▬▬ *SANT'ANDREA AL QUIRINALE*** IV, E2

Bernini once told his son that, of all his architectural works, Sant'Andrea was the only one which gave him 'pleasure deep in his heart'. At the end of his life, the old man came here often, forgetting his troubles in the contemplation of his greatest work.

The church was commissioned by Cardinal Camillo Pamphili for the novices of the Jesuit order and was built between 1568 and 1571. Its site was somewhat narrow, a problem which Bernini solved by adopting an elliptical floorplan with the main entrance and high altar on its minor axis.

The façade

The façade is dominated by a rounded portico supported by columns; the curve of this portico is accentuated by the concave tendency of the side walls, which describe a quarter-circle, in anticipation of the curvilinear interior. The coping of the portico gives a subtle illusion of passing beneath the Corinthian pilasters to meet the cornice of the oval wall surrounding the chapels. Above the portico, a series of exuberant bas-reliefs surround the coat of arms of the Pamphili family.

The interior

The interior of Sant'Andrea is elliptical, with rectangular side-chapels at intervals; these increase the apparent size of the building. The extremities of the major axis are marked by pilasters, which prevent the eye from straying into the depths of the side-chapels and instead direct it along the sequence of colossal pilasters, as far as the fluted pink-and-white columns of the central portico, which opens onto the high altar.

Above the altar hangs a painting by Jacques Courtois representing the *Martyrdom of St Andrew*. The canvas is supported by angels fluttering between gilded beams of sunshine and lit by a skylight which is invisible from the entrance.

Before you leave this beautiful little church, spare a moment for the sacristy (off the passage to the right of the choir) with its *trompe l'œil* ceiling.

▬▬ *SAN CARLO ALLE QUATTRO FONTANE*** IV, D3

This tiny church is not only Borromini's greatest masterpiece, but also the prototype for most of the innovations of European Baroque architecture.

In 1611, the Spanish Order of the Trinity, an institution dedicated to the collection of funds for ransoming Christians from the Moors, acquired a small plot of land at the corner of the strada Pia (today's via XX Settembre) and the strada Felice (now the via delle Quattro Fontane). The strada Pia had been built by Pius IV (1559-1565); the strada Felice, linking Santa Maria Maggiore and Trinità dei Monti, was the work of Sixtus V (1585-1590). In 1634, the procurator of the order commissioned Borromini—then a little known and inexpensive architect—to build the monastery of San Carlo. Borromini began with an edifice to house the monks (1634), then constructed a cloister (1635) and a small church (1638-1641). Due to a lack of funds, the church's façade was not completed until 1665.

The façade

The façade produces an undulating effect, created by the play of convexity and concavity and a powerful entablature separating two lines of tall columns. This dominant theme is subtly transposed to the façade's upper level. Here the central bay is concave, and the convex tendency is re-affirmed by a small oval structure and a balcony with graceful Borromini-style balusters with triangular bases.

The façade of San Carlo constitutes the most perfect example of the Baroque era's aspiration towards the expression of movement in architecture. As such, it is Borromini's greatest legacy to his profession.

The interior

The interior prolongs and amplifies the effect created by the façade. Borromini's complex design, which he refused to reveal and which gave rise to many imitations, appears to have been based on an ingenious combination of ellipse, octagon and cross.

The crypt

Beneath the church there is a fine crypt, which can be entered through a door to the left of the main doors. This crypt has the same dimensions as the church but is far simpler in conception. On its left is the charming octagonal chapel in which Borromini at one time hoped to be buried.

The cloister**

Entrance is by way of a door to the right of the high altar. With this small, perfectly proportioned masterpiece, Borromini rejected the rectangular pattern of the Renaissance in favour of a shape using parallelograms. This design created the illusion of a larger area.

As you leave the church, note the fine **doorway of the monastery** at n° 23 via del Quirinale, crowned by a monumental concave pediment. At the **crossroads of the Quattro Fontane,** the meeting place of the two former pilgrim ways (strada Pia and strada Felice) since the end of the 16th century, there is a wonderful view over Michelangelo's Porta Pia and the three obelisks of Trinità del Monti, the piazza del Quirinale and the piazza dell'Esquilino. The four fountains, which were installed here at the end of the 16th century, represent the Tiber, the Nile and the goddesses Juno and Diana.

▬▬ *PIAZZA SAN BERNARDO* IV, D3

This piazza contains a fountain that was designed by Domenico Fontana in 1585. An apocryphal story relates that he died of remorse after having produced a work of such ugliness. On one side of the piazza stands the church of **San Bernardo,** built at the close of the 16th century.

On the other side of the piazza is the church of **Santa Susanna.** Its main interest lies in its façade, which was built by Carlo Maderno in 1603. It marks an important stage in the history of Roman religious architecture, providing a foretaste of the Baroque. For the first time, a church façade was designed to emphasize its dynamic possibilities.

A bit further on, you will come to the church of **Santa Maria della Vittoria,** which was built between 1610 and 1612 from plans by Maderno. The façade, built between 1625 and 1638 by Giovanni-Battista Soria and commissioned by Cardinal Scipio Borghese, is an uninspired copy of Maderno's Santa Susanna. The extraordinary **Cornaro Chapel**** is in the left transept. Executed between 1647 and 1652, it is among Bernini's most important achievements as a sculptor. Its decoration illustrates St Teresa of Avila's account of her moment of extreme ecstasy. On either side of the chapel, kneeling cardinals of the Cornaro family observe this scene, seeming to discuss its theological implications.

▬▬ *PORTA PIA** IV, BC5

Realized between 1562 and 1564, the Porta Pia was Michelangelo's last architectural project. The master was 87 years old when he drew up the plans for this monument, the practical purpose of which was to close off a given area, the Rome of Pius IV. Symbolically, however, the raising of the Porta Pia marked the end of the Renaissance, and many of the remarkable ideas embodied in it (such as the curious crenellations, the broken curving pediment within another pediment of triangular shape, and the blind window-embrasures) were later seized upon and developed by Bernini, Borromini and others in the 17th century.

The external façade of the gate, facing via Nomentana, was rebuilt in the

19th century by the architect Virginio Vespignani. Via Nomentana follows the line of the old consular highway to Nomentum (Mentana). It crosses a residential district where a number of green areas have been preserved, notably the gardens of the **Villa Torlonia** (designed by Giuseppe Valadier at the beginning of the 19th century and used as a private residence by Mussolini) and of the **Villa Paganini,** on the other side of via Nomentana.

SANT'AGNESE FUORI LE MURA* II, B5

This church was founded in AD 342, on a site above the catacombs which reputedly contained the body of the martyr St Agnes. Traces of the original basilica still survive but the present building began as a small chapel, built over the saint's grave; it was reconstructed during the 7th century and restored several times thereafter.

At the end of the courtyard, on the right, a broad flight of marble steps, with walls covered in stone fragments from the catacombs, leads to the narthex of the church. The interior is divided into three naves by 14 ancient columns. Above the side-naves, the 7th-century platforms show a strong Byzantine influence. The **mosaic** in the apse (also 7th-century Byzantine) represents St Agnes, in the robes of an empress, in company with Pope Symmachus, who restored the chapel in the early 6th century, and Pope Honorius, who carries a scale model of the new church.

The catacombs
Entrance to the catacombs of Sant'Agnese (2nd-3rd centuries) is at the rear of the left-hand nave. *Open daily 9am-noon, 3.30-6.30pm.*

SANTA COSTANZA** II, B4

This church was built at the beginning of the 4th century and was originally the mausoleum of St Constance and St Helena, the daughters of the Emperor Constantine. It was later used as a baptistry, until its conversion to a church in the 13th century.

This fine example of early Christian architecture was much admired by Renaissance architects, who wrongly assumed it was a converted Roman temple. The church is round, with a diameter of 74 ft/22.5 m. Its central area, which was originally covered by a dome, rests on 12 pairs of superb granite columns, pillaged from older buildings. A pillared portico (now demolished) once encircled the ring gallery, which today is covered by a barrel vault with magnificent 4th-century mosaics. These depict bucolic scenes against a light background, along with fruit, foliage and geometrical motifs in the ancient style. The mosaics in the small side-apses are from the 5th and 7th centuries. The niche at the rear contains a copy of the porphyry sarcophagus of St Constance, the original of which is now at the Vatican (Museo Pio-Clementino).

PIAZZA DEI CINQUECENTO IV, D4

The final leg of this itinerary commences on piazza dei Cinquecento, which commemorates 500 soldiers who fell at Dogali (Eritrea) in 1887. On one side of the piazza is the **Termini railway station***, built before World War II by the architect Angiolo Mazzoni (note the austere arcades, facing the piazza). The magnificent façade of the station was completed in 1950 by Eugenio Montuori and Leo Calini.

TERME DI DIOCLEZIANO** (Baths of Diocletian) IV, D4

The remains on the far side of piazza dei Cinquecento give only a vague idea of the sheer scale of the original Baths of Diocletian. Built between AD 298 and 306, they once covered an area of 34 acres/14 hectares and could accommodate up to 3000 people. They were laid out, like most other Roman baths, around the basic features of hot, warm and cold pools, with

The Quirinal, formerly the papal summer residence, is now the seat of the president of the republic.

porticos for strolling, exercise rooms and libraries. The marble facing that once covered the brick masonry has disappeared, along with most of the floor mosaics. In the 16th century, Michelangelo was commissioned by Pius IV to build the church of Santa Maria degli Angeli and a convent on this site.

▬▬ *SANTA MARIA DEGLI ANGELI* IV, D4

The site of this church was formerly one of the halls of the Baths of Diocletian. It was constructed between 1563 and 1566 by Michelangelo, then altered by Vanvitelli in 1749. The Greek-cross interior is broad and well-lit, but Michelangelo's original plan has otherwise completely succumbed to later restoration. On the right of the passage leading to the transverse nave is an imposing **statue of St Bruno***, of which Pope Clement XIV remarked that it would undoubtedly talk if not forbidden to do so by the rules of its order. This statue is the work of the French sculptor, Jean-Antoine Houdon (1766).

The huge transverse nave gives some idea of the size of the ancient Roman bath house that was its predecessor. It is hung with 17th- and 18th-century paintings, of which *Mass of St Basil* by Pierre Subleyras and *Fall of Simon the Magician* by Pompeo Batoni are particularly noteworthy. Both hang on the left-hand wall on the nave's left side.

In the choir are a fresco representing the *Martyrdom of St Sebastian* by Domenichino (16th century) and a *Baptism of Jesus* by Carlo Maratta (17th century).

▬▬ *PIAZZA DELLA REPUBBLICA* IV, D4

This piazza, with its sweep of buildings (1896-1902) by George Koch, is one of the most successful accomplishments of the 'Classical' school of the late 19th century. The **Naiad Fountain***, at its centre, is the work of Antonio Guerrieri and Mario Rutelli. The piazza opens onto via Nazionale, which was built in 1867 to link piazza Venezia with the Termini railway station. Today, via Nazionale is one of Rome's busiest shopping streets.

XI
AUGUSTAN AND BAROQUE ROME

Fontana del Tritone, Palazzo Barberini, Trinità dei Monti, Villa Medicis, Pincio, Villa Borghese, Santa Maria del Popolo, Mausoleum of Augustus, Ara Pacis

T his itinerary, which covers north-central Rome, takes in a selection of palazzos, monuments and works of art that have little in common but their geographical proximity.

Via del Tritone, a noisy street dating from the 19th century, links via del Corso to the Fontana del Tritone, one of Rome's celebrated Baroque fountains. This monument bears the arms of the Barberini family, whose magnificent palazzo stands close by. The itinerary continues down via Sistina, opened by Sixtus V at the end of the 16th century. Leaving the hubbub of the commercial areas behind, it passes through piazza Trinità dei Monti, with its memorable view across the rooftops of Rome, to the romantic Pincio and the Villa Borghese with one of the city's largest parks.

The next stop is piazza del Popolo. Santa Maria del Popolo, one of the churches on this splendid piazza, contains several masterpieces from the Renaissance and Baroque eras. The itinerary then concludes with the Ara Pacis and the mausoleum of Augustus, two remarkable monuments that have survived from the early empire.

Access

Map IV, D1. Bus: 52, 53, 56, 58, 58b, 60, 61, 62, 71, 81, 90b, 95, 115.

▬ *VIA DEL TRITONE* IV, D1-2

Via del Tritone, which was opened in the last century, is one of Rome's busiest roads. It links the Corso with the north-eastern areas of Rome.

▬ *FONTANA DEL TRITONE (Fountain of Triton)* IV, D2

This famous monument was commissioned by Pope Urban VIII Barberini in 1642, and executed by Bernini. The superb sculpted group is supported by four dolphins and features a triton perched on a shell. The effect is charming and fairy-like, a triumph of the Baroque imagination.

▬ *PALAZZO BARBERINI* IV, D3

Palazzo Barberini, begun in 1625 by Carlo Maderno, was commissioned by Pope Urban VIII, who wished to build a palace that would be commensurate with his family's newly acquired importance. When Maderno died,

Bernini took charge and, with the collaboration of Borromini, he completed the palace in 1633.

The building was situated at some distance from the (then) centre of Rome. Maderno rejected the usual quadrilateral layout, with a central courtyard, in favour of a larger version of the 16th-century country villa as typified by the Villa Farnesina—a central courtyard with wings on either side giving onto a large garden.

The main façade, with its Classical positioning of the three orders of architecture, is remarkable for its upper windows. The two windows of the top floor at either end of the central edifice were designed by Borromini (1630) and are among his earliest contributions to Roman architecture. Bernini was responsible for the flight of stairs on the left, while the spiral staircase on the right is by Borromini.

The recently restored palazzo houses the National Gallery of Antique Art (see p. 180).

▬▬ *VIA SISTINA* IV, D2

This street is named after Pope Sixtus V, who carried out a project to connect all the basilicas and churches visited by pilgrims with a system of roads focussed on Santa Maria Maggiore. Via Sistina was designed to link Santa Maria Maggiore with Trinità dei Monti, and Santa Maria del Popolo with the gate of the same name, through which pilgrims from northern Europe entered the city. Today, via Sistina is lined with elegant shops, art galleries and luxury hotels.

At the top of the via Sistina, spare a moment for n° 30 via Gregoriana (on the left), the house of Federico Zuccaro (1540-1609). The windows and doors of this strange building are all sculpted in the form of gaping monsters.

▬▬ *PIAZZA DELLA TRINITÀ DEI MONTI* IV, C1

From this small piazza, there is a delightful **view**** of hanging gardens, with their cream-coloured parasols and luxuriant vegetation, and beyond, the brown-and-ochre rooftops and domes of the city. The obelisk, erected here by Pius VI at the end of the 18th century, is a Roman imitation from imperial times. It used to be in the gardens of Sallust.

▬▬ *TRINITÀ DEI MONTI* IV, C1

This church was founded in 1495 by Charles VIII, King of France, for the Order of Minims created in the same century by St Francis de Paule. Consecrated by Sixtus V in 1585, it was pillaged during the Napoleonic occupation and later restored by Louis XVIII (1816). The church is one of five French churches in Rome.

In the second chapel on the left is a *Descent From the Cross**, the masterpiece of Daniele da Volterra, a pupil of Michelangelo. The *Assumption,* in the third chapel on the right, is by the same artist.

Viale della Trinità dei Monti leads upwards from here to the Pincio, offering further fine views across the city. The fountain (1588), which occupies the terrace in front of the entrance of the Villa Medici, has inspired many painters, notably Corot *(Vasque de la villa Médicis).*

▬▬ *VILLA MEDICI*** IV, C1

The gardens of the Villa Medici are open Oct-June, Sat and Sun 10am-1pm. The villa itself is closed to the public, but regular exhibitions and conferences are organized here throughout the year.

The Villa Medici, built at the close of the 16th century, is the headquarters of the Académie de France. It is probably the best preserved of the great

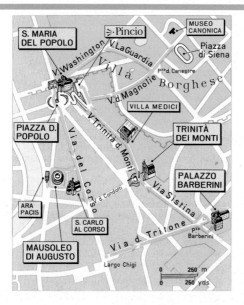

suburban mansions constructed in the style of Peruzzi's Villa Farnesina (see p. 140).

Commissioned by Cardinal Ricci di Montepulciano in 1540, the property was acquired and enlarged by Cardinal Ferdinando di Medici in 1576. The Académie de France, founded by Colbert in 1666, was transferred to the Villa Medici in 1803 by Napoleon, who felt that French artists would be better equipped to do credit to the Empire if given a chance to study the traditions of antiquity and the Renaissance. Until fairly recently, the academicians were the winners of the much-coveted Grand Prix de Rome; today, they tend to be painters, sculptors, filmmakers, art historians and musicians, chosen by committee and housed in the Villa Medici for one or two years.

The exterior façade is somewhat austere, but the one which gives onto the gardens is a remarkable example of Mannerist architecture. There seems to be only one rule governing the profusion of niches, festoons, friezes, bas-reliefs and stuccos: namely, an aversion to unadorned masonry. The magnificent gardens are planted with mature pines, live oaks and cypresses and studded with statues and vestiges from antiquity.

▬▬▬ IL PINCIO   IV, B1

The little hill known as Il Pincio owes its name to the Pinci family, which possessed gardens here in the 4th century. The Roman architect Giuseppe Valadier laid out the park during Napoleon's occupation of the city (1809-1814), and today its fountains, statues and avenues of oaks and parasol pines are much appreciated by the inhabitants. Incomparable sunsets may be seen from the terrace.

From here, the itinerary doubles back, eventually turning right down **viale dell'Obelisco,** in the middle of which stands the elegant obelisk dedicated by Hadrian to his youthful lover, Antinous. At the end of the viale dell'Obelisco, the itinerary turns left down **viale dell'Orologio,** with its curious 19th-century water-clock (on the left). Returning to viale dell'Obelisco, it crosses the bridge spanning **viale del Muro Torto** (named after a particularly sinuous stretch of Aurelian's wall nearby), after which you will find yourself in the gardens of the Villa Borghese.

The elegant form of the Trinità dei Monti rises up behind the Locanda.

VILLA BORGHESE* IV, AB1-3

The gardens of the Villa Borghese constitute the city's most extensive park, and as such are much appreciated by Romans, who come here throughout the year to enjoy the lawns, the romantic avenues, the pools and fountains.

The palace and gardens, designed in the 17th century for Cardinal Scipio Borghese, were altered and enlarged at the turn of the 18th century. The property was purchased by the King of Italy just after 1900 and presented as a gift to the city of Rome.

After the piazzale delle Canestre, follow viale Pietro Canonica. The avenues on your left lead to the delightful **Giardino del Lago** (lake garden), which was laid out at the end of the 18th century. The diminutive Temple of Aesculapius, in the middle of the lake, is a neo-Classical copy of a Greek temple. On the other side of the viale Canonica is the Temple of Diana, dating from the same period. Piazza di Siena, nearby, is the venue for the Rome International Horse Trials. At the end of viale Canonica is the Museo Canonica (on the left), which contains works by the sculptor of the same name (1869-1959).

This park also includes a **zoological garden** (the most important zoo in Italy) and several museums (see pp. 180, 182). More information about the Villa Borghese is given in another itinerary in this guide (see p. 168).

Leaving the Villa Borghese by the main entrance, you will find yourself in piazza Flaminio. On the right is via Flaminia, which follows the line of the ancient Roman road built by Caius Flaminius. This road crosses the entire Italian peninsula, terminating at Rimini. The majestic Porta del Popolo is on the left.

PORTA DEL POPOLO (People's Gate) III, B5

This great gate was set in Aurelian's wall in place of the Porta Flaminia. The outer façade (1562-1565), by Niccolo di Baccio Bigio, was commissioned by Pius IV who wished to impress travellers and pilgrims arriving from the north. The inner façade was reconstructed by Bernini in 1655 for Queen Christina of Sweden's state visit to Rome after her conversion to Catholicism. The hills and star on the façade were the emblem of the reigning pope, Alexander VII Chigi.

PIAZZA DEL POPOLO** III, C5

Piazza del Popolo boasts the hanging gardens of Il Pincio on its left, Giuseppe Valadier's hemispherical benches on its right, a central obelisk, and a number of fountains and allegorical statues. In all, it represents the neo-Classical zenith of three centuries of urban planning.

The backdrop to this magnificent piazza is supplied by two Baroque churches, **Santa Maria in Montesanto** (on the left) and **Santa Maria dei Miracoli** (on the right). Both were designed by Rainaldi and completed by Bernini and Carlo Fontana (1661-1677), but their likeness is only superficial. The site of Santa Maria in Montesanto imposed an elliptical floorplan and a 12 sided dome, while Santa Maria dei Miracoli is circular, with an octagonal dome. Nonetheless, Rainaldi and Bernini contrived to create an optical illusion of perfect symmetry.

These small Baroque churches stand between three long streets which fan out behind them towards different areas of Rome. The middle street, **via del Corso,** was formerly via Lata, the street that linked the piazza with the Capitol district. It is now lined with fashionable clothes shops. **Via di Ripetta,** the street on the right, was constructed by Leo X (1513-1521) to give access to the Campo Marzio and Ponte San Angelo from the north. On the left is **via del Babuino,** constructed in the reign of Clement VII (1523-1534) and today a centre for art and antique dealers.

The granite obelisk (79 ft/24 m high) in the middle of piazza del Popolo once stood before the Temple of the Sun in Heliopolis during the reign of Ramses II of Egypt (13th century BC). The Emperor Augustus had it brought to Rome and erected in the Circus Maximus, and in 1587, on the orders of Sixtus V, it was moved to its present position by Domenico Fontana.

SANTA MARIA DEL POPOLO*** III, B5

The sober façade of Santa Maria del Popolo belies the fact that it is Rome's most extraordinary microcosm of Italian art from the Renaissance to the Baroque eras.

The church itself, built by an unknown architect under Sixtus IV (1472-1477), replaced an earlier, 13th-century edifice which had been paid for by 'the people of Rome', hence the origin of its name 'Maria del Popolo'. In the 16th century, it was enriched with additions by Bramante, who lengthened the apse, and by Raphaël, who designed the Chigi Chapel. In the 17th century, Bernini was commissioned to restore and embellish the church; he was followed by Carlo Fontana, who added the Cybo Chapel (1682-1687) to complement Raphaël's contribution.

The façade is one of the finest surviving examples of the early Renaissance style in Rome. The interior was designed as a Latin cross with side-chapels. The stucco saints on the points of the arches were added during the Baroque restoration. The paving incorporates a number of tombstones from the Middle Ages and the Renaissance.

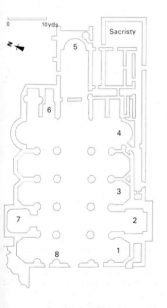

Santa Maria del Popolo

Della Rovere Chapel (1)

This chapel, the first in the right-hand nave, is fronted by an elegant balustrade bearing the arms of the della Rovere family (*rovere* means oak, thus the tree emblem). The chapel is decorated inside with frescos* (1485-1489) by Pinturicchio: note *The Life of St Jerome* and the fine *Adoration of the Christ Child*, with its sweet-faced virgin, simple graceful postures and richly detailed landscape.

On the left is the remarkable tomb* of Cristoforo and Domenico della Rovere, the nephews of Sixtus IV, by Andrea Bregno (late 15th century) and Mina da Fiesole (the medallion of the Virgin is by da Fiesole).

Cybo Chapel (2)

This Baroque chapel on a Greek-cross plan surmounted by a dome is the work of Carlo Fontana (1682-1687). Its marble decoration is some of the most ambitious ever executed in Rome.

The apse (5)

This apse was one of Bramante's first projects in Rome (early 16th century). There are fine frescos* on the ceiling by Pinturicchio (*Coronation of the Virgin, The Evangelists, The Sibyls and the Fathers of the Church*). On either side of the apse are the magnificent tombs* (circa 1505) of Cardinal Girolamo Basso della Rovere and Cardinal Ascanio Sforza, by Andrea Sansovino.

Basso della Rovere Chapel (3)

This chapel, the second in the right-hand nave, is covered with superb frescos* of scenes from the life of the Virgin (school of Pinturicchio, late 15th century). On the right is the tomb of Giovanni della Rovere (school of Andrea Bregno, late 15th century). In the left is a fine bronze recumbent figure by Vecchietta (late 15th century).

First chapel to the right of the choir (6)

This chapel contains two famous paintings by Caravaggio, *The Conversion of St Paul*** and *The Crucifixion of St Peter*** (1600). These two paintings are so powerful that they make Caracci's *Assumption* (above the altar in the same chapel) seem thoroughly tepid.

Chigi Chapel (7)

This chapel the second in the left-hand nave, was designed by Raphaël for the Sienese banker Agostino Chigi and built between 1510 and 1515. Raphaël also drew the cartoons for the **mosaics*** of the dome (1516) and designed the graceful *Jonah** (on the left of the altar) and *Elijah** (on the right of the entrance).

In two niches are *Habbakuk and the Angel** (on the right of the altar) and *Daniel** (to the left of the entrance)—these were sculpted (1655-1661) by Bernini. Over the altar hangs a *Birth of Mary* (1533-1534), by Sebastiano del Piombo. Against the walls are the tombs of Agostino and Sigismondo Chigi, reworked by Bernini in the 17th century.

To the right of the main entrance (8), the funerary monument (1672) fashioned by Ghisleni for his own tomb is typical of the religious atmosphere in Rome during the Baroque era.

▬▬ MAUSOLEO DI AUGUSTO* *(Mausoleum of Augustus)* III, D5

On his return from Egypt in 29 BC, Augustus undertook the construction of a huge dynastic mausoleum similar in style to those of the great Greek sovereigns. Its architectural original was not so much an Etruscan *tumulus*, to which it is sometimes compared, but more like the circular tomb of Alexander the Great at Alexandria (also in the form of a mound), which Augustus had visited in 30 BC.

When his monument was completed, Augustus placed in it the ashes of his nephew Marcellus, along with those of his sister Octavia, his son-in-law Agrippa, and Agrippa's sons. After Augustus's death, his wife Livia, her son Tiberius, and Agrippina eventually followed him to the same resting place (Agrippina's funeral urn is now to be seen in the Capitol Museum). During the Middle Ages, the dilapidated mausoleum became one of the fortresses of the Colonna family, after which it was used successively as a limestone quarry, a vineyard, a garden and, finally, in the 19th century, a concert hall. The concert hall was closed in 1936 when the monument was restored.

The tomb of Augustus was a cylindrical edifice 285.5 ft/87 m in diameter, composed of a series of concentric walls topped by a barrow planted with cypresses. In the centre of this barrow stood a huge bronze statue of Augustus. The entrance was marked, in the Egyptian style, by two granite obelisks (now in piazza Quirinale and piazza del Esquilino). A passage led through to the circular funeral chamber in the middle of which stood the emperor's tomb, vertically beneath his statue atop the monument. The ashes of the other members of his family were placed in three niches in the walls of the same chamber.

From **piazza Augusto Imperatore,** a deplorable product of fascist urbanism, there is a fine view of the **dome of San Carlo al Corso** (designed by Pietro di Cortona in 1668).

▬▬ ARA PACIS AUGUSTAE* III, D5

Open winter, daily 10am-4pm; summer Tues-Sat 10am-1pm, 3-6pm, Sun 9am-1pm.

The allegorical figure of River and Rome's symbol, the wolf, adorn the gardens of Il Pincio.

This altar (13-9 BC), erected by the Senate to mark the pacification of Spain and Gaul, is typical of Roman art during the golden age of Augustus. It was unearthed piece by piece from under the foundations of Palazzo Fiano near San Lorenzo in Lucina between 1568 and 1937, patiently reconstructed in 1937-1938, and finally installed in a special building between via di Ripetta and the bend in the Tiber. The altar itself is set within a two-doored marble chamber. The upper portion of the interior of this chamber is decorated with garlands and flowers, which rest on the sculpted skulls of bulls, the symbolic remains of sacrifice.

On the outer surface of the wall opposite the entrance, the following scenes are represented: on the left, the shepherd Faustulus discovering the twins Romulus and Remus, who are being suckled by the she-wolf; on the right, Aeneas performing a sacrifice to his household gods. The two doorless sides of the chamber bear a frieze representing a cortège that includes Augustus and his family—they are apparently going to the consecration of the altar.

On the inside, facing the entrance, on the left, are allegorical figures representing Earth (with two children), Water (astride a sea-monster) and Air (riding a swan). The space on the other side (now blank) probably held an image of the goddess Roma. The lower areas on the wall are covered by a frieze of plants and foliage.

The altar and its chamber do not really form an architectural unit, and the decorative motifs of the chamber seem to have been juxtaposed without much attention to stylistic harmony. There is unity in the altar's 'message' to the world: namely, that the continuation of peace is dependent on the will of imperial Rome as directed by Augustus, who, like Rome, is descended from the mythical Aeneas because of his adoption by the Julian dynasty. Hence, the history of the world and that of Rome are providentially united in the person of Augustus.

XII
AROUND THE VILLA BORGHESE

Via Veneto, Villa Borghese, Villa Giulia

This itinerary follows the celebrated via Veneto as it winds between piazza Barberini and Villa Borghese. Via Veneto is lined with palazzos, cafés and luxury shops.

The Villa Borghese (see p. 164) was built in the 17th century for Cardinal Scipio Borghese. Today, it houses a sculpture museum (exhibiting works by Bernini and Canova, among others) and an art gallery (with paintings by Pinturicchio, Raphaël, Botticelli, Dürer, Titian and Caravaggio). The nearby Galleria d'Arte Moderna contains examples of every trend in Italian art since the beginning of the 19th century. In the north-west corner of the Borghese gardens, you will find the charming Villa Giulia, a Renaissance mansion in which the collections of the National Etruscan Museum are displayed.

Access

Map IV, D2. Bus: 52, 53, 56, 58, 60, 61, 62, 90, 95. Metro: Barberini.

▬▬▬ *SANTA MARIA DELLA CONCEZIONE* IV, D2

This church was built in 1624 for Cardinal Antonio Barberini, brother of Pope Urban VIII. It contains a number of fine 17th-century paintings. Over the altar in the first chapel on the right, there is a remarkable canvas by Guido Reni, *St Michael Killing the Dragon* (1632). In the second chapel on the right, there is Giovanni Lanfranco's *Adoration of the Shepherds* (1631) and, in the third chapel on the right, Domenichino's *Death of St Francis*. The first chapel on the left is notable for Pietro di Cortona's *Ananias Restoring the Vision of St Paul* (1631).

Under the church is the Capuchin cemetery, whose five chapels are gruesomely strewn with the skulls and bones of over 4000 Capuchin monks.

▬▬▬ *CASINO OF THE VILLA LUDOVISI* IV, C2

If you find yourself in this part of Rome at the right time, the casino of the Villa Ludovisi *(open Sun 9-10am)* is really worth a visit. It is the only vestige of the huge 17th-century Villa Ludovisi, which was demolished in the late 19th century to make way for the via Veneto residential district.

The caretaker (who should be tipped) will show you the magnificent **fresco of Aurora**★★ (1621) by Il Guercino, executed a few years after Guido Reni's painting of the same subject at the casino of the Palazzo Rospigliosi-Pallavicini (see p. 154).

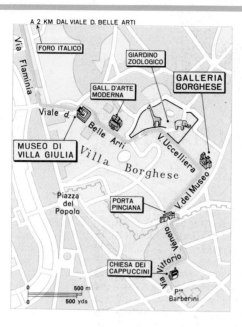

A 2 KM DAL VIALE D. BELLE ARTI

GARDENS OF THE VILLA BORGHESE IV, AB1-3

Pass through the Porta Pinciana (IV, B2), and you will find yourself facing the main entrance of the Villa Borghese (see p. 164). This entrance bears the Borghese family's emblem of the eagle and the dragon.

Casino Borghese IV, A3

The casino was built between 1613 and 1615 by the architect Vasanzio for Cardinal Scipio Borghese, nephew of Pope Paul V. He wanted a house on the same lines as the Villa Farnesina, with a central loggia. The two upper floors are pierced by niches containing statues. Today, the casino houses the superb Borghese Collection (see p. 180).

Zoological Garden IV, A2-3

Open daily 8am-sunset.

The Rome zoo occupies some 42 acres/17 hectares of the Villa Borghese.

Palazzo delle Belle Arti III, A6

This palazzo contains the National Museum of Modern Art *(open Tues-Sun 9am-2pm)*. This gallery has the world's largest collection of works by Italian painters and sculptors of the 19th and 20th centuries (see p. 179).

VILLA GIULIA III, A5-6

This villa was built between 1551 and 1553 for Pope Julius III, who intended to use it as a summer residence. The façade of the central part of the building, which faces the garden, was designed by Giacomo Barozzi da Vignola. It is attached to a graceful, semicircular portico, the arches of which are decorated with *trompe l'œil* pergolas. The portico opens onto a courtyard, at the rear of which a fine loggia by Ammanati leads through to a second courtyard. The villa houses the collections of the National Etruscan Museum (see p. 182).

XIII
FROM VIA APPIA ANTICA TO EUR

Via Appia Antica, or the Appian Way, is perhaps the most famous of Rome's ancient thoroughfares. Shaded by parasol pines and cypresses, it is lined with funerary monuments of all shapes and styles—a constant reminder of the presence of the dead. Further evidence can be found in the nearby catacombs, a huge network of underground galleries in which early Christians were buried.

The second part of this itinerary includes a visit to EUR, the extraordinary satellite town built south of Rome in the late 1930s. The grandiose scale of this project captures the megalomania of the Mussolini era.

Access

Map II, EF4-5. Bus: 118, 218.

▬▬ VIA APPIA ANTICA II, EF4-5

The via Appia Antica starts at Porta San Sebastiano. Begun in 312 BC by the censor Appius Claudius, a member of an illustrious Roman family, the road was intended to link Rome with Campania and to consolidate Roman domination of Magna Graecia (southern Italy). While some highways, such as the via Salaria (literally, 'salt road'), were named after their purpose, and others, such as the via Tiburtina ('the Tibur or Tivoli road') were named after their destination, the Appian Way was the first Roman highway to be named after its builder.

The original road was 13 ft/4 m wide, with pavements on either side for pedestrians and animals. It also had drainage ditches and, after the 2nd century BC, was paved with broad basalt slabs.

Posting stations with fresh horses were sited at regular intervals along the way. There were plenty of roadside inns as well, but their unsavoury reputation was such that richer citizens like Cicero maintained private pieds-à-terre for each stage of the journey.

In Rome, like the rest of the ancient world, strict laws prohibited burials within the city walls. The busy Appian Way, just outside town, thus became a favourite burial site for Romans of all classes. During the last years of the empire, these tombs were used as hideouts by bandits, who turned them into fortresses for holding captured travellers for ransom. Little by little, the Appian Way was abandoned in favour of less dangerous routes across the Alban hills.

The Appian Way and its surroundings were subsequently despoiled for building materials. It was not until the 16th century that humanist scholars and artists like Raphaël began to look more closely at the ruined tombs and to save those which had not already been destroyed. By the 19th century, the romantic taste for ancient ruins was attracting visitors from all over Europe. The ancient road became a promenade, where people came to stroll in nostalgic contemplation of the ruins.

The road between Porta San Sebastiano and Casal Rotondo is 5 mi/8 km long and not all of it is especially interesting. If you have no car, take bus n° 118 from the Coliseum to the **catacombs of San Callisto,** which stops by the entrance to the catacombs. From here, continue on foot beyond the **tomb of St Cecilia Metella.** From here on there are many spectacular ruins as far as Casal Rotondo. The distance between the tomb of St Cecilia Metella and Casal Rotondo is about 3 mi/5 km.

If you have a car, the best route is to turn left after Casal Rotondo, then left again into via Appia Pignatelli, which leads to the **Catacombs of Domitilla.**

The catacombs

In ancient times, the word 'catacomb' meant the site of the Necropolis of St Sebastian (*ad catacumbas,* 'by the ravine'). The other underground Christian cemeteries were known as *koimètèria,* or 'dormitories', because death for the Christian signifies no more than a temporary sleep. In the 16th century, 'catacombs' became the generic name for communal underground cemeteries (Jewish catacombs also exist).

Like the pagans, Christians began by burying their dead close to the surface, but later took to using tunnels. The first Christian necropolises were installed in the cellars of patrician families who had converted. Later, a whole series of galleries spread out from these cellars, the walls of which contained specially dug cavities for the corpses. These cavities *(loculi)* would be closed off by slabs of marble or terracotta. The catacombs were rarely used as places of worship and never served as hiding places for persecuted Christians.

In the 3rd century, the deacon (later Pope) Callistus began a reorganization of Christian burial places and bought land specifically for this purpose. Rich and poor, masters and slaves alike were buried in these new cemeteries. This practice lasted until Constantine was reconciled to Christianity in AD 313, and private burial grounds became the norm for wealthier Roman converts. From the 4th century onwards, the martyr cult began to supersede the cult of the dead. Constantine and his successors built basilicas over the tombs of the most venerated saints: St Peter's at the Vatican, St Paul's on the road to Ostia and the basilica of the Apostles (San Sebastiano) on the via Appia. This new cult also led to renewed interest in the catacombs around the more sacred tombs, because the early faithful wished to be buried close to their martyrs.

With successive invasions, Rome grew more and more depopulated and insecure. In the 6th century, the catacombs ceased to be used for burial. From the 7th to the 9th centuries, constant barbarian incursions led the popes to transfer the relics of the martyrs to sites within the city walls. The Pantheon, rechristened St Mary of the Martyrs, housed the ashes of many saints at this time. The catacombs were forgotten until their rediscovery by the militants of the Counter-Reformation in the 16th century. Among these militants was San Filippo Neri, founder of the Philippine Order, who often went into the catacombs to pray and meditate. Yet, no systematic investigation of their contents was undertaken until the 19th century.

The catacombs have retained much of their original decoration, in which themes such as scrolls of vine leaves, cupids, birds and rustic scenes were clearly borrowed from pagan art. These decorations gradually assumed more specific symbolism: for example, a dolphin saving a shipwrecked mariner represents Christ the Saviour. Biblical themes made their appearance later: Jonah and the whale signify the Resurrection, and Noah's Ark is interpreted as mankind's hope of salvation. From the 4th century onwards, private catacombs were used by the rich, with the result that heavily decorated burial vaults began to proliferate, many borrowing freely from pagan mythology.

Domine Quo Vadis II, E4

This small church, close to Porta San Sebastiano, marks the spot where, according to legend, St Peter encountered Christ while fleeing from his persecutors in Rome. 'Domine, quo vadis?' ('Lord, where goest thou?') the Apostle asked. Jesus replied: 'To Rome, to be crucified a second time.' A chastened Peter returned to the city, where he duly met his martyrdom.

Catacombs of San Callistus* II, E4

Open Thurs-Tues 8.30am-noon, 2.30-5.30pm. Guided tours.

These catacombs were the church's first officially sanctioned cemetery, arranged by the deacon Callistus at the beginning of the 3rd century. When Callistus became pope in AD 217, he further enlarged the necropolis, which became the tomb of nearly all the 3rd-century pontiffs. Only the second of its four levels is open to the public today, though some 12 mi/20 km of tunnels have so far been explored.

The first stage of the guided tour includes the **popes' crypt,** discovered in 1855, where the martyr popes of the 3rd century (Pontian, Anterus, Fabian, Lucius and Entychian) were buried. The letters MPT, which accompany the names Pontian and Fabian, are the main consonants in the Greek word for 'martyr'.

A neighbouring crypt once contained the tomb of St Cecilia; note the marble copy of Stephano Maderno's famous sculpture from the church of Santa Cecilia (Trastevere) and the 7th- and 8th-century frescos on the walls. Nearby, in a series of five chambers, early 3rd-century frescos depict the themes of baptism, penitence and the Eucharist. The vault of the deacon Severus contains an interesting inscription dated AD 298, in which the bishop of Rome is referred to as 'pope' for the first time in recorded history.

San Sebastiano II, E4

This basilica, founded in the 4th century, was first dedicated to the Apostles, Peter and Paul. Their remains were temporarily hidden in the cemetery under the church during the persecutions of the Emperor Valerian in AD 258. The body of St Sebastian, who was martyred in the reign of Diocletian, was later buried here and the church assumed his name from the 9th century onwards. At the beginning of the 17th century, at the request of Cardinal Scipio Borghese, it was rebuilt by Flaminio Panzio and Giovanni Vasanzio.

In the first chapel on the left is a fine 17th-century **statue of St Sebastian** by Giorgetto, a pupil of Bernini. According to tradition, Sebastian was a Roman officer who was martyred by being shot full of arrows. Left for dead, he was rescued and nursed back to health by a woman, only to be flogged to death in AD 290. During the Middle Ages, it was firmly believed that his relics, when carried through the streets in solemn procession, were a protection against the plague. He remains one of Rome's most deeply venerated saints.

Catacombs of St Sebastian** II, E4

Open daily 8.30am-noon, 2.30-5pm (6pm in summer). Guided tours.

The catacombs of St Sebastian are the only ones which have remained open throughout their history—hence, they are in very poor condition. Nevertheless, they are of considerable interest: note, in particular, three 1st-century **mausoleums** with pediments and brick façades, close to the ravine after which the catacombs are named. These mausoleums, though pagan in origin, were converted to Christian use during the second half of the 2nd century. The first of them, to the left, has a **vault*** covered in very beautiful white stucco. The vault of the second (in the centre) is decorated with rosettes; the peacock at the bottom of the steps was a pagan symbol for immortality. Finally, the mausoleum on the right is covered with beautiful and delicate **frescos***; look for the bird pecking at fruit in a bowl and the splendid gorgon's head on the ceiling.

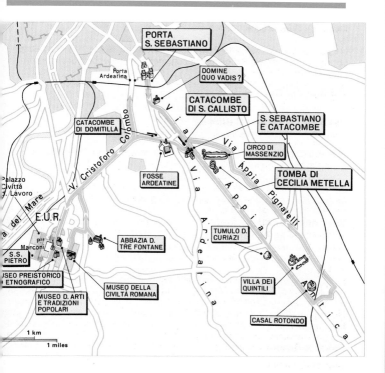

The nearby *triclia* was used for funeral banquets. The graffiti on the wall is in honour of St Peter and St Paul. It dates from the late 3rd century and has even been claimed as proof that relics of the two saints were buried in this gallery.

Circus of Maxentius II, E5

Open Wed, Fri and Sun 9am-2pm, Tues, Thurs and Sat 9am-2pm, 5-8pm.

The ruins of the Circus of Maxentius can be seen on the left-hand side of the Appian Way. This monument was built in AD 309 and dedicated to Romulus, the young son of the Emperor Maxentius who died that year. The circus was 1641 ft/500 m long and 295 ft/90 m wide; it was used for chariot races and was the original site of the great obelisk which Bernini later transferred to his fountain in piazza Navona. The **Tomb of Romulus,** which stands in front of the circus, was once surrounded by a broad piazza and portico; the tomb itself, with its cylindrical base 108 ft/33 m across, is similar to the Pantheon in design.

Tomb of Cecilia Metella II, F5

Open Tues-Sat 9.30am-3.30pm, Sun 9am-1pm.

This fine structure (1.9 mi/3 km from Porta San Sebastiano, on the left) is a cylindrical mausoleum with a diameter of 65 ft/20 m. It originally contained the remains of Cecilia Metella, the wife of Crassus. Cecilia's father ruled Rome together with Caesar and Pompey in 60 BC.

The monument has retained its original ornamentation of limestone blocks with a frieze of shields. In the 14th century, the tomb of Cecilia Metella was used as a keep by the adjacent fortress of the Caetani family, which stood astride the Appian Way. The battlements on its top date from this period.

Beyond this tomb, the modern Appian Way becomes a one-way street, and the bus route deviates to via Cecilia Metella (a bar, a restaurant and a fountain mark the turnoff). This is unquestionably the most beautiful section of the Appian Way, which from here on is lined by magnificent tombs, parasol pines and cypresses against a peaceful backdrop of Roman countryside.

Tumulo dei Curiazi II, F5

On the right-hand side of the road, about 1313 ft/400 m beyond the crossroads of the Appian Way, via Erode Attico and via di Tor Carbone, you will see a broad *tumulus*. This is said to be the tomb of one of the Curiatii, killed in the legendary duel of the three Albans (the Curiatii) and the three Romans (the Horatii), during the reign of Tullus Hostilius (673-642 BC).

A little further on, after the mediaeval farmhouse of Santa Maria Nuova and an impressive pyramid-shaped mausoleum, you will see two more *tumuli* on the right-hand side of the road. These mounds, which are surrounded by pines and cypresses, are said to be the tombs of the Horatii.

Villa dei Quintili II, F5

This villa, on the left-hand side of the Appian Way, was the centre of a huge agricultural estate dating from the reign of Hadrian (2nd century). The Emperor Commodus confiscated the property in AD 182, after having killed its owners, the Quintili brothers, who were distinguished soldiers and writers of great merit. Beside the road at this point, there are also the remains of some ancient baths, converted into a fortress during the Middle Ages, as well as a ruined amphitheatre and a hippodrome. The aqueduct that supplied Rome with water passed behind this villa—note the vestiges of a huge cistern at its side.

Casal Rotondo II, F5

The Casal Rotondo, a bit further along on the left-hand side of the road, is the largest tomb on the Appian Way. Built under the republic and enlarged during the early years of the empire, this cylindrical mausoleum was at one time faced with limestone. Today, it is part of an old farmhouse. Note the magnificent ruins of aqueducts on its left.

Ardeatine Pits II, E4

After the Casal Rotondo, turn left and left again along via Appia Pignatelli. From here, go back to San Sebastiano, turning left at the junction of via Appia Antica and right along via delle Sette Chiese. The road passes alongside the Ardeatine Pits (on the left), where 335 Italians were executed by the Nazis on March 24, 1944.

Catacombs of Domitilla II, E4

Entrance at n° 282 via delle Sette Chiese. *Open daily 8am-noon, 2.30-5pm (5.30pm in summer).*

The catacombs of Domitilla form a gigantic network of galleries leading off the private cemetery of Domitilla, a kinswoman of the Emperor Domitian. These catacombs have retained a number of important traces of early Christian art. The tour begins in a basilica with three naves, partially joined to the catacombs; it is dedicated to St Nerea and St Achillea, martyred under Diocletian in the late 3rd century. From here, you can enter the underground cemetery. The Hall of the Flavians (1st century) is the oldest part, containing many frescos. A tunnel leads from this area to a second large vault with vestiges of 2nd-century frescos. Further on is an area dating from the 3rd and 4th centuries which contains more frescos.

▄▄▄ *EUR* VII

When you leave the catacombs of Domitilla, take via delle Sette Chiese to the left as far as piazza dei Navigatori (II, E4). Then take the n° 97 bus. If you are coming from Rome, catch the n° 97 bus or the metro (line B) as far as the Marconi stop. By car, take the via Cristoforo Colombo (II, E4-F3) left from the piazza dei Navigatori.

The construction of EUR (Esposizione Universale di Roma), a monstrous urban development to the south of Rome, was begun in 1937. Its completion was intended to coincide with the 1942 Rome Universal Exhibition, which never took place because of the exigencies of World War II. This was Mussolini's great project. Its purpose was twofold: to mark the first 20 years of Italian fascism and to create a symbol of his regime's Mediterranean ambitions by extending the capital southwards to the coast.

Work was resumed in 1951. During the following decade, damaged buildings were repaired, new ones were added, and major banks, ministries and corporations set up their headquarters in the district, which has excellent metro and road links to the centre of Rome.

The monumental architecture of this new capital stands in stark contrast to that of Rome. Despite efforts to humanize the area with green spaces, pedestrian precincts, residential quarters and fountains, EUR has remained massive, symmetrical and dreary.

There are a number of important museums in this area:

- Museo preistorico ed etnografico (Prehistoric and Ethnographic Museum), see p. 176.

- Museo d'arti e tradizioni popolari (Museum of Popular and Traditional Art), see p. 179.

- Museo della civiltà romana (Museum of Roman Civilization), see p. 178.

Palazzo della Civilta del Lavoro (Palace of the Civilization of Work) VII, AI-2

As you enter EUR, you will see the Palazzo della Civiltà del Lavoro to the left of piazza delle Nationi. This building, which was designed in 1938 by de Guerrini, La Paluda and Romano, is frequently called the Square Coliseum, or even Mussolini's Coliseum. With its six floors of blind arcades and its abundant statuary, it is among the most important examples of pre-war Roman architecture.

Palazzo dello Sport (Palace of Sports) VII, C2

The sports stadium, which is to the south of EUR proper, was built for the 1960 Olympic Games. Its immense 327 ft/100 m dome is the work of Pier Luigi Nervi.

Abbazia delle Tre Fontane (Abbey of the Three Fountains) VII, B3

This abbey was founded on the spot where the Apostle Paul is said to have been martyred. Tradition states that when the saint's head was cut off, it bounced three times on the ground, causing three springs to well up. The three churches of the Abbazia delle Tre Fontane commemorate this miracle.

The churches stand in a garden scented by eucalyptus. The first church that you will come upon is **Ss. Vicenzo e Anastasio,** which was founded in the 19th century. On its right is **Santa Maria Scala Coelî,** reconstructed in 1583 on an octagonal plan by Giacomo della Porta. At the back of the garden is **San Paolo alle Tre Fontane,** which was founded in the 8th century and rebuilt in 1599 (also by della Porta).

THE MUSEUMS OF ROME

F rom the 16th century onwards, the princes of Rome patronized the arts. In their palaces, they amassed vast collections and these collections were protected by a papal law known as the *fidéicommis,* which made artistic possessions indivisible among heirs for four generations.

Today, the works of hundreds of painters and sculptors are displayed in the churches, museums and galleries of Rome. In addition to great names of the Renaissance and Baroque eras such as da Vinci, Bernini, Raphaël, Titian, Michelangelo, Bellini Uccello, Botticelli, Tintoretto, Caravaggio and Carpaccio, the Vatican possesses works by modern artists like Braque, Munch, Chagall, Dali, Rouault, Foujita, Kandinsky and Picasso. The range is vast, extending from the earliest years of Rome to the most contemporary work. In addition, new masterpieces from the past are constantly being discovered—recently, stuccos and frescos comparable to those at Pompeii and Herculaneum were excavated beneath the Villa Farnesina.

Visitors setting out to discover even a few of the artistic treasures of Rome will require solid guidelines to avoid being overwhelmed and eventually disheartened by the task. This section of the guide offers a list of the principal Roman collections, as well as detailed descriptions of Rome's five great museums.

▬▬ ROME'S MAJOR COLLECTIONS

Prehistory
• **Luigi Pigorini Museum of Prehistory and Ethnography,** viale Lincoln 1, VII, B2, ☎ 591 0702. Metro: EUR. *Open Tues-Sat 9am-2pm, Sun 9am-1pm. Admission charge.*
This museum, covering Italy from the Stone Age to the Iron Age, is considered one of the world's great prehistoric museums.

Egyptian art
• **Museum of Oriental Antiquity,** at the Vatican, viale Vaticano, 1st floor, III, D1, ☎ 69 80. Bus: 23, 32, 47, 64, 492, 990, 994. Metro: Ottaviano. *Open Mon-Sat 9am-2pm, final Sun of each month.*
This museum houses objects of varying quality. Note the statue of Queen Tuaa, mother of Ramses II, and the reproduction of a tomb from the Valley of the Kings (see p. 183).

Said to have suckled Romulus and Remus, the wolf has been Rome's symbol since antiquity.

Etruscan art

● **National Etruscan Museum,** Villa Giulia, piazza di Villa Giulia 9, III, A5, ☎ 360 1951. Bus: 1, 2, 2b, 19b, 26, 30, 30b, 48, 95, 202, 203, 910, 911. Metro: Flaminio. *Open Tues-Sat 9am-2pm, Sun 9am-1pm, 3-7pm. Admission charge.*

This museum houses weapons, vases, jewelry and sculpture from a little-known civilization (see p. 182).

● **Vatican Etruscan Museum,** 2nd floor

A collection comparable to that of Villa Giulia but with better examples of ancient metalwork and Greek ceramic art (see Vatican Museums p. 184).

Greek art, Roman art

● **Vatican Museums:** Braccio Nuovo, Galleria Chiaramonti, Museo Pio-Clementino, Gregorian Museum (1st floor); Candelabra Gallery, viale Vaticano, III, D1, ☎ 69 82. Bus: 23, 32, 47, 64, 492, 990, 993, 994. Metro: Ottaviano. *Open Mon-Sat 9am-2pm; July-Sept 30 and Easter holidays, Mon-Sat 9am-5pm. Closed Sun except last Sun of month.*

The Museo Pio-Clementino is especially interesting (see p. 184).

● **Capitol Museums,** piazza del Campidoglio, VI, A5, ☎ 67 101. Bus: 46, 57, 90, 90b, 92, 94, 95, 116, 716, 718, 719. *Open Wed and Fri 9am-2pm, Sun 9am-1pm, Tues and Thurs 5-8pm, Sat 9am-2pm, 8.30-11pm. Admission charge.*

These museums are situated on one of Rome's most beautiful piazzas. Designed by Michelangelo, they contain some priceless pieces (see p. 182).

● **National Museum of Rome** or **Museum of the Baths,** via Terme di Diocleziano, IV, D4, ☎ 46 0530. Bus: 3, 4, 38, 38b, 57, 64, 65, 75, 93c, 163, 170, 310, 319. Metro: Termini, Repubblica. *Open Tues-Sun 9am-1pm. Admission charge. At present, only the great cloister and one or two rooms on the first floor are open.*

The Ludovisi Collection includes an excellent replica of the *Athena* at the Parthenon. Room III contains a *Discobolus* by Myron.

● **Museum of Roman Civilization,** piazza Agnelli 13 VII, B3, ☎ 592 6135. Metro: EUR, Marconi. *Open Tues-Sat 9am-2pm, Sun 9am-1pm, also Tues and Thurs 5-8pm. Admission charge.*

This museum consists entirely of copies. Its main interest lies in a moulding of Trajan's Column and a large-scale model of imperial Rome.

● **Forum and Trajan's Markets,** via IV Novembre 94, IV, F2. Bus: 57, 64, 65, 70, 87, 94, 186. Metro: Colosseo. *Open Tues-Sat 9am-1.30pm, Sun 9am-1pm, also Tues, Thurs and Sat 4-6.30pm. Admission charge.*

The only vestige of this site, which was impressive in antiquity, is Trajan's Column.

● **Wall Museum,** Porta San Sebastiano, V, F4, ☎ 457 5284. Bus: 118, 218. *Open Tues-Sun 9am-1pm, also Tues and Thurs 4-7pm. Admission charge.*

This small museum retraces the history of Aurelian's wall and includes a few sectors of the original wall.

Early Christian art

● **Gregorian Museum,** 1st floor of Vatican Museums.

This is a very fine collection, mostly of interest to students of epigraphy. It contains sarcophagi and mosaics from the catacombs and the first basilicas (see p. 188).

● **Capitol Museum,** Palazzo dei Conservatori.

This museum also contains a collection of epigraphic segments, not quite as rich as the Gregorian Museum (see p. 182).

High Middle Ages and Byzantine art

● **Museum of the High Middle Ages,** viale Lincoln 1, VIII, B2, ☎ 592 5806. Metro: EUR, Marconi. *Open Tues-Sat 9am-2pm, Sun 9am-1pm. Admission charge.*

Late art of antiquity (5th century) and pre-Romanesque (7th-10th centuries) are the principal focus of this museum.

12th-18th-century painting

● **Vatican Art Gallery** (Pinacoteca)

This gallery houses 500 paintings, along with tapestries, classified by school and chronology (see p. 188).

● **Capitoline Museum Art Gallery,** Palazzo dei Conservatori.

This gallery includes chiefly 15th- and 16th-century Venetian paintings (see p. 182).

15th-century painting

● **Chapel of Nicolas V,** Vatican Palace.

This sanctuary was painted by Fra Angelico (see p. 186).

● **Side walls of the Sistine Chapel,** Vatican Palace.

These walls are a Renaissance masterpiece, representing eight years of work. Many great artists have painted scenes from the Old and New Testaments here (see p. 187).

● **Borgia Apartments,** Vatican Palace.

Formerly the apartments of Pope Alexander VI, these rooms are covered in beautiful frescos (see p. 186).

16th-century painting

● **The Raphaël Rooms,** Vatican Palace.

These are the former private apartments of Pope Julius II, situated just above those of Alexander VI; also has rooms containing masterpieces by Raphaël (see p. 184).

● **Sistine Chapel,** Vatican Palace.

The ceiling was designed and painted by Michelangelo, an arduous task which took him four years to complete. The frescos celebrate God's creation of the world and include 200 characters from the Bible. One of mankind's timeless masterpieces (see p. 187).

● **Farnesina,** Villa della Lunara, VI, A2. Bus: 23, 41, 65, 280. *Open Sat and Sun 9am-1pm.*

Built between 1508 and 1511, this Renaissance villa and landscape was decorated by Raphaël and his assistants. Among other things, it contains two magnificent frescos: the *Legend of Psyche* and *Galatea with Water Spirits* (see p. 140).

15th-18th-century painting

● **Borghese Gallery,** via Pinciana, IV, A3, ☎ 85 8577. Bus: 34, 52, 53, 56, 57, 319, 910. Metro: Spagna.

A must for anyone visiting Rome. Amid gloriously verdant surroundings, a collection of world-famous masterpieces assembled by generations of art patrons (see p. 180).

● **National Gallery of Antique Art,** Palazzo Barberini, via Quattro Fontana 114, IV, D2, ☎ 475 0184. Bus: 52, 53, 56, 58, 58b, 60, 61, 62. Metro: Barberini. *Open Tues-Sat 9.15am-7pm, Sun 9am-1pm. Admission charge.*

This gallery celebrates the pure Baroque style, includes a famous ceiling and a series of 30 rooms containing all the great names in Italian painting, as well as El Greco and Flemish and German masters (see p. 180).

● **Galleria Doria-Pamphili,** piazza del Collegio Romano 1, IV, E1, ☎ 679 4365. Bus: 26, 44, 46, 56, 60, 61, 64, 65, 70, 75, 81, 87, 90, 95, 116, 170, 710.

This is a remarkable collection, mostly Baroque, which includes many works by foreign artists, particularly of the Flemish and Dutch schools (see p. 123).

● **Galleria Colonna,** via del Pilotta 17, IV, E2, ☎ 679 4362. Bus: 56, 60, 62, 85, 90, 90b, 96, 116. *Open Sat 9am-1pm. Admission charge.*

This private gallery in a magnificent 18th-century palazzo offers a brief history of Italian and foreign painting from the 15th to the 18th centuries, including Carracci, Lotto, Tintoretto, Ghirlandaio, Luini, Bronzini, Ribera and Van Dyck.

19th- and 20th-century painting and sculpture

● **National Museum of Modern Art,** viale delle Belle Arti 131, III, A6, ☎ 80 2751. Bus: 19, 19b, 30, 30b, 90b, 95, 490. *Open Tues-Sat 9am-2pm, Sun 9am-1pm, also Tues, Thurs and Sat 3-7pm. Admission charge.*

All the great movements in painting from the 19th century to the present are included here.

Popular and traditional art

● **National Museum of Popular and Traditional Art,** piazza Marconi 8, VII, B2, ☎ 591 1848. Metro: EUR, Marconi. *Open Tues-Sun 9am-1pm, also Wed 4-7pm. Admission charge.*

Popular folklore, customs and art from Italy's various provinces make a lively, original display here.

● **Folklore Museum,** piazza S. Egidio 1b, VI, B2, ☎ 581 6563. Bus: 56, 60, 65, 97, 23, 280. *Open Tues-Sat 9am-1.30pm, also Tues and Wed 5-8pm. Admission charge.*

This is a waxwork museum dealing with Roman life and traditions.

● **International Crêche Museum,** via Tor de'Conti 31a, V, A1, ☎ 678 7135. *Open daily 4-8pm. Visit by appointment only.*

This museum contains countless images of the Christ Child.

● **Museum of Souls in Purgatory,** lungotevere Prati 18, III, D4, ☎ 654

0517. *Open by appointment only,* contact Chiesa del Sacro Cuore (same address).

This is a typically Roman museum, exhibiting clothing and wooden tablets with traces of burns that are said to have been caused by the ghosts of souls in Purgatory. This establishment is specially designed to inflame the imaginations of unrepentant sinners; it contains objects which will probably induce you to lead the life of a saint for the rest of your days.

NATIONAL GALLERY OF ANTIQUE ART, PALAZZO BARBERINI

Via Quattro Fontane 13, IV, D3, ☎ 475 0184. Bus: 52, 53, 56, 58b, 60, 61, 62. Metro: Barberini. *Open Tues-Sat 9.15am-7pm, Sun 9am-1pm. Admission charge.*

The recently restored Palazzo Barberini (16th century) is in the heart of the ministerial district, next to the Quirinal and not far from the Trevi Fountain. This pure Baroque ensemble is enclosed by via Barberini, via dei Quattri Fontane, via XX Settembre and via Nicola da Tolentino and houses an extraordinary collection of paintings.

On entering the palace, you will first see the marvelous ceiling by Pietro di Cortona, *The Triumph of Divine Providence.* On the second floor (left-hand staircase), 14 rooms contain examples of the various Italian schools and their most brilliant protagonists: Filippo Lippi's *Virgin and Child,* a remarkable *Tryptych of the Last Judgment* by Fra Angelico, P. di Cosimo's *Mary Magdalene,* and Raphaël's *La Fornina.* There are also portraits by Lotto and Bronzino, canvases by Tintoretto and Titian and two superb paintings by El Greco, as well as a selection of Flemish and German paintings and some remarkable works by 18th-century French artists. There is an exquisite 18th-century suite of private apartments on the second floor.

BORGHESE MUSEUM AND GALLERY★★★

Villa Borghese, via Pinciana, IV, A3, ☎ 85 8577. Bus: 34, 52, 53, 56, 57, 319, 910. Metro: Spagna (exit Villa Borghese, on piazzale Brasile). *Open Tues-Sat 9am-2pm, Sun 9am-1pm.*

The Villa Borghese, at the northern end of the capital, is one of the largest and most beautiful of Rome's public gardens. Laid out in the 17th century and improved in the 18th, the broad shady avenues of the Villa Borghese are a welcome refuge from the heat, dust and din of the surrounding streets.

Try to allow enough time and energy for a leisurely visit to the Borghese Museum and Gallery. The collection now on display at the **casino Borghese,** assembled mostly by Cardinal Scipio Borghese, includes many of the greatest masterpieces of the Italian Baroque period. Among these are Bernini's *David,* Titian's *Sacred and Profane Love* and *Venus Blindfolding the Eyes of Love,* Caravaggio's *Madonna of the Stableboys* and Raphaël's vigorous *Deposition From the Cross.* There are also masterpieces by Botticelli, Dürer, Cranach, Lotto, di Cortona, Rubens, Correggio, Carpaccio and Veronese.

Borghese Museum

The museum section of the casino Borghese contains a remarkable collection of sculpture, among them Bernini's *Apollo and Daphne* and *David,* Canova's *Pauline Borghese,* and a large number of pieces that have survived from antiquity.

At the time of writing, the gallery section was closed for restoration.

The abduction of Proserpina, Bernini's masterpiece in the Borghese Gallery.

CAPITOL MUSEUMS: PALAZZO DEI CONSERVATORE AND PALAZZO NUOVO

Piazza del Campidoglio, VI, A5, ☎ 67 101. Bus: 46, 57, 90, 90b, 92, 94, 95, 116, 716, 718, 719. *Open Tues-Sat 9am-2pm, Sun 9am-1pm, also Tues and Thurs 5-8pm, Sat 8.30-11pm. Admission charge, single ticket for all sections of the museum.*

The Palazzo dei Conservatore and the Palazzo Nuovo on the Capitoline hill open onto a broad piazza designed by Michelangelo (see p. 76). Between them, these two museums possess one of the world's oldest art collections, dating as an entity from the 15th century.

In the Palazzo Nuovo, the Gladiator Room contains a fine statue of a *Dying Gaul* and a somber, magnificent *Bust of Brutus*. In the other rooms two objects stand out—a Hellenistic Venus and a vivid, delightful mosaic of doves.

The Palazzo dei Conservatore is richer than its neighbour, possessing an immense store of great art. Its paintings and sculpture are far too numerous to be listed here, but we especially recommend the following: the famous *She-Wolf With Romulus and Remus,* Domenichino's *Sibyl* and Caravaggio's *St John the Baptist*. Room II contains a quite exceptional grouping of 15th- and 16th-century canvases.

The following list summarizes the various sections of the Capitoline museums.

Palazzo dei Conservatore

● Rooms 1-19: antique and Christian art—steles, friezes, vases, sarco-phagi, bas reliefs, etc.

● Braccio Nuovo: seven rooms containing objects excavated before 1950—frescos, mosaics, etc.

● Museo Nuovo: busts of poets, philosophers, emperors; Greek and Hellenistic fragments; painting section with works by Lotto, Titian, Velásquez, Caravaggio, Cortona, Guerchino.

Palazzo Nuovo

● Courtyard: three rooms with objects relating to the Eastern cults—Mithras, Isis, Cybele.

● First floor: antique sculptural groups.

NATIONAL ETRUSCAN MUSEUM OF THE VILLA GIULIA

Piazza di villa Giulia 9, III, A5, ☎ 360 1951. Bus: 1, 2, 2b, 19b, 26, 30, 30b, 48, 95, 202, 203, 910, 911. Metro: Flaminio. *Open Tues-Sat 9am-2pm, Sun 9am-1pm, also Wed 3-7pm. Admission charge.*

The Villa Giulia, which adjoins the Villa Borghese, houses a very important collection of Etruscan art.

The museum was reorganized and modernized during the 1950s. Objects grouped regionally and chronologically exhibit every technical variation in the working of bronze. In addition, two private collections are exhibited here—those of the Castellani and Barberini families.

We especially recommend the enigmatic *Apollo of Veies,* a masterpiece characteristic of Ionian and Etruscan art, the terracotta sarcophagus of a couple united in death, and the many ceramics and other precious objects discovered in the necropolises of Rome.

The origins of the Etruscans are fiercely debated, but their presence in the 9th and 8th centuries BC between the Tiber and the Arno is indisputable.

Originally, the Etruscans were hut-dwellers, mainly occupied with pastoral and agricultural pursuits. They buried their dead, along with various possessions and objects, in deep pits.

In the second half of the 8th century BC, the Greeks came to Campania, in search of metals and minerals. From the Greeks, the Etruscans acquired more luxurious objects and knowledge of important technical innovations in metallurgy, ceramics and agriculture. Henceforward, they practised crop rotation and cultivated vines and olive trees.

In the 7th century BC, the Etruscans occupied Latium, founded a number of new cities (among them Rome) and participated in maritime commerce. Etruscan pottery spread throughout the peninsula and into Central Europe.

In the 5th century BC, Etruscan power declined. Defeated by the Greeks and expelled from Rome, their commercial activities narrowed to the coastal towns, while the regions of the interior developed agriculture and increasingly relied on trade with districts beyond the Apennines. Each town had its own relationship with the Romans, and each in turn was conquered and absorbed. By the time of Augustus, Etruria was no more than a part of the empire.

Etruscan art draws on many different sources, but some of the surviving objects have specific characteristics: for example, sarcophagi, filiform statuettes, black ceramic known as *bucchero*, objects carved from bone, urns, amphorae, jewelry and fragments of temple decoration.

● Ground floor: tombs from Vulci, Bisenzio, Veies and Cerveteri (with superb sarcophagi).

● First floor: Etruscan art, votive statuettes, the Castellani collection, Greek and Etruscan ceramics and fragments from various excavations.

● Gardens (between the nympheum and the right-hand wing of the museum): reconstruction of the Temple of Alatri (2nd and 3rd century BC).

▬▬ *VATICAN MUSEUMS*

Viale Vaticano, III, D1, ☎ 6982. Bus: 23, 32, 47, 64, 492, 990, 993, 994. A bus leaves from the Ufficio Informazione Pellegrini e Turisiti (Tourist and Pilgrim Information Office) on St Peter's Square every 30 minutes from 9am-12.30pm. Tickets may be bought on the bus, which carries 38 passengers. Metro: Ottaviano. *Open Mon-Sat 9am-2pm, July 1-Sept 30 and Easter holidays, Mon-Sat 9am-5pm. Closed Sun except the last Sun of month and during major religious festivals.*

Practical information

— The museums offer a cassette guide of the Sistine Chapel and the Raphaël Rooms, along with publications, posters, reproductions, postcards and slides. These can be obtained at different places within the museums.

— Wheelchairs are available near the cloakroom (next to the ticket office).

— Toilets, telephones and first-aid stations can be found at regular intervals throughout the museums.

— The museums have a foreign exchange counter and post office, as well as a cafeteria and a snack bar (close to the painting section, or Pinacoteca).

— Certain rooms are closed from time to time to the public (consult the noticeboard at the viale Vaticano entrance).

The Vatican Museums are visited by over two million people every year. There are 11 museums, five art galleries, and 1400 display rooms and chapels. Some of the palaces within the Vatican complex were specially built to house the masterpieces of the collection. Traditionally, popes have shown a keen interest in the creative arts.

1) Egyptian and Oriental Antiquities Museum

This museum houses works of widely differing quality, including sarcophagi, mummies, statues, papyri, Roman copies.

2) Chiaramonti Museum

This museum occupies part of the main gallery and is divided into sections with odd numbers on the left and even numbers on the right. It exhibits sarcophagi dating from the 1st century, a Renaissance portrait of Cicero and a Lapidary Gallery (special permission required) containing over 5000 Roman and Christian inscribed tablets.

3) Braccio Nuovo***

This section was installed at the beginning of the 19th century to house works returned by France under the conditions of the Treaty of Vienna (1816): statues of *Augustus****, *Apollo Playing the Lyre***, *The Wounded Amazon*** and *The Nile***.

4) Pio-Clementino Museum***

This museum concentrates on Greek and Roman sculpture: the statue of *Laocoön****, *The Belvedere Torso****, *The Belvedere Apollo****, *The Venus of Cnidos*** and *The Sleep of Ariadne***.

5) Etruscan Museum

This museum was founded by Gregory XVI in 1837. It contains objects unearthed from a tomb in southern Etruria (*Mars***, late 5th century BC).

6) Bige Room*

This section was built in the 18th century and contains a Roman chariot in marble** from the 1st century, as well as statues of *Apollo** (n° 614), *Diana** (n° 622), *Pericles** (n° 616) and a *Discus-Thrower** (n° 618).

7) Candelabra Gallery**

This gallery exhibits fine candelabras (2nd century) and Roman works from the 2nd, 3rd and 4th centuries.

8) Tapestry Gallery

This gallery houses 16th-century Flemish and 17th-century Italian tapestries.

9) Geographical Maps Gallery**

This gallery contains 40 maps, painted as frescos and exceptional for their period, which represent Italy at the close of the 16th century. These maps were assembled by the scholar Ignazio Danti, and created by his brother Antonio. The map of Latium of the left-hand wall offers a fascinating glimpse of Rome at that time.

10) Towards the Raphaël Rooms

After the maps gallery, there is a series of rooms containing 15th-, 16th-and 17th-century tapestries.

11) The Raphaël Rooms***

These rooms were originally the private apartments of Pope Nicolas V (1447-1455) and were decorated by Piero della Francesca, Signorelli and Perugino. Pope Julius II (1503-1513), who refused to live in the apartments of Alexander VI Borgia one floor below, commissioned Raphaël (then only 25) to redecorate these rooms. Raphaël continued his work throughout the pontificates of Julius and his successor, Leo X; the result was a succession of huge compositions in which the painter developed his understanding of light and colour and expressed his own neo-Platonic ideas. The influence of Michelangelo (then working nearby in the Sistine Chapel) is strongly evident.

(a) The Room of the Borgo Fire (1514-1517)

This room is covered entirely with frescos representing four spectacular events which took place during the pontificates of Leo III and Leo IV. The main fresco, *The Borgo Fire** shows Leo IV quenching a fire that broke out in AD 847 in the districts adjoining the basilica (the Borgo). On the right wall is *The Coronation of the Emperor Charlemagne by Leo III** in AD 800, at St Peter's, with assembled bishops and cardinals.

On the left wall is *The Battle of Ostia** (AD 846), in which Leo IV won a victory against the Saracens.

On the wall by the windows is *The Justification of Leo III**. The pope is

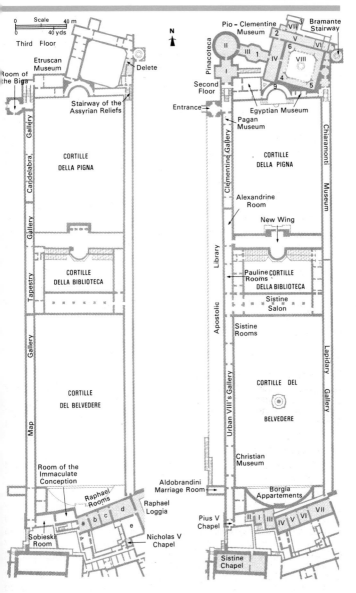

Vatican Museums

seen rebutting the attacks of the nephews of Adrian I, in the presence of Charlemagne and the assembled clergy.

On the ceiling is *The Glorification of the Trinity*★ by Perugino, Raphaël's master.

(b) The Signature Room (1509-1511)

This room was used by Julius II as an office and library. On the ceiling are four medallions indicating the subjects of the scenes which decorate the walls: theology, poetry, philosophy and justice.

On the right wall is *The Controversy of the Holy Sacrament*★★★.

On the facing wall is *The School of Athens*★★★. The greatest philosophers of antiquity are represented discoursing in groups or meditating.

Mount Parnassus, or *The Triumph of Poetry*★★★ is inspired by Greek mythology. Apollo, playing his lyre, is shown surrounded by the nine muses, along with a group of celebrated humanists and poets.

The wall of *Justice*★★ is illustrated with three separate scenes. In the window niche are the three cardinal virtues: Prudence (at centre), Strength (with a helmet, at left) and Temperance (at right) showing the reins of her power.

The angel figures refer to the theological virtues: Charity gathers acorns, Hope carries a torch, and Faith points toward Heaven.

Below, Gregory IX (in the likeness of Julius II) carries a volume of the Decretals (1227), an allusion to Canonical Law; likewise, the Emperor Justinian is seen with a copy of the Pandectes (AD 530), an allusion to his greatest achievement as a lawgiver.

The images in this room demonstrate Raphaël's preoccupation with the three principal themes of neo-Platonism: truth, evidenced by the Triumph of the Church and the School of Athens, beauty, by Mount Parnassus, and justice.

(c) The Heliodorus Room (1512-1514)

Various episodes in the church's history are evoked here. In this room, Raphaël paid particular attention to the dramatic possibilities of the Classical style.

Heliodorus Driven From the Temple★★★ — Heliodorus, having looted the Temple of Jerusalem, is smitten to the ground by three angels.

The Mass at Bolsena★★ shows a miracle authenticated by Urban IV in 1263.

Leo the Great Halting Attila★★ (AD 452).

The Liberation of St Peter★★★ — at centre, St Peter is awakened by a shining angel.

The ceiling is covered with *trompe l'œil* tapestries illustrating sundry biblical themes related to the frescos: the burning bush, the sacrifice of Isaac, Jacob's dream and Noah leaving the ark.

(d) The Constantine Room

This room was decorated (1517-1524) by J. Romain and G. Penni. On the ceiling, Christ is seen displacing a broken idol (in this case, the god Hermes). Elsewhere, scenes of major historical events elaborate on the theme of celebration and glorification of the church.

— Facing the entrance is *The Apparition of Christ to Constantine*.

— To the right is *Constantine's Victory Over Maxentius* (at the Bridge of Milvius, AD 311). The emperor is shown under the protection of three angels.

— On the wall of the entrance is *The Baptism of Constantine by Pope Sylvester*.

— By the windows is *The Donation of Constantine*, which commemorates Constantine's transfer of temporal power to the pope.

12) The Raphaël Loggias *(closed to the public)*

These are decorated with scenes from the Old and New Testaments.

13) The Fra Angelico Chapel (1448-1450)

Pope Nicolas V commissioned Fra Angelico to create this chapel, celebrating the two martyr saints, Stephen and Lawrence.

Leaving the Raphaël Rooms, cross the tiny chapel of Urban VII. Here, you have a choice—continue to the left to the Sistine Chapel or go to the right to the Borgia Apartments.

14) The Borgia Apartments

This first-floor suite of rooms was decorated by Pinturicchio for Pope

Alexander VI Borgia (1492-1498). Today, these apartments contain part of the papal collection of modern religious art.

15) The Sistine Chapel

The Sistine Chapel is named after Pope Sixtus IV (1471-1484). It is 131 ft/40 m long, 44 ft/13.5 m wide, slightly more than 66 ft/20 m high with a barrel vault. It was in great part decorated by Umbrian and Florentine painters. Michelangelo painted the ceiling frescos between 1508 and 1512, completing the *Last Judgment* above the altar between 1536 and 1541.

As the chapel of the papal palace, the Sistine was principally used for the celebration of special masses. It was also in the Sistine Chapel that the cardinals assembled to elect a new pope.

The paintings are currently being restored as part of a project which will be completed in 1992. The work has aroused a virulent campaign of protest, though it is hard to understand why anyone would regret the passing of the old, smoke-blackened surfaces when today it is possible to see the original magnificent colours of Michelangelo, colours that lie at the origin of the entire Mannerist movement.

(a) The side walls

Above the painted draperies on these walls are scenes from the Old and New Testaments. The order (beginning at the altar) is as follows:

On the left:

- *Moses's Journey Into Egypt**** (Perugino and Pinturicchio)
- *Moses and the Young Women* (Jethro)
- *Scenes From Moses's Youth*** (Botticelli)
- *The Crossing of the Red Sea* (Rosselli)
- *The Ten Commandments* (Rosselli)
- *Punishment of Korah, Dathan and Abiron** (Botticelli)
- *Moses Passing His Staff to Joshua; Death of Moses*** (Signorelli)

On the right:

- *The Baptism of Christ**** (Perugino and Pinturicchio)
- *The Healing of the Lepers and the Temptation of Christ*** (Botticelli)
- *Vocation of the Apostles Peter and Andrew*** (Ghirlandaio)
- *The Sermon on the Mount*** (di Cosimo and Rosselli)
- *Christ Presenting St Peter With the Keys of Heaven*** (Perugino)
- *The Last Supper* (Rosselli)

Above the *Last Judgment,* note the 24 portraits of the early popes.

(b) The ceiling frescos***

The ceiling, an intricate web of arches and cornices, is about 2691 sq ft/ 250 sq m in area. Its entire surface is covered in painted figures, all larger than life, numbering exactly 300. Together, they illustrate the creation of the world and the history of mankind prior to the Redemption of Christ.

The central part of the ceiling is occupied by nine separate scenes. These are (from the altar end):

The origin of the world:	• God divides the light from the darkness
	• Creation of sun, moon and plantlife
	• God divides the earth from the waters
The origin of man:	• Creation of Adam
	• Creation of Eve
The origin of evil:	• Original sin; Adam and Eve expelled from Eden
	• The sacrifice of Noah
	• The flood
	• The drunkenness of Noah

(c) The Last Judgment***

This greatest of frescos was begun in 1534 and completed in 1544. The restoration now in progress has succeeded in bringing Michelangelo's colours back to their original brightness, which had been darkened by the accumulated deposit of smoke from candles and incense burners and by the glues used to hold the paint in place.

Many of Michelangelo's contemporaries disapproved of the many nude figures included in his composition and, at the height of the Counter-Reformation, Daniele da Volterra was commissioned to clothe the naked figures.

Today, this dispute has surfaced again: should Volterra's additions be removed or should they now be considered as part of the original work?

The Last Judgment contains no architectural divisions. The figures are merely placed against a grey-blue background, in which the various registers are defined by clouds.

● In the top area are angels bearing the instruments of the Passion of Christ.

● Christ occupies the centre; around him are the Virgin and a throng of Apostles, patriarchs and martyrs carrying the symbols of their martyrdom: St Lawrence with a gridiron, St Bartholomew with a knife, St Catherine with a wheel, St Sebastian with arrows and St Blaise with a rake.

● On either side are angels blowing trumpets or carrying books. The elect rise into heaven and (on the right) the damned are thrust into the eternal abyss.

● In the lower right-hand corner, the damned are crowded into a boat and hurled into the waters of Hell by Charon. At left is a scene of the resurrection of the dead.

This fresco clearly marks the end of Renaissance optimism, which was irremediably broken by the sack of Rome in 1527. There is no doubt that Clement VII, who commissioned the work, wished to commemorate the terrible days of 1527; but it is also certain that Michelangelo was expressing his own pain and suffering, while at the same time affirming his deep Catholic faith. The mass of agonized, tortured bodies he portrays is clearly intended to strike fear into the viewer and to remind him of the ineluctable approach of death.

16) The Great Gallery

The Aldobrandini Wedding Room: a superb fresco** (1st century AD) representing two groups of people busy with preparations for a wedding.

Gallery of Urban VIII: the apparatus once used to apply the pope's seal to papal bulls is by one of the windows in this gallery.

The Sistine Room (1587): this was formerly the library reading room. Its 16th-century decoration celebrates the book collection and pontificate of Sixtus V (1585-1590) and illustrates some of his decrees. From time to time there are temporary exhibitions here of manuscripts and documents from the Vatican Library.

17) The Pinacoteca (Picture Gallery)

The paintings in the Pinacoteca (which may be reached by crossing the Cortile delle Pinacoteca from the Great Gallery) are grouped chronologically, school by school. Noteworthy are Gozzoli's *Virgin and St Thomas*** (15th century); *The Angel Musicians*** by Melozzo da Forli (18th century); Cranach's *Pietà*** (15th-16th centuries); Raphaël's *Transfiguration*** (16th century); Leonardo's *St Jerome*** (15th-16th centuries) and Caravaggio's superb *Christ Descending From the Cross*** (16th-17th centuries).

18) The Gregorian Museum

The lighting in this modernized museum is remarkable. It is divided into four sections:

Section one: copies of Greek originals made during the era of Imperial Rome.

Section two: Roman sculptures from the 1st and 2nd centuries AD.
Section three: sarcophagi illustrated with scenes from mythology.
Section four: Roman sculpture from the 2nd and 3rd centuries AD.

At the top of the stairs on the left are mosaics of athletes and judges of races, excavated from the Baths of Caracalla.

19) Pio-Cristiano Museum

This museum contains an outstanding statue of the *Good Shepherd*, as well as sarcophagi decorated with garlands and scenes from the Old and New Testaments.

20) Ethnological and Missionary Museum

This museum houses collections illustrating the world's religions.

21) History Museum

This museum includes a collection of carriages belonging to the various popes and uniforms of the now disbanded papal army corps.

ENVIRONS OF ROME

If you have time, the countryside surrounding Rome is well worth a visit: Ostia Antica, the majestic Villa Adriana, the lovely fortified villages of the Castelli Romana, the Villa d'Este and the bizarre Etruscan necropolis at Cerveteri. All are in Rome's immediate vicinity.

OSTIA ANTICA***

(13.5 mi/22 km south of Rome).

Access

By metro: from Termini to Ostia Antica.

By train: from the Termini railway station or from the Roma-Ostiense station, VI, F4.

By car: leave Rome by way of Porta San Paolo, station, VI, F4, taking via Ostiense and via del Mare; at Ostia, follow the signs to Scavi di Ostia.

Ostia Antica was founded in the 4th century BC and, despite the ravages of time, it still looks like a model town, built along regular lines which have been respected in subsequent reconstructions over the centuries.

The original settlement was a military camp guarding the mouth of the Tiber. Ostia served as an arsenal and seaport for Rome during the Punic Wars, and afterwards became a great clearing house for Empire trade: ivory from Africa, Phoenician glass, purple dyes from Syria, Ephesian oysters, fabrics, silks and spices from the Orient, wax from the Black Sea, incense from Arabia, papyrus, obelisks and dates from Egypt, North African grain, Dalmatian gold, Spanish oil, amber from the Baltic, wool from Gaul, geese from Bologna, marble from Tuscany.

To protect Ostia from attack, first Sully, then Claudius and Trajan surrounded it with massive ramparts.

The town reached the height of its wealth during the second century AD, when its population exceeded 100,000 people of every race and creed. These included sailors, dock workers, fishermen, ferrymen, merchants, civil and military administrators, hotel-keepers, customs officials and others whose livelihoods derived from the bustling seaport.

Ostia's decline coincided with that of the empire. It was here that St Augustine and his mother, Monica, had their famous discussion on eternal life, as reported in the *Confessions*. During the 4th century, Ostia was gradually engulfed in the mud washed down by the Tiber, and the roofs of its houses collapsed beneath the weight of windborne sand and dust. The town disappeared completely and was not rediscovered until 1909.

The ruins of Ostia Antica

Open Tues-Sun 9am-1 hour before sunset, closed holidays. Admission charge.

The most evocative features of this extraordinary site are the Porta Romana, the square of the Corporations, the Forum, the Capitol and the House of the Fishes, with its marbles, mosaics and frescos. A bar, postcards and information can be found behind the theatre.

The Museum of Ostia

Open Mon-Sat 9am-2pm.

This museum complements a tour of Ostia Antica. The various objects unearthed in excavations provide a vivid portrait of daily life in the seaport, populated by artisans and people who followed a variety of cults.

The modern village

(North-west of the excavations)

The village of Ostia was founded by Gregory IV in AD 830, close to the remains of the old town. The tower and fortifications are reminders of the threat of pirates and other independent raiders.

▬ *CASTELLI ROMANI***

(South-west of Rome)

The Castelli Romani are small towns on the sides of the Alban hills *(Colli Albani)* between the two volcanic lakes of Albano and Nemi. Allow half a day for the following itinerary.

Access

By metro: Subaugusto (line A), piazza di Cinecittà, II, E6

By car: along via Tuscolana, II, D5.

By bus: ACOTRAL line (via di Portonaccio, ☎ 57 531).

Frascati*

(13 mi/21 km south-east of Rome)

This town, celebrated for its wines and patrician villas, is dominated by the impressive **Villa Aldobrandini*** *(open 9am-1pm; apply to tourist office),* which is fronted by a magnificent avenue of oaks. This villa was built by Giacomo della Porta between 1598 and 1609.

Villa Falconieri* *(closed to the public),* built between 1545 and 1548, was enlarged by Borromini in the 17th century.

Guided tours are available at the Frascati Tourist Office, piazza Marconi 1, ☎ 942 0331.

Tusculum**

(4 mi/6 km south-east of Frascati)

A panoramic road skirts the park of the Villa Aldobrandini, leading to what remains of Tusculum, where Cicero maintained one of his eight villas in the 1st century BC. Cicero relates that he used to rise early, write letters, enjoy the view of the plains stretching below and receive friends who came to talk politics and philosophy. The site also includes an amphitheatre.

From the top of the hill, there is a superb view of Rome (the dome of St Peter's is visible) and, to the right, the Villa d'Este at Tivoli.

Grottaferrata

(1.5 mi/3 km from Frascati, 15 mi/24 km south-east of Rome)

This little town is mainly famous for its **abbey***, which was founded by St Nilus in the 11th century and fortified in the 15th century.

Excavation work unearthed delicate mosaics in Ostia, an important seaport during the Punic Wars.

The church *(open Mon-Sat 9am-12.30pm, 4-7pm, Sun 11am)* was redecorated in the 17th century to contain the holy relics of the orthodox monks. The result is very successful.

In the side-chapel on the right are frescos* by Domenichino illustrating the lives of St Nilus and St Bartholomew.

Rocca di Papa*

(18.5 mi/30 km from Rome)

The road continues through the chestnut woods and pastures of the Alban hills to Rocca di Papa (2300 ft/700 m above sea level). This town, which has preserved an interesting mediaeval quarter, is built around a wide hollow at the foot of Monte Cavo.

Monte Cavo**

The summit of Monte Cavo (3105 ft/946 m) can be reached by road through magnificent woodland. The temple here was dedicated to Jupiter, and there is a magnificent view of Rome, the Roman countryside, Tusculum, the Castelli Romani and the lakes.

Lake Albano* is 6 mi/10 km around and 558 ft/170 m deep at its centre. It is surrounded by wooded slopes, with Castel Gandolfo on one bank.

Nemi*

(22 mi/36.5 km south-east of Rome)

From Lake Albano, take via dei Laghi through oak woods until you reach the road leading to Nemi, an austere little village perched on the slope above a lake.

Here, the **Ship Museum** (closed for repairs) contains replicas of two large ships commissioned by the Emperor Caligula in the 1st century AD.

At Nemi, you can eat strawberries at any time of year, and an annual strawberry festival is held in June.

Genzano di Roma

(26 mi/42 km south-east of Rome)

Genzano is famous for its flower festival, which takes place on Corpus Christi day. The 17th-century **Palazzo Cesarini*** is also of interest.

Ariccia

(28 mi/45 km south-east of Rome)

This little town is dominated by the imposing façade of the **Chigi Palace***. Opposite is Bernini's church of **Santa Maria dell'Assunta**. Ariccia is also the home of *porchetta,* suckling pig roasted with aromatic herbs.

Albano Laziale and Castel Gandolfo

(29 mi/47 km south-east of Rome)

At Ariccia, you join the via Appia Nuova, which leads back to Rome by way of Albano Laziale, on the banks of Lake Albano, and Castel Gandolfo, a peaceful little town best known as the site of the **papal summer residence** *(closed to the public).* This palazzo built by Carlo Maderno, was constructed on the town's central piazza between 1624 and 1629. The nearby church of **San Tomaso da Villanova** (1661) was designed by Bernini. In summer, the pope gives audiences in the square.

From here, you re-enter Rome by way of Porta S. Giovanni, II, D4.

▰▰ *PALESTRINA**

(23.5 mi/38 km east of Rome)

Access

By train: from the Latium railway station, via Giolitti, IV, E5; for information, ☎ 4775.

By car: via Prenestina, then via Casilina, from Porta Maggiore, V, AB6.

By bus: ACOTRAL line, n° 4 (terminus opposite entrance of the Termini railway station, IV, D2).

Palestrina, called Praenesta in ancient times, was formerly known for its gigantic **Temple of Fortune*** (1st century BC) which, in its time, had a frontage of over 656 ft/200 m along the moutainside. The town was also the birthplace of the composer Palestrina. The **Palazzo Barberini** (1640) and the **Museo Prenestino Barberiniano** (Etruscan and Roman art) are noteworthy.

▰▰ *VILLA ADRIANA****

(18 mi/29 km east of Rome)
Open Tues-Sun 9am-1 hour before sunset. Admission charge.

Access

By car: via Tiburtina, II, C4-5-6 or the toll-road, Aquila Autostrada, II, C6.

By bus: ACOTRAL line, n° 2 (via Gaeta terminus, off piazza Cinquecento, IV, C5).

The Villa Adriana is a masterpiece of ancient Roman architecture, in perfect harmony with the surrounding countryside. It was constructed by the

Emperor Hadrian between AD 118 and 130, on the site of an earlier country house. For political reasons, Hadrian spent most of his life travelling. He settled here during his final years, dividing his time between politics, encounters with philosophers and intellectuals, and solitary meditation. His collections, musical instruments and library were all assembled at the Villa Adriana.

The palace precinct, which covers a total of 370 acres/150 hectares, takes advantage of the landscape to create a subtle division between private, quiet areas for personal use and areas for public ceremonies. No edifice overpowers another. There is perfect harmony between the landscape and the complex of buildings, a harmony which produces an effect of extraordinary calm.

The Villa Adriana is bounded to the north-east by the **Valley of Tempe** and to the south-west by the **Tower of Roccabrune.** Originally, its buildings lay along two axes: that of the north (the Hall of the Philosophers, the library courtyard, the imperial palace and the piazza d'Oro) and that of the west (Pecila, stadium, baths, praetorium and canopus). The buildings to the north were best for the cool hours of the morning and evening, while those to the west received the afternoon sunshine, yet remained cool because of their many pools, fountains and shady porticos.

Piranesi left a magnificent series of 18th-century engravings of the Villa Adriana, and most of what he recorded may still be seen today. The tour of the palace begins with the circular Temple of Venus, then continues through the Pecila, the Maritime Theatre, the Triclinia, the hostelry chambers, the cryptoporticus, the imperial palace, the piazza d'Oro with its audience chamber, the larger and smaller bath houses, the Canopus and the Serapeum.

The Villa Adriana was destroyed by barbarian invasions and ransacked for building materials during the Middle Ages. Today, it is difficult to visualize its former luxury under Hadrian, when it was filled with marble, green jasper, porphyry, stucco, painted frescos, mosaics and innumerable statues (some of which are preserved in the Pio-Clementino Museum in the Vatican, see p. 184). Nonetheless, it is easy to recognize the harmony of place and position that Hadrian held so dear.

▬ *VILLA D'ESTE***

(20 mi/32 km east of Rome)
Open Mon-Sat 9am-1 hour before sunset.

Access

Same as for the Villa Adriana (see p. 193), but continue to Tivoli.

Cardinal Ippolito d'Este was the grandson of Pope Alexander VI and the son of Alfonso d'Este, Duke of Ferrara. In 1550, he became Governor of Tivoli and its surroundings, and commissioned the architect Ligorio to build a villa and lay out magnificent gardens beside the town. The work began in 1550 and was completed in 1569.

The entrance to the villa is via the **cloister** of the former convent building, around which Ligorio planned the new palace; there follows a series of 10 rooms, the cardinal's private apartments.

On the level below are the formal reception rooms, with a **main salon** in the centre. On the ceiling of this salon is Zuccaro's splendid *Assembly of the Gods*★. Munziano's plan of the villa can be observed, painted on one of the walls.

The main salon leads through to the **loggia,** which looks out across the gardens, part of the town and the adjacent hills.

The Gardens**

The gardens of the Villa d'Este, with gushing fountains and lovely statuary, were imitated all over Europe at the end of the Renaissance. Their most celebrated features include the Little Rome fountain, the Cento fontane avenue, the Oveto fountain and the extraordinary organ fountain.

Villa Gregoriana

Beyond Tivoli, the magnificent **cascades*** of the Villa Gregoriana are well worth a visit.

CERVETERI**

(27 mi/44 km west of Rome)

Access

By car: along via Aurelia, I, C2, or along autostrada A12 to Civita Vecchia, II, F2.

By bus: ACOTRAL line, n° 11 (from via Lepanto terminus on the corner of via G. Cesare).

Cerveteri was a major Etruscan city during the 8th century BC. Vestiges of Etruscan and mediaeval ramparts survive in the town. The **Palazzo Ruspoli** (16th century) contains a **museum of Etruscan antiquities** *(open Tues-Sun 10am-4pm).* The extraordinary necropolis is 1 mi/1.6 km north of Cerveteri.

Etruscan necropolis**

Open Tues-Sun 9am-1 hour before sunset. Admission charge.

This strange monument consists of huge circular *tumuli* surrounded by tall cypresses and thick vegetation. The tombs (6th century BC) bear the names of their decorative elements, e.g., the **tomb of the reliefs****, the **tomb of the painted animals****, the **tomb of the stuccos**** and the **tomb of the sarcophagi****.

ROME ADDRESSES

T his section includes a list of hotels and restaurants, classified by neighbourhood. Entries are ordered alphabetically under each heading, with map references. Bars, snack-bars and nightclubs are listed after the hotels and restaurants.

The section concludes with a carefully selected, alphabetical list of shops, classified by the items they sell.

SYMBOLS USED

Hotels

The hotels and *pensiones* (boarding houses) fall into several different categories and the prices quoted reflect the minimum cost of a single room and the maximum cost of a double room with breakfast included.

▲▲▲▲ Luxury hotel

▲▲▲ First-class hotel

▲▲ Moderately priced

▲ Inexpensive hotel

Prices may vary within a given category according to the amenities offered, i.e., location, view, terrace, etc. Prices should be viewed as approximate indications only. You should request the exact price when reserving.

Restaurants

Prices given for restaurants are calculated on the basis of an à la carte meal, including hors-d'œuvres (*antipasti*), two main dishes (*primo piatto* and *secundo piatto*), dessert, beverage and cover charge (*coperti*). As in cafés, you should always leave a tip in addition to the service charge shown on the bill.

LLLL: Deluxe

LLL : Expensive

LL : Moderate

L : Inexpensive

CONTENTS

HOTELS AND RESTAURANTS

Vatican, Prati, Monte Mario

Hotels

▲▲▲ **Cavalieri Hilton,** via Caldolo 101, II, B2, ☎ 3151, telex: 610296. Bus: 903, 913, 991. Credit cards accepted, 387 rooms, air-conditioning, parking, sauna, swimming pool, gymnasium, garden, terraces. Away from the city centre, superb view of Rome.

▲▲▲ **Visconti Palace,** via Cesi 37, III, C4, ☎ 3684, telex: 680407. Bus: 34, 77, 49, 910. Credit cards accepted, 247 rooms, air-conditioning, no restaurant.

▲▲ **Giulio Cesare,** via degli Scipioni 287, III, B4, ☎ .31 0244, telex: 613010. Metro: Ottaviano or Leponte. Credit cards accepted, 86 rooms, air-conditioning, parking, no restaurant. Very quiet, close to St Peter's and the Vatican Museums.

▲ **Colombus,** via della Conciliazione 33, III, E2, ☎ 656 5435, telex: 620096. Bus: 23, 34, 41. Credit cards accepted, 107 rooms, parking, gardens. In a 15th-century cardinal's palace with antique furniture, round the corner from St Peter's.

Restaurants

LLL **San Luigi,** via Mocenigo 10, III, B1, ☎ 35 0912. Bus: 51, 907. Closed Sun evening and Mon. Credit cards accepted. Neapolitan and Milanese cooking, excellent wine list, refined atmosphere.

LL **Antico Falcone,** via Trionfale 60, III, B1, ☎ 35 3400. Bus: 31, 70. Closed Tues. Charming ambience in a 15th-century building.

LL **Cucurucù,** via Capoprati 10, II, B2, ☎ 35 4434. Bus: 32, 186. Closed Sun evening and Mon. Overlooking the Tiber, a delightful restaurant serving Roman cuisine.

LL **Girarrosto Toscano,** via Campania 29, III, C2-3, ☎ 49 3759. Bus: 492. Closed Wed. Lively atmosphere, copious helpings, reservations necessary.

LL **Hostaria da Cesare,** via Crescenzio 13, III, D3, ☎ 656 1227. Bus: 39, 49. Closed Sun evening and Aug. Credit cards accepted. A charming trattoria, seafood specialities.

LL **Il Matriciano,** via dei Gracchi 55, III, C2, ☎ 95 5246. Bus: 492. Closed Wed in winter, Sat in summer. A delightful trattoria.

Campo dei Fiori, Largo Argentina, Farnese, Campidoglio

Hotels

▲▲ **Cardinal,** via Giulia 62, III, F3-4, ☎ 654 2719, telex: 612373. Bus: 98, 98c, 881. Credit cards accepted, 73 rooms, garden. Located on one of Rome's most beautiful streets, quiet ambience, friendly service.

▲▲ **Della Torre Argentina,** corso Vittorio Emanuele 102, III, F5, ☎ 654 8251. Bus: 44, 710. Credit cards accepted, 32 rooms, no dogs allowed. Centrally located.

▲▲ **Tiziano,** corso Vittorio Emanuele 110, III, E3-F4, ☎ 687 5087. Bus: 44, 98, 98c, 710, 881. Credit cards accepted, 50 rooms.

Restaurants

LLLL **Da Piperno,** via Monte de' Cenci 9, VI, AB4, ☎ 654 0629. Bus: 24, 774. Closed Sun evening and Mon, Christmas, Easter and Aug. Located in the former stables of Palazzo Cenci Bolognetti. Classic Roman cuisine, reservations necessary.

LLL **Girone VI,** vicolo Sinibaldi 2, on the corner of via di Torre Argentina, III, F5, ☎ 654 2831. Bus: 44, 70. Closed Sun. Italian nouvelle cuisine, reservations necessary.

LL **La Carbonara,** Campo dei Fiori 23, III, F4, ☎ 656 4783. Bus: 46, 62, 64. Closed Tues in winter, Sat in summer. Traditional Roman cuisine, lively ambience, terrace.

LL **Carmelo il Velino,** via Monserrato 32, III, F4, ☎ 654 2636. Bus: 46, 62, 64. Closed Sun. Elegant restaurant, with Sicilian specialities and a wide choice of fish dishes.

LL **Da Giggetto,** via del Portico d'Ottavia, VI, A4, ☎ 656 1105. Bus: 57, 90, 774, 780. Closed

Mon and three weeks in July. In the heart of the Jewish ghetto with terrace overlooking the Temple of Octavia, Da Giggetto is famous for its Jewish specialities.

LL **Hostaria da Costanza,** piazza del Paradiso 65, VI, A3, ☎ 656 1717. Bus: 61, 65. Closed Sun. Located in a wing of the Theatre of Pompey, close to parliament buildings. Excellent meat and fish dishes.

LL **La Piccola Cuccagna,** via della Cuccagna, III, F4, ☎ 654 1502. Bus: 42, 62, 64. Closed Sun. Old-fashioned decor, seasonal cuisine.

LL **Polese,** piazza Sforza Cesarini 40, III, F4, ☎ 656 1709. Bus: 42, 62, 64. Closed Tues and Aug 15-31. An unpretentious, delightful trattoria with air-conditioning and a shady terrace. Traditional Genoese and Roman cuisine.

LL **Vecchia Roma,** piazza Campitelli 18, VI, A4, ☎ 656 4604. Bus: 90. Closed Wed and two weeks in Aug. Comfortable, intimate ambience, with a superb terrace. Seasonal cuisine and highly original salads.

Piazza Navona, Pantheon, Piazza Colonna

Hotels

▲▲ **Colonna Palace,** piazza di Monteciterio 12, III, E6, ☎ 678 1341, telex: 621467. Bus: 52, 53, 58, 58b, 61, 71, 85. Credit cards accepted, 100 rooms, air-conditioning, no restaurant. Located on a beautiful piazza.

▲▲ **Raphael,** largo Febo 2, III, E4. ☎ 656 9051. Bus: 41, 46b. Credit cards accepted, 85 rooms. This exclusive hotel is patronized by the Italian intelligentsia and particularly by ex-prime minister Bettino Craxi. When Craxi is in residence, the hotel is kept under tight security.

▲ **Cesari,** via di Pietra 89a, III, E6, ☎ 679 2386. Bus: 46, 92, 94. Credit cards accepted, 50 rooms, no restaurant. Convenient central location.

▲ **Portoghesi,** via dei Portoghesi 1, III, E5, ☎ 656 4231. Bus: 26, 70, 81, 87. 27 rooms, air-conditioning. Simple, well-run hotel, close to piazza Navona.

▲ **Sole al Pantheon,** via del Pantheon 63, III, F5, ☎ 679 3490. Bus: 44, 56, 60. 28 rooms. This has been an inn since the 15th century. Charming, excellent location.

Restaurants

LLLL **Fortunato,** via del Pantheon 55, III, F5, ☎ 679 2788. Bus: 26, 90. Closed Sun. Credit cards accepted. Spacious restaurant with view of the Pantheon, patronized by Italian politicians. Seasonal dishes, excellent wine list.

LLLL **Hostaria dell'Orso,** via dei Soldati 25, III, E4, ☎ 656 4250. Bus: 26, 70. Closed noon, Sun and Aug. Credit cards accepted. 15th-century building, very luxurious. Roman cuisine, good wine list, efficient service.

LLLL **La Majella,** piazza Sant' Apollinare 45, III, E5, ☎ 656 4174. Bus: 26, 70. Closed Sun and one week in Aug. Credit cards accepted. Terrace, efficient service and excellent, inventive cuisine.

LLLL **Quattre Colonne,** via dell Posta 4, III, F5, ☎ 654 7152. Bus: 46, 62. Closed Sun. Credit cards accepted. An excellent fish restaurant, air-conditioning.

LLLL **La Sacrestia,** via del Seminario 89, III, F5, ☎ 679 7581. Bus: 26, 90. Closed Wed. Roman cuisine.

LL **Il Drappo,** vicolo del Malpasso 9, III, F3-4, ☎ 65 7365. Bus: 62, 64. Closed Sun and two weeks in Aug. Probably the best Sardinian restaurant in Rome, elegant and comfortable. Reservations necessary.

L **Il Baffeto,** via del Governo Vecchio 144, III, F4. Bus: 46, 62, 64. The pizzas here are so delicious that you forget all about the drab surroundings. Always crowded so it is advisable to go very early or very late.

Piazza del Popolo, Corso, Piazza di Spagna

Hotels

▲▲▲ **D'Inghilterra,** via Bocca di Leone 14, III, D6, ☎ 67 2161, telex: 614552. Metro: Spagna. Credit cards accepted, 105 rooms, no restaurant. One of Rome's most exclusive hotels, recently renovated.

A drink at a café terrace is a wonderful way to experience Rome's unique charm.

Liszt, Hemingway and Henry James all stayed here. The top-floor rooms have terraces.

▲▲▲ **Le Plaza,** via del Corso 126, III, D6, ☎ 67 2101, telex: 624669. Metro: Spagna. Credit cards accepted, 207 rooms, air-conditioning, no restaurant. Turn-of-the-century decor, stained-glass windows, old-fashioned charm.

▲▲ **Valadier,** via della Fontanella III, D5, ☎ 361 0592. Metro: Spagna. Credit cards accepted, 41 rooms, air-conditioning. Pleasantly decorated with Liberty prints.

▲ **Locarno,** via della Penna III, C5, ☎ 361 0841. Metro: Flaminio. Close to piazza del Popolo, patio, comfortable rooms.

▲ **Pensione Forte,** via Margutta 61, III, C6, ☎ 678 6109. Metro: Spagna. An informal, family-run hotel.

Restaurants

LLLL **El Toulà,** via della Lupa 29, III, DE5, ☎ 678 1196. Bus: 81, 90. Closed Sat noon, Sun and Aug. Credit cards accepted. Fine furniture and service, excellent cuisine, good choice of wines. Reservations necessary.

LLLL **Porto di Ripetta,** via di Ripetta 250, III, C5, ☎ 361 2376. Metro: Flaminio. Closed Sun and Aug 10-30. Credit cards accepted. Attentive service, exquisite Roman cuisine and a solid wine list.

LLL **Ranieri,** via Mario de' Fiori 26, III, D6, ☎ 679 1592. Metro: Spagna. Closed Sun and two weeks in Aug. Credit cards accepted. The turn-of-the-century surroundings are more impressive than the food. Reservations necessary.

LL **Beltramme,** via della Croce 39, III, D6. Metro: Spagna. Closed Sun and two weeks in Aug. Old-fashioned, simple Roman cooking, always crowded.

LL **Buca di Ripetta,** via di Ripetta 36, III, C5, ☎ 361 9391. Metro: Spagna or Flaminio. Closed Sun evening, Mon and Aug. A lively, country-style trattoria, serving authentic Roman cuisine.

LL **Il Buco,** via Sant'Ignazio 7-8, III, F6, ☎ 679 3298. Bus: 56, 60, 90. Closed Mon and Aug. Credit cards accepted. Traditional Tuscan cooking, pleasant atmosphere, excellent service and wine list.

LL **La Campana,** vicolo della Campana 18, III, E5, ☎ 656 7820. Bus: 26, 70. Credit cards accepted. A 400-year-old trattoria serving Roman cuisine, traditional but never heavy.

LL **Dal Bolognese,** piazza del Popolo 1, III, C5, ☎ 361 1426. Metro: Flaminio. Closed Sun evening and Aug. Terrace, attentive service, Bolognese cuisine. Reservations necessary.

LL **Da Mario,** via della Vite 56, III, D6, ☎ 678 3818. Metro: Spagna. Closed Sun, Sat in summer and Aug. Delightful atmosphere and decor, Tuscan cuisine, renowned for fresh game dishes.

LL **L'Eau Vive,** via Monterone 85, III, F5, ☎ 654 1095. Bus: 26, 90. Closed Sun and Aug. In a 16th-century palace, a variety of international dishes are served by Catholic mission-worker waitresses from all over the world. A restaurant much favoured by higher dignitaries of the Vatican. Reservations necessary.

LL **La Fontanella,** largo Fontanella Borghese, III, D5, ☎ 678 3849. Metro: Spagna. Closed Mon. Credits cards accepted. Tuscan cuisine, with game in season, terrace. Reservations necessary.

LL **Leoncino,** vicolo del Leoncino 28, III, D5. Metro: Spagna. An authentic pizzeria with a regular local clientele.

LL **Otello alla Concordia,** via della Croce 81, III, D6, ☎ 679 1178. Metro: Spagna. Closed Sun. Picturesque trattoria, with a shady terrace under an arbour.

LL **La Rampa,** piazza Mignanelli 18, III, D6, ☎ 678 2621. Metro: Spagna. Closed Sun, Mon noon. Terrace, Roman cuisine.

LL **Re degli Amici,** via della Croce 33b, III, D6, ☎ 679 5380. Metro: Spagna. Closed Mon and last three weeks in June. Credit cards accepted. Cheerful trattoria, with Roman cuisine, pleasant decor and efficient service.

LL **La Rossetta,** via della Rossetta 9, III, F5, ☎ 656 1002. Bus: 26, 90. Closed Sun, Mon noon and Aug. Credit cards accepted. Excellent Sicilian specialities in one of Rome's finest fish restaurants.

LL **Taverna Giulia,** vicolo dell'Oro 23, III, E3, ☎ 656 9786. Bus: 46, 98. Closed Sun and Aug. Credit cards accepted. Renowned for its Ligurian specialities and excellent wine cellar. Reservations necessary.

Barberini, Trintà, Trevi

Hotels

▲▲▲▲ **Hassler Villa Medici,** Trinità dei Monti 6, IV, C1, ☎ 679 2651, telex: 610208. Metro: Spagna. Credit cards accepted, 108 rooms, air-conditioning, parking. Beautifully furnished rooms, restaurant with magnificent view.

▲▲▲ **Bernini-Bristol,** piazza Barberini 23, IV, D2, ☎ 46 3051, telex: 610554. Metro: Barberini. Credit cards accepted, 125 rooms, air-conditioning. Rooms have fine views.

▲▲ **Delle Nazioni,** via Po, III, E6, ☎ 679 2441, telex: 614193. Metro: Barberini. Credit cards accepted, 74 rooms, air-conditioning, parking, no restaurant. Decor is ultra-modern.

▲ **Gregoriana,** via Gregoriana 18, IV, D2, ☎ 679 4289. Metro: Barberini or Spagna. 19 rooms, air-conditioning, no restaurant. A former convent, well-located, quiet. Excellent quality at reasonable prices.

▲ **Pensione Suisse,** via Gregoriana 56, IV, D2, ☎ 678 3649. Metro: Barberini or Spagna. Credit cards accepted, 28 rooms. Very well located.

▲ **Scalinata di Spagna,** piazza Trinità dei Monti 17, IV, C1-2, ☎ 679 3006. Metro: Spagna. 14 rooms, always booked well in advance. Close to Il Pincio and the Villa Medici, beautiful view from the terrace, a hotel full of charm.

▲ **Trinità dei Monti,** via Sistina 91, IV, C2, ☎ 679 7206. Metro: Spagna. Well located.

Restaurants

LLLL **Hassler Roof,** piazza Trinità dei Monti 6, IV, C1, ☎ 679 2681. Metro: Spagna. Closed Sun. Credit cards accepted. Terrace offering exceptional views across the city, international cuisine.

LLL **Casina Valadier,** via Casina Valadier, III, C6, ☎ 679 4189. Metro: Spagna. Closed Mon. Credit cards accepted. Located between the Villa Medici and the Villa Borghese. Terrace with view across Rome, attentive service.

LLL **Moro,** vicolo delle Bollette 13, III, E6, ☎ 678 3495. Metro: Barberini. Closed Sun and Aug. Plenty of charm, game in season, excellent cuisine.

LL **La Cantinella da Emilio,** via Crispi 19 IV, D2, ☎ 679 5069. Metro: Spagna. Closed Wed and Aug. An excellent trattoria, Sardinian specialities.

LL **Il Corsaro,** via del Boccaccio 6, IV, D2, ☎ 475 9915. Metro: Barberini. Closed Mon and Aug. Pleasant, intimate atmosphere, specializing in fish dishes.

LL **Crispi,** via Crispi 29 IV, D2 ☎ 679 2481. Metro: Spagna. A friendly restaurant, traditional Roman cuisine.

L **Il Giardino,** via Zucchelli 29, IV, D2, ☎ 46 5202. Metro: Spagna. Closed Mon. An excellent unpretentious trattoria, small garden, prompt service, Roman cuisine.

Veneto, Ludovisi, Parioli

Hotels

▲▲▲▲ **Ambasciatori Palace,** via Veneto 70, IV, C3, ☎ 47 493, telex: 610241. Metro: Barberini. Credit cards accepted, 149 rooms, parking. Beautifully furnished hotel.

▲▲▲▲ **Eden,** via Ludovisi 49, IV, C2, ☎ 474 3551, telex: 610567. Metro: Barberini. Credit cards accepted, 110 rooms, air-conditioning. Terrace restaurant, fine view across the Villa Medici and the Quirinal.

▲▲▲▲ **Excelsior,** via Veneto 125, IV, C3, ☎ 4708, telex: 610232. Metro: Barberini. Credit cards accepted, 363 rooms, air-conditioning. Sumptuous with wide range of services, piano bar.

▲▲▲ **Jolly,** corso d'Italia 1, IV, B3, ☎ 8495, telex: 612293. Bus: 56, 57, 319, 490, 495. Credit cards accepted, 200 rooms, air-conditioning. Modern, functional, opposite the Villa Borghese.

▲▲▲ **Lord Byron,** via G. de Notaris 5, II, B3, ☎ 360 9541, telex: 611217. Bus: 26, 52. Credit cards accepted, 55 rooms, air-conditioning. Overlooking the gardens of the Villa Borghese, refined, peaceful ambience.

▲▲▲ **Regina Carlton,** via Veneto 72, IV, C3, ☎ 47 6851, telex: 620863. Metro: Barberini. Credit cards accepted, 125 rooms. Impeccable service.

▲▲ **Borromini,** via Lisbona 7, II, B4, ☎ 84 1321, telex: 621625. Bus: 168. Credit cards accepted, 75 rooms, air-conditioning, parking, no restaurant.

▲▲ **Eliseo,** via di Porta Pinciana, IV, C2, ☎ 46 0556, telex: 610693. Metro: Barberini. Credit cards accepted, 50 rooms, air-conditioning. Terrace restaurant, fine view across the Villa Borghese gardens.

▲▲ **Victoria,** via Campania 41, II, B3, ☎ 47 3931, telex: 610212. Bus: 56, 57, 319. Credit cards accepted, 110 rooms. Terrace and view across the Villa Borghese gardens, excellent service.

▲ **Degli Aranci,** via Oriani 11, II, B3. ☎ 87 0202. Bus: 26, 168, 910. Credit cards accepted,. 42 rooms. Excellent value for money.

▲ **Panama,** via Salaria 336, II, B4, ☎ 86 2558, telex: 620189. Bus: 19, 30, 168. 43 rooms, air-conditioning.

▲ **Rivoli,** via Taramelli 7, II, B3, ☎ 87 0141, telex: 614615. Bus: 26, 52. Credit cards accepted, 49 rooms. Very quiet hotel.

Restaurants

LLLL **Relais le Jardin,** via G. de Notaris 5, II, B3, ☎ 360 9541. Bus: 26, 52. Closed Sun. Credit cards accepted. Discreet service and refined atmosphere. Traditional Roman and nouvelle cuisine. Reservations necessary.

LLLL **Sans Souci,** via Sicilia 20, IV, C2, ☎ 49 3504. Metro: Barberini.

Closed noon, Mon and Aug. Credit cards accepted. International and Italian cuisine. Reservations necessary.

LLL **Andrea,** via Sardegna 26, IV, BC3, ☎ 49 3707. Metro: Barberini. Closed Sun and Aug. Credit cards accepted. A terrace restaurant serving Abruzzi and Roman cuisine.

LLL **Il Caminetto,** viale Parioli 89, II, B3, ☎ 80 3946. Bus: 26. Closed Thurs and Aug 12-18. Credit cards accepted. Traditional Roman cuisine.

LLL **Canceletto,** via Alamanno Morelli 1, II, B4, ☎ 87 4334. Bus: 4. Closed Sun. Refined decor, quiet ambience, attentive service and excellent cuisine.

LLL **Colline Emiliane,** via degli Avignonesi 22, IV, D2, ☎ 475 7538. Metro: Barberini. Closed Fri and Aug. Credit cards accepted. Emilian cuisine, game in season.

LLL **Coriolano,** via Ancona 14, IV, B5, ☎ 844 9501. Metro: Barberini. Closed Sun and Aug 3-Sept 2. An elegant, comfortable restaurant with terrace serving game in season and excellent homemade pasta. Reservations necessary.

LLL **Fogher,** via Tevere 13b, IV, B4, ☎ 85 7032. Bus: 3, 4, 56, 57. Closed Sun. Credit cards accepted. Dinner under the plane trees in summer. Venetian and Northern Italian cuisine.

LLL **La Gola,** viale Parioli 103, II, B3, ☎ 80 5136. Bus: 3, 53. Closed Sun. Credit cards accepted. Charming decor including terrace, excellent service, Roman cuisine at its most refined.

Coliseum, Forum

▲▲ **Forum,** via Tor de'Conti 25, IV, F2, ☎ 679 2446/7/8, telex: 622549. Metro: Colosseo. Credit cards accepted, 81 rooms, air-condition ing, parking. A former palace, frequented by businessmen and politicians. Exceptional location, gardens with views of the Forum and the Palatine hill.

▲ **Richmond,** largo Corrado Ricci 36, V, A1, ☎ 678 3797. Metro: Colosseo. Credit cards accepted, 13 rooms, air-conditioning.

LLLL **Ai Tre Scalini Da Rossano e Matteo,** via Ss. Quattro 30, V, B3, ☎ 73 2695. Metro: Colosseo. Closed Sat noon, Sun evening and Mon in July and Aug. Credit cards accepted. Behind a modest exterior, very refined ambience and cuisine. Reservations necessary.

LLL **Gladiatore,** piazza del Colosseo 15, V, B2, ☎ 73 6276. Metro: Colosseo. Closed Wed. Credit cards accepted. A cheerful restaurant with terrace, high-quality traditional Roman cuisine.

LLL **Hostaria al Fori,** largo C. Ricci 2/4, V, A1, ☎ 678 6133. Metro: Colosseo. Closed Tues. Credit cards accepted. Pizzeria with terrace.

LLL **Mario's Hostaria,** piazza del Grillo 9 IV, F2. Metro: Colosseo. Closed Sun. Delightful terrace, traditional Roman cuisine. Reservations necessary.

San Giovanni in Laterano, Santa Maria Maggiore, Termini

▲▲▲▲ **Grand Hotel,** via V.E. Orlando 3, IV, D3, ☎ 4709, telex: 610210. Metro: Repubblica. Credit cards accepted, 168 rooms, air-conditioning. Marble, painted ceilings, antique carpets—one of Rome's great hotels.

▲▲▲ **Mediterraneo,** via Cavour 15, IV, E4, ☎ 46 4051. Metro: Termini. Credit cards accepted, 272 rooms, air-conditioning. Classical furnishings, excellent service.

▲▲ **Londra e Cargill,** piazza Salustio 18 IV, C4, ☎ 47 3871, telex: 622227. Metro: Repubblica. Credit cards accepted, 105 rooms, air-conditioning, parking. New interior in a 19th-century palazzo.

▲▲ **Massimo d'Azeglio,** via Cavour 18, IV, E4, ☎ 46 0646, telex: 610556. Metro: Termini. Credit cards accepted, 210 rooms, air-conditioning. Refined 19th-century elegance.

▲▲ **Quirinale,** via Nazionale 7, IV, D3, ☎ 4707, telex: 610332. Metro: Repubblica. Credit cards accepted, 193 rooms, air-conditioning, no dogs allowed. Built by the architect of the Rome Opera House, to which it is attached.

▲ **Britannia,** via Napoli 64, IV, E3, ☎ 46 3153, telex: 611292. Metro: Termini. Credit cards accepted, 32 rooms, air-conditioning.

▲ **Napoleon,** piazza Vittorio Emanuele 105, V, A4, ☎ 73 7646, telex: 611069. Metro: Vittorio. Credit cards accepted, 82 rooms, air-conditioning.

▲ **Nord-Nuova Roma,** via G. Amendola 3, IV, E4, ☎ 46 5441, telex: 610556. Metro: Termini. Credit cards accepted, air-conditioning, parking. Part of the same chain as the Massimo d'Azeglio, with similar high-quality service, although simpler and more modestly priced.

Restaurants

LLL **Massimo d'Azeglio,** via Cavour 14, IV, E4, ☎ 47 5401. Metro: Termini. Credit cards accepted. Refined, 19th-century atmosphere, traditional and inventive cuisine.

LL **Cannavota,** piazza San Giovanni 20, V, C4, ☎ 77 5007. Bus: 4, 13, 16, 85, 118. Closed Wed and Aug 1-30. Family restaurant, large tables, substantial servings.

LL **La Matriciana,** via del Viminale 40-44, IV, E4-5, ☎ 46 1775. Metro: Repubblica or Termini. Closed Sat and Aug 11-16. Credit cards accepted. Roman cuisine.

LL **Pulcino Ballerino,** via degli Equi 66, IV, F6, ☎ 49 0331. Bus: 11, 71. Your meat is cooked at your table on a *pietra ollare* (hot stone).

LL **Ricci,** via Genova 32, IV, E3, ☎ 46 4412. Bus: 57, 64, 65. Metro: Repubblica. Closed Mon. One of the best pizzerias in Rome.

LL **Taverna Flavia,** via Flavia 9, V, C4, ☎ 474 5214. Bus: 16, 37, 63. Closed Sun and Aug 15-20. A favourite with actors during the great days of Cinecittà.

L **Elettra,** via Principe Amadeo 74, IV, E4, ☎ 47 5397. Metro: Termini. Closed Fri evening, Sat and Aug 12-Sept 3. Elettra has been serving a loyal clientele in this little restaurant for over 50 years, traditional Roman cuisine.

Trastevere

Restaurants

LLL **Alberto Ciarla,** piazza S. Cosimato 40, VI, C2, ☎ 581 8668. Bus: 26, 44, 56, 75. Closed noon, Sun and Aug. Credit cards accepted. Superb fish restaurant with terrace. Reservations necessary.

LLL **Sabatini,** vicolo Santa Maria in Trastevere 18, VI, B3, ☎ 581 8307. Bus: 23, 56, 65. Closed Tues. Credit cards accepted. Typical Roman hostaria serving fish specialities. Efficient service, terrace. Reservations necessary.

LL **Galeassi,** piazza S. Maria in Trastevere, VI, B3, ☎ 580 3775. Bus: 23, 56, 65. Closed Mon. Credit cards accepted. Fish specialities, terrace, cheerful ambience.

LL **Romolo,** via di Porta Settimania 8, VI, AB2, ☎ 581 8284. Bus: 23, 65, 280. Closed Mon and Aug. A typical trattoria serving Roman cuisine, with friendly staff and pleasant terrace.

L **Turiddù al Mattatoio,** viale Galvani 64, VI, E3, ☎ 575 0447. Closed Wed and Aug 10-31. A family-run trattoria, serving popular Roman dishes.

▬▬ *FOREIGN SPECIALITIES*

Arab cuisine

Chef du Village, via del Governo Vecchio 125-127, VI, A2, ☎ 656 8693. Closed noon. Eclectic cooking and atmosphere. Reservations necessary.

Brasseries

Birreria Viennese, via della Croce 21, III, D6, ☎ 679 5569. Closed noon and Wed. The best brasserie in Rome: Bavarian and Austrian specialities.

Chinese cuisine

La Giada, via IV Novembre 137/1, IV, F2, ☎ 679 8384. Closed Mon. Expensive, but well worth the money.

French cuisine

Chez Albert, vicolo della Vaccarella 11, III, E5, ☎ 656 5549. Closed Sun. Intimate surroundings, specialities of Southern France, excellent wines.

Jewish cuisine

Luciano, via Portico d'Ottavia 16, VI, A4, ☎ 656 1613. Closed Sat. One of Rome's most authentic Jewish restaurants.

▬ *RESTAURANTS OPEN AFTER MIDNIGHT*

Antica Pesa, via Garibaldi 18, VI, B2, ☎ 580 9236. Open Mon-Sat until 2am. A typical Trastevere tavern with pleasant garden, Roman cuisine.

Le Cabanon, vicolo della Luce 4/5, VI, E2. Open Mon-Sat until 2am. French and Oriental cuisine, music after 11pm.

Canto del Riso, via della Cordonata 21, IV, E2, ☎ 361 0430. Open Wed-Mon until 1am. Every rice combination under the sun.

Spaghetteria, via Arno 80b, II, C5, ☎ 85 5535. Open Tues-Sun until 3am. All kinds of pasta.

▬ *WINE BARS*

La Bottiglieria Cavour, via Cavour 313, IV, FE3-4. Open Mon-Sat 8pm-midnight. Always crowded.

Enoteca di Piazza Navona, piazza Navona 72 III, F5. Well-stocked cellar—over 10,000 bottles from vineyards all over Italy.

Il Goccetto, via dei Banchi Vecchia 14, III, F3. Closed Sun. 18th-century ceiling, remarkable choice of wines and fine oils.

Trimani, via Goito 20, IV, C4, ☎ 475 5851. Rome's longest-established wine merchant.

▬ *ICE CREAM PARLOURS*

Fiocco di Neve, via del Pantheon 51, V, B2. Excellent homemade ice cream.

Giolitti, via degli Uffici del Vicario 40, III, E5, ☎ 679 4206. Closed Mon. Perhaps the best ice cream shop in Rome. Giolitti has been popular for decades.

Palazzo Freddo, via Principe Eugenio 65, V, A5, ☎ 73 7804. Consistent high quality since 1880.

Ristoro della Salute, piazza del Colosseo 2a, V, A2. A favourite meeting place for Rome's younger generation in the evening; remarkable selection of fruit ices.

Tre Scalini, piazza Navona, III, F5, ☎ 65 9148. Closed Wed. Known for its legendary *tartufo* (truffles).

▬ *CAFÉS AND SNACK-BARS*

Antico Caffè della Pace, via della Pace 3, III, F4. Mirrors, marble and wood decor; popular meeting place in the evening.

Argentina, largo di Torre. Argentina 15, III, F5. Café and restaurant. Open Mon-Sat until 2am.

Bar, viale delle Milize, III, B2-3 Open Mon-Sat until 4am.

Caffè Greco, via Condotti 86, III, D6, ☎ 678 2554. Closed Sun. This has long been a meeting place for intellectuals, beautiful 18th-century decor.

Chez Toi, via Cicerone 56b, III, BC4. Open daily until 3am.

Doria, via Doria 2/4, III, C1. Open Mon-Sat until 2.30am.

Gran Caffè Adriano, piazza Cavour 21b, III, D4. Open Tues-Sun until 2.30am.

Rosati, piazzale Clodio 25/26, III, A1. Open Thurs-Tues until 2.30am.

Tazza d'Oro, via degli Orfani 84, III, F5, ☎ 678 9792. Closed Sun. The best espresso in Rome.

Tritone, via del Tritone 144, IV, D1-2. Open Mon-Sat until 2.30am.

▬ *NIGHTCLUBS*

La Cabala, via dell'Orso, III, C5, ☎ 656 4221.

Capriccio, via Liguria 38, IV, C2, ☎ 474 4587.

La Clef, via Marche 13, IV, C3, ☎ 46 1730.

Saint Moritz, via Sicilia 57, IV, C3, ☎ 475 9160.

▬ *JAZZ CLUBS*

Big Mama, vicolo San Francesco a Ripa 18, VI, B3, ☎ 58 2551. A classic jazz club.

Billie Holliday Jazz Club, via degli Orti di Trastevere 43, VI, D2, ☎ 581 6121. Small club catering to true jazz fanatics.

Mississippi Club, via del Masche-rino 92, III, D2, ☎ 654 0348. Dixieland and Italian groups.

Music Inn, via Giulia 81, III, F3, ☎ 654 4934. Closed Tues and Thurs. Jazz, reggae, rock samba.

Saint Louis, via del Cardello 13a, VI, A1, ☎ 474 5076. Closed Sun. Excellent jazz.

▬ *DISCOTHEQUES*

Histeria, via Giovanelli 3, IV, A4, ☎ 86 4587. Favourite nightspot for young people.

Olimpo, piazza Rondanini 36, III, E5 ☎ 654 7314. The 'in' discotheque.

Piper 80, via Tagliamento 9, II, B4, ☎ 85 4459. Excellent music.

▬ *PIANO BARS*

Club 84, via Emilia 84, IV, C2, ☎ 475 1538. With restaurant.

Privilege, via S. Nicola da Tolentino 22, IV, D3, ☎ 4746 6888.

Tartarughino, via della Scrofa 2, III, E5, ☎ 678 6037. A slightly older clientele from the theatre, cinema and politics.

▬ *SHOPPING*

Department stores

Coin, piazzale Appio, II, D4, ☎ 757 3241.

La Rinascente, via del Corso, on the corner of piazza Colonna, III, E6, ☎ 679 7691; piazza Fiume, IV, B4.

Standa, via Cola di Rienzo 173/181, III, C3, ☎ 38 6450 ; via di Trastevere 62, VI, C3; via Tibertina 421/431, II, C6.

Upim, via del Tritone 172, IV, D2, ☎ 678 3336; piazza Santa Maria Maggiore, IV, F4; via Nazionale 211, IV, E3; via Ottaviano 48, III, C2.

Antiques

Rome's best-known antique stores are on via del Babuino, III, C5-6, and via Giulia, III, F3. Via Giulia is known for its 16th- to 18th-century paintings.

On via del Babuino:

A. Ferrante (nos 42-43), ☎ 678 3613.

Apolloni (n° 133, rare silver), ☎ 679 2429.

A. Efrati (n° 80).

A. di Castro (n° 146), ☎ 679 5792.

On via Giulia:

S. Longhio (n° 107).

Monetti (n° 169), ☎ 687 7436.

Other antique stores include:

F. di Castro, piazza di Spagna 5, ☎ 679 2269, and **G. Cohen,** via Margutta 83, III, C6, ☎ 678 4311 (for fine antique carpets). Less exclusive stores may be found around Palazzo Farnese and the Cancelleria, III, F4, where furniture is restored and sold on via Giulia and via del Babuino.

Jewellers

The most reputable jewellers and goldsmiths are concentrated around piazza di Spagna, III, D6. In the via Condotti: **Bruggi** (n° 78); **Bulgari** (n° 10), ☎ 679 3876; **Buccellati** (n° 31) and **Cartier** (nos 78-79). On via Frattina, III, D6 **Fumanti** (n° 1) and **Martini** (n° 33). **Fürst,** via Veneto 42, IV, C2, ☎ 48 3992, specializes in emeralds and rubies.

Many more modest Roman jewellers and goldsmiths specialize in the imitation or sale of old jewelry. Among these are **Corradini,** via Bocca di Leone 53, and **R. Cecconi,** via del Pellegrino 95, III, F4, ☎ 654 0577.

Hats

Argenti, via del Corso 47, III, F6, ☎ 38 6764. All types of men's felt hats and panamas.

Vigano, via Cavour 75, IV, E3-F4. For those partial to Stetsons, bowlers or borsalinos.

Shoes

For women

Barrila, via Condotti, III, D6, ☎ 679 3916, ready-to-wear or made-to-measure, fabulous leather but very expensive. **Fausto Santini,** via Frattina 120, III, D6, ☎ 678 4114, youthful shoes. For less expensive shoes, try **Cervone,** via del Corso 38, and **Shoe Shop,** via del Corso 138, III, F6, ☎ 679 4928. **Salato,** via Veneto 149, IV, CD2-3, ☎ 679 5646, is renowned for its embroidered leather and **Albanese,** via Lazio 19, IV, B2, ☎ 48 6898, specializes in supple leather. Other high-quality shops are **Carrano,** via Borgognona 2a, ☎ 679 1580, and

Moro, via Palestro 11, IV, D5, for made-to-measure shoes.

For men

Capodarte, via Sistina 14, IV, D2, ☎ 475 9681, a touch of fantasy in shoes of the highest quality. **Barrila,** via Condotti, ☎ 679 3916; **Cenci,** via Campo Marzio 4, III, E5, ☎ 678 4537, English and Italian shoes. **Magli,** via del Gambero 1, ☎ 679 3802, a chain of shops selling classic, conservative shoes at reasonable prices. **Zenith,** via del Tritone 97, IV, D1-2, conservative, expensive shoes.

Engravings

Casalli, via della Rotonda 81, III, F5.

Maresca, via Crescenzio 54, III, D2-3.

Old Master Drawings, via del Seminario 117, III, F5-6.

Piazza Borghese, art market Mon-Sat mornings, III, D5.

Bookshops

The following stores offer the widest selection:

Feltrinelli, via del Babuino 41, III, C6; ☎ 679 3360. via V.E. Orlando 83, IV, D3.

La Rinascità, via delle Botteghe Oscure 1, IV, F1.

Rizzoli, largo Chigi 15, IV, D1, ☎ 883 0202.

In addition, specialist bookshops can be found all over Rome.

Art and architecture

Dedalo, viale G. Rossini 20, II, B4.

Rizzoli and **Feltrinelli** (see above), also offer a wide selection of books on art.

Books in English

Anglo-American Paperbacks, piazza di Spagna 29, III, D6, ☎ 678 3890.

Lion Bookshop, via del Babuino 181, III, C6, ☎ 360 5838.

Clothing

For children

La Bancarella, piazza Buenos Aires 18, IV, A5. Superfashionable.

Bimbex, viale Libia 80-82, II, B4-5, ☎ 839 5953. Wide choice.

Capriccio, via Piave 25, IV, BC4, ☎ 831 0772.

La Cigogna, via Frattina 138, III, D6, ☎ 679 1912. Eight other premises throughout Rome. Expensive.

Tablo, piazza di Spagna 96, III, D6, ☎ 679 4468. Elegant and expensive.

For women

Giorgio Armani, via del Babuino 102, III, CD5-6, ☎ 679 3777. A Roman institution, for men and women.

Fendi, via Borgognona 39, III, D6, ☎ 679 7641.

Missoni, via Borgognona 38b, III, D6, ☎ 679 7971. Incomparable textures, colours and patterns.

Gianni Versace, via Bocca di Leone 26, III, D5, ☎ 678 0521. One of the great Italian designers.

Three other great fashion houses on via Bocca di Leone, III, D5, are **Trussardi, Valentino,** ☎ 679 5862, and **Ungaro,** ☎ 678 9931. **Ferragamo** is located at via Condotti 73/74, III, D5.

More moderately priced stores include:

Bamba de Clercq, via dell'Oca 39, III, C5. All types of knitwear.

Camomilla, piazza di Spagna 85b, III, D6, ☎ 679 3551.

For men

Giorgio Armani, see above.

Battistoni, via Condotti 61a, III, D6, ☎ 678 6241. Elegant ready-to-wear

and made-to-measure clothes for a select clientele.

Gucci, via Condotti 67, III, D6, ☎ 679 1882. Among Rome's most prestigious men's stores.

Gianfranco Ferré, via Borgognona 6, III, D6. Haute couture.

Gianni Versace, via Borgognona 29, III, D6, ☎ 679 5292.

More moderately priced stores include:

Cenci, via Campo Marzio III, E5, ☎ 678 4537. Classic British chic since the 1930s.

Degli Effetti, piazza Capranica, III, E5, ☎ 679 1650. Contemporary clothes.

Energie, via del Corso, III, F6, Teenage fashions.

Leather goods

Beltrami, via Condotti 19, III, D6, ☎ 679 1330. Snakeskin and crocodilian bags, shoes and belts, all handmade.

Campanile a Sparatella, via Condotti 58, III, D6. Leather goods for men and women.

Gucci, via Condotti 8, III, D6, ☎ 678 9340; **Gucci Boutique,** via Borgognona 25, III, D6, ☎ 678 3232. World-famous leather goods.

Sirni, via dei Porthogesi 33, III, D5. Beautiful bags.

Around Campo de Fiori, III, F4, you will find plenty of shoes, bags and suitcases at more moderate prices.

USEFUL VOCABULARY

Common words and phrases

Yes	*Si*
No	*Non*
Mr.	*Signore*
Mrs.	*Signora*
Good morning	*Buongiorno*
Good evening	*Buona sera*
Good night	*Buona notte*
Goodbye	*Arrivederci*
Excuse me	*Scusi*
Please	*Per favore*
Thank you	*Grazie*
You're welcome	*Prego*
Why?	*Perchè?*
Far	*Lontano*
Near	*Vicino*
Again	*Ancora*
Can you tell me?	*Puo dirmi?*
Do you have...?	*Ha...?*
I don't understand	*Non capisco*
Speak slowly	*Parli lentamente*
A lot	*Molto*
A little	*Poco*
Too much	*Troppo*
Enough	*Abbastanza*
All, everything	*Tutto*
Nothing	*Niente*
How much?	*Quanto costa?*
It's too expensive	*E'troppo caro*

Numbers

One	*Uno*
Two	*Due*
Three	*Tre*
Four	*Quattro*
Five	*Cinque*
Six	*Sei*
Seven	*Sette*
Eight	*Otto*
Nine	*Nove*
Ten	*Dieci*
Eleven	*Undici*
Twelve	*Dodici*
Thirteen	*Tredici*
Fourteen	*Quattordici*
Fifteen	*Quindici*
Sixteen	*Sedici*
Seventeen	*Diciassette*
Eighteen	*Diciotto*
Nineteen	*Diciannove*
Twenty	*Venti*
Twenty one	*Ventuno*
Twenty two	*Ventidue*
Thirty	*Trenta*
Forty	*Quaranta*
Fitty	*Cinquanta*
Sixty	*Sessanta*
Seventy	*Settanta*
Eighty	*Ottanta*

Ninety	*Novanta*
One hundred	*Cento*
Two hundred	*Duecento*
One thousand	*Mille*
Two thousand	*Duemila*
Three thousand	*Tremila*
One million	*Un milone*
One billion	*Un milliardo*

Time

Monday	*Lunedi*
Tuesday	*Martedi*
Wednesday	*Mercoledi*
Thursday	*Giovedi*
Friday	*Venerdi*
Saturday	*Sabato*
Sunday	*Domenica*
Spring	*Primavera*
Summer	*Estate*
Autumn	*Autunno*
Winter	*Inverno*
Today	*Oggi*
Yesterday	*Ieri*
Day before yesterday	*Ieri l'altro*
Tomorrow	*Domani*
Day after tomorrow	*Dopo domani*
The morning	*Il Matino*
In the afternoon	*Nel pomeriggio*
The evening	*La sera*

At the station or airport

To arrive	*Arrivare*
To change	*Cambiare*
Closed	*Fermata*
To leave	*Partire*
Left luggage	*Deposito*
Luggage	*Bagagli*
Platform	*Binario*
Porter	*Facchino*
Sleeping berth/Couchette	*Cuccetta*
Station	*Stazione*
Suitcase	*Valigia*
A ticket for	*Un biglietto per...*
Ticket inspector	*Controllore*
Timetable	*Orario*
What time does... arrive?	*A che hora arriva*
What time does... leave?	*A che hora parte*

By car

Attention, take care	*Attenzione*
Automobile	*Macchina*
Carwash	*Lavaggio*
Danger	*Pericolo*
Entrance	*Ingresso*
Exit	*Uscita*
Forbidden	*Vietato*
Fuel	*Benzina*
Greasing	*Lubrificazione*
No parking	*Divieto di sosta*
Oil	*Olio*

Parking	*Parcheggio*
Roadworks in progress	*Lavori in corso*
Slippery road	*Fondo Sdrucciolevole*
Tyre	*Pneumatico*
Tyre pressure	*Gonfiaggio*
Toll	*Pedaggio*

In town

Alley	*Vicolo*
Avenue	*Viale*
Cemetery	*Campo santo, Cimitero*
Church	*Chiesa*
Cloister	*Chiostro*
Courtyard	*Cortile*
Garden	*Giardino, orto*
Main square	*Piazzale*
Market	*Mercato*
Museum	*Museo*
Palace	*Palazzo*
Promenade	*Passeggiata*
Ruins	*Rovine*
Square	*Piazza, largo*
Stairway	*Scala*
Street	*Via*
To the right	*A destra*
To the left	*A sinistra*
Way, Promenade	*Corso*

At the hotel

Inn	*Locanda*
Hotel	*Albergo*
Family boarding house	*Una pensione familiare*
I want a room...	*Vorrei una camera*
With one bed, with two beds	*A un letto, a due letto*
Double bed	*Letto matrimoniale*
Bedroom with bath	*Camera con bagno*
On the street	*Sulla strada*
On the courtyard	*Sul cortile*
What is the price, service and tax included?	*Qual'e il prezzo, servizio e tasse comprese?*
Everything understood?	*Tutto compreso?*
English breakfast	*Colazione all'inglese*
What time is lunch served?	*A che ora il pranzo?*
And dinner?	*E la cena?*
Wake me at... o'clock	*Mi svegli alle ore...*
The bill, please	*Il conto, per favore*

At a restaurant

Appetizers (Hors d'œuvre)	*Antipasti*
Course, plate	*Piatto*
Fork	*Forchetta*
Glass	*Bicchiere*
Knife	*Coltello*
Meal	*Pranzo*
Menu	*Menu*
Place-setting	*Coperto, posata*
Simple restaurant	*Trattoria*
Spoon	*Cucchiaio*

Food

Apple	*Mela*
Bread	*Pane*
Butter	*Burro*
Cake	*Dolce*
Cheese	*Formaggio*
Chicken	*Pollo*
Egg	*Uovo*
Fish	*Pesce*
Fruit	*Frutta*
Grape	*Uva*
Ham	*Prosciutto*
Ice cream	*Gelato*
Ice cube	*Ghiacciolo*
Lamb	*Agnello, abbachio*
Mustard	*Mostarda*
Mutton	*Castrato*
Omelette	*Frittata*
Orange	*Arancia*
Pasta	*Pasta*
Peach	*Pesca*
Pepper	*Pepe*
Pork	*Maiale*
Potato	*Patata*
Rice	*Riso*
Salad	*Insalata*
Salt	*Sale*
Sausage	*Salame*
Sugar	*Zucchero*
Veal	*Vitello*

Drinks

Beer	*Birra*
Chocolate	*Cioccolata (in tazza)*
Coffee	*Caffé*
Coffee with cream	*Cappuccino*
Diluted Coffee	*Caffé lungo*
Fruit juice	*Succo di frutta*
Mineral water	*Acqua minerale*
Red wine	*Vino rosso*
Tea	*Té*
Water	*Acqua*
White wine	*Vino bianco*
Wine list	*Lista dei vini*

▰▰▰ *GLOSSARY OF ARCHITECTURAL TERMS*

Aedicule: The architectural frame of a bay, usually consisting of two columns bearing an entablature and a pediment.

Apse: Rounded or rectangular extremity of a church, at the end of the choir.

Ambo: A raised desk or pulpit, as in early Christian churches, used during the reading of the epistle and the gospel, and when making announcements to the people.

Architrave: The lowest division of the entablature, resting immediately on the columns.

Basilica: Under the Romans, a large oblong building with a broad nave separated from side aisles by rows of columns, and often with a semicircular apse at one end, used as a hall of justice and public meeting place. Later, this term applied to a Christian church with this same form. It is also an honorific title conferred by the pope on a church, without reference to its architectural form (eg. Sant'Agnese, San Giovanni in Laterano).

Campanile: A bell-tower, often divided horizontally into several levels.

Chevet: The apse, or termination of the apse, of a church, particulary the apsidal end of a church when it consists of a main apse and several secondary apses or chapels radiating from it.

Corbel: A supporting projection of stone, wood, etc., on the face of a wall, on which rest cornices or lintels.

Corinthian: Capital carved with acanthius leaves.

Cosamati: A group of sculptors and marbleworkers who came to Rome in the 13th and 14th centuries. The Cosmati also worked with enamel, mosaic and porphyry.

Crypt: Space beneath the choir, used as a repository for the relics of a saint. It is entered by a flight of steps.

Entablature: All of the elements supported by a column (architecture, frieze, cornice).

Greek Cross (floorplan): A church built in the shape of a cross with branches of equal length (like the cross of St George).

Latin Cross (floorplan): A church in which the nave is longer than the transept.

Monolithic: Made from a single stone block.

Narthex: Vestibule or portico forming the entrance of early Christian churches.

Nympheum: Natural or artificial grotto harbouring a spring or fountain. The design of Renaissance nymphea was inspired from antiquity.

Order: A column (base, shaft and capital) with an entablature, viewed as the characteristic element of a particular architectural style (Doric, Ionic, Corinthian, Tuscan or Composite).

Pendentive: A triangular segment of the lower part of a hemispherical dome, between two adjacent penetrating arches.

Peristyle: A range of columns surrounding a building, court or the like.

Pilaster: A square or rectangular pillar, with capital and base, engaged in a wall from which it projects.

Presbytery: The part of a church appropriated to the clergy, usually around the bishop's throne.

Pronaos: Colonnaded area in the front of a temple.

Scola Cantorum: Space defined by a low wall in front of the choir of a church, where the choristers stand.

Stucco: A dried mixture of plaster and ground marble, often sculpted or decorated.

Titulus: A private chapel converted for Christian services.

Transept: The transverse portion of a cruciform church.

Travertine: A form of limestone deposited by springs, used for building.

Triumphal Arch: Monumental arch at the entrance to the choir, decorated with paintings or mosaics.

Tufa Volcanic: A porous volcanic limestone. The catacombs were cut through stone of this type.

Tympanum: A semicircular or triangular surface, usually sculpted above the door of a church.

▬▬▬ SUGGESTED READING

Ackerman, J.S. *The Architecture of Michelangelo* (University of Chicago, 1986).

Barrow, Reginald H. *The Romans* (Penguin, 1975).

Bowder, Diana. *Who Was Who in the Roman World* (Cornell University Press, 1980).

Bowen, Elizabeth. *A Time in Rome* (Knopf, 1959).

Bull, George. *Inside the Vatican* (St Martin, 1983).

Christ, Karl. *The Romans: An Introduction to their History and Civilization* (University of California Press, 1984).

Clark, Eleanor. *Rome and a Villa* (Atheneum, 1982).

De Tolnay, Charles. *Michelangelo* (Princeton University Press, 1970).

Gibbon, Edward. *The History of the Decline and Fall of the Roman Empire* (Modern Library, 1932).

Hofmann Paul. *Rome: The Sweet Tempestuous Life* (Congdon & Weed, 1982).

Krautheimer, Richard. *Rome: Profile of a City 312-1308* (Princeton University Press, 1980).

Lanciani R. *The Golden Days of the Renaissance in Rome* (New York, 1906).

Luttwack, Edward N. *The Grand Strategy of the Roman Empire from the First Century A.D. to the Third* (Johns Hopkins, 1977).

Masson, Georgina. *Companion Guide to Rome* (Prentice Hall, 1983).

Meade, C. Wade. *Ruins of Rome: A Guide to the Classical Antiquities* (Palatine Pubns., 1980).

Morton, H.V. *A Traveller in Rome* (Dodd, Mead, 1984).

Oliphant, Mrs. *The Makers of Modern Rome* (Norwood Edns., 1978).

Partner, Peter. *Renaissance Rome: A Portrait of a Society 1550-1559* (University of California Press, 1977).

Plutarch, *Fall of the Roman Republic,* trans. by Rex Warner (Penguin, 1975).

Scullard, H.H. *Festivals and Ceremonies of the Roman Republic* (Cornell University Press, 1981).

Starr, Chester G. *Ancient Romans* (Oxford University Press, 1971).

Stendhal. *Rome, Naples, and Florence* (George Braziller, 1959).

Stinger Charles. *The Renaissance in Rome* (Indiana University Press, 1984).

Symonds, J.A. *The Renaissance in Italy* (London, 1906).

Vickers, Michael. *The Roman World* (Phaidon Press, 1981).

Ward-Perkins, J.B. *Roman Imperial Architecture* (Penguin, 1981).

Wheeler, Mortimer. *Roman Art and Architecture* (Thames and Hudson, 1985).

Wittkower, R. *Art and Architecture in Italy 1600-1750* (Pelican History of Art, Penguin, 1959).

INDEX